T0319718

Foreign Firms, Technological Capabilities and Economic Performance

To the memory of the late Linsu Kim and Ishak Shari

Foreign Firms, Technological Capabilities and Economic Performance

Evidence from Africa, Asia and Latin America

Rajah Rasiah

Professor and Deputy Director, Asia Europe Institute,
University of Malaya, Kuala Lumpur, Malaysia

With contributions from Geoffrey G. Gachino, Jorge Monge, Henry Tamale, Ganesh Rasagam and Thabo Gopane

Edward Elgar
Cheltenham, UK • Northampton, MA, USA

Published by
Edward Elgar Publishing Limited
Glensanda House
Montpellier Parade
Cheltenham
Glos GL50 1UA
UK

Edward Elgar Publishing, Inc.
136 West Street
Suite 202
Northampton
Massachusetts 01060
USA

A catalogue record for this book
is available from the British Library

ISBN 1 84376 986 7 (cased)

Typeset by Manton Typesetters, Louth, Lincolnshire, UK.
Printed and bound in Great Britain by MPG Books Ltd, Bodmin, Cornwall.

Contents

Contributors

Rajah Rasiah holds a Ph.D. in Economics from Cambridge University. He is currently Professor and Deputy Director of the Asia Europe Institute at the University of Malaya in Kuala Lumpur, Malaysia. He has undertaken consultancies in over 20 countries for the World Bank, UNIDO, UNDP, ADB, Harvard Institute of International Development, ILO, JETRO, DFID, UNCTAD and the state of Rhine-Westphalia.

Geoffrey Gachino is a Ph.D. candidate at the MERIT–UNU–INTECH doctoral programme. He holds a M.Phil. in economics from University of Ghana. He is currently on leave from Kenya's Ministry of Planning and National Development where he is employed as an Economic Statistician.

Jorge Monge holds a Ph.D. in Engineering. He is currently President of CODETI and Mason Fellow at Harvard University. He has carried out consultancies in 15 countries in Latin America, the Caribbean, Africa, Eastern Europe and the Middle East for CIDA, IDRC, ILO, OAS, SSRC, UNCTAD and the World Bank.

Henry Tamale holds an M.Phil. in Development Studies from Cambridge University. He is currently the Deputy Director at the Currency Department of Bank of Uganda, and is a fellow of the Cambridge Commonwealth Society.

Ganesh Rasagam holds a Master's degree in Engineering from the Asian Institute of Technology. He is currently a Development Specialist in the Private Sector of the World Bank. He has extensive consultancy experience working with the Asian Development Bank, UNDP, USAID and World Bank in 18 African and Asian economies.

Thabo Gopane is pursuing a Ph.D. in Economics at Georgia State University. He is currently Project Manager at South Africa's Ministry of Trade and Industry. He served as the executive director of McRade until 2003.

Preface

This book is the culmination of extensive research carried out in the continents of Africa, Asia and Latin America between February 2002 and August 2003. Using a methodology drawn from the technology capability framework, but adapting and simplifying it extensively to extract common cross-industry parameters for undertaking statistical analysis, the individual chapters examine differences in technological and performance indicators in Kenya, South Africa, Uganda, Indonesia, Malaysia and Brazil. The chapter on Costa Rica examines the development of firms linked to Intel. The former uses statistical analysis to compare technological, local sourcing and performance dynamics of foreign and local firms in selected industries, while the latter examines Intel's impact on the development of small- and medium-scale suppliers in Costa Rica. The results offer a common synthesis. First, foreign firms tend to enjoy higher human resource and process technology capabilities in the most underdeveloped economies of Kenya, Indonesia and Uganda. Second, local firms enjoy similar human resource and process technology levels as foreign firms in the industries selected in Brazil, Costa Rica, Malaysia and South Africa. Third, institutional and systemic strength matters in explaining the relative strength of participation of foreign firms in R&D activities. Domestic and regional markets, infrastructure and incentives, natural resources and human capital have been important in stimulating significant R&D activities in foreign firms in selected industries of these economies.

A number of institutions and individuals have been involved in this study, without whose help it would not have seen the light of day. Generous contribution for the project came from UNU–INTECH, which financed the entire study in Africa and Latin America, and the Asian Development Bank, which financed the Asian part of the study. The Costa Rican study received partial support from the Organisation of American States and the Social Science Research Council. We wish to thank these organisations for their generous help. Research support was provided by the Human Science Research Council (HSRC) in Pretoria (South Africa), Bank of Uganda in Kampala (Uganda), Central Bureau of Statistics, Nairobi (Kenya), DCT Consultancy, Penang (Malaysia), University of Indonesia, Jakarta (Indonesia), Unicamp, Campinas (Brazil) and Cooperation for International Development (CODETI), San José (Costa Rica). The following individuals assisted in engaging discussions and data collection: Miriam Altman, Eric Wood, Anthony Black, Rashad Cassim, Geoff Parr, George Djolov, Jochen Lorentzen, Werner Johnson, Mike Peet, Justin Barnes, Clive Williams, Brian Brink, Nico and David Moshapalo in South Africa; Ruy Quadros, Rubia Quintao, Flavia Luciane Consoni, Antonio Correa Lacerda, Marco Rodrigues, Severino de Oliveira, Sylvio Napoli, Guilherme Aguilar Patriota, Andre Furtado, Paulo Negreiros Figueiredo, Jorge Katz and Victor Do Prado in Brazil; Humphrey Njoroge Muhu, Isaac K. Ndegwa, Noah Odaa, Shem Maina Chituyi, Benjamin C. Chesang, Francis K. Rotich, Robert S. Bwire, Timothy K. Tiampati, Robert Gatimu Kiboti, Moses K. Kiambuthi, Stephen Odua, Shamji M. Patel, D.P. Shah, T.G. Coulson, Kathiga and J.S. Bedi in Kenya; Naveen Krishnan, Sikander Lalani, Sam Kanakulya-Lubinga, Patrick Banya, Richard Kiwomero and Leonard Musisi in Uganda; Roberto Brenes, Rosa Adolio and Mirtha Navarro in Costa Rica; O.K. Lee, Y.H. Tan, Koh Tsu Koon, Toh Kin Woon, Y.B. Jong, Lim P.L., Anna Ong, Zawawi Ismail, Boonler Somchit, Ahmad Konchong, Tengku Azman, Tengku Mahaleel, Kamal Salih, Nungsari Ahmad, Paul Low, Selvaratnam V., Thillainathan R., Norlela Ariffin, Shamsulkubahriah Ahmad, Jaya Gopal, Colin Chang, Chia Swee Huat, Palasandaram and Mohamad Arif Nun in Malaysia; and Ari Kuncoro and M. Sinivasan in Indonesia.

We are also grateful for extensive comments from a number of respected scholars. John Dunning, Sanjaya Lall, Rajneesh Narula, Pierre Mohnen, Kiichiro Fukasaku, Rene Belderbos, Prasada Reddy and Moses Ikiara offered incisive comments on most of the chapters. Paulo Negreiros Figueiredo, Lynn Mytelka, Anthony Bartzokas, John van den Elst, Dieter Ernst, Gary Gereffi, Eric Hersberg, Richard Doner, Slavo Radosevic, Rajiv Kumar, Kaushelesh Lal, Banji Oyeyinka, Padmashree Gehl Sampath, Frederich Sachwald, Michael Best, Justin Barnes, Eric Wood, Jorge Katz, the late Linsu Kim, Colin Chang, Brian Ritchie, Paul Lubeck, Shin Jang-Sup and Pedro Martinez Lara offered comments on individual chapters. In addition, the Costa Rican chapter has benefited from comments by Gary Gereffi, Dieter Ernst and Eric Hershberg. We are also grateful to the comments from others who attended the International Workshop, 'Foreign Firms, Technological Capabilities and Economic Performance', organised by UNU–INTECH in Maastricht on 19–20 June 2003.

We are also grateful for the able support of Marc Vleugels, Ad Notten, Yvonne de Groot, Eveline in de Braek, Jacqueline van Kesteren and Mourik Young at UNU–INTECH. Last but not least we wish to thank all others who have helped directly or indirectly in the fieldwork as well as in the preparation of this book. I am deeply indebted to Krishna Kumari, Dayita Priya and Dharmin Kumar for graciously carrying the work left behind at home and giving me tremendous moral support in the preparation of this book. Needless to say, they bear no responsibility for any errors of fact or interpretation in the book.

Foreword

There has been a great deal of research recently on technological capabilities and their implications for industrialisation in developing countries. There has also been considerable work on the impact of foreign direct investment (FDI) for poor host economies, with a new branch of research emerging on the growth of global production networks and the 'fragmentation' of production in developing countries. For the most part, however, the two lines of research have proceeded independently, using different methodologies, data and approaches. In the context of technology, the FDI analysis has mainly focused on the transfer of technology and spillovers to local firms, with relatively little attention to capability development within foreign affiliates.

The technology capability literature has also not pursued in any great depth the differences between foreign and local firms. One of the fundamental problems with this literature has been that it is very difficult to quantify capabilities in a way that allows comparisons between companies. Attempts have been made to find meaningful measures of capabilities but clearly much more remains to be done. Progress in this is important for development policy: with growing disillusionment towards neoliberal approaches of simply 'letting in the market', countries feel the need to understand what capabilities are, how they develop and how to develop them.

This book by Rajah Rasiah and colleagues is a major step forward in this direction. It bases the analysis of foreign and local firms in a range of developing countries squarely on measuring and comparing technological capabilities. This is a significant advance in methodological terms. It also yields very interesting results. What adds to the interest is the range of countries covered, from industrially advanced nations like Brazil, South Africa and Malaysia, to relatively backward ones such as Kenya and Uganda. The book is thoroughly researched, rigorous in its analysis and comprehensive in its coverage of the literature.

The results offer interesting insights into how local and foreign firms differ in their technological competence, and, more interestingly, into what influences their technological activity. It appears that foreign firms have better skills and technological capabilities in most countries, but this is not uniform. In the more advanced economies, local firms are relatively strong.

The book will be of wide interest. It will inform the debate on the role of FDI in industrial and technological development, offering a balanced and original analysis of the behaviour and strengths of foreign affiliates in a range of countries. It will be an important contribution to the technological capability literature, showing how the rather amorphous concept of 'capabilities' can be made more tractable and measurable. It will illustrate why industrial development has succeeded in some countries and failed in others. It will clarify the context in which technology development takes place, and so offer insights to policy makers on how to improve that context. It is a major credit to the main author, Rajah Rasiah, who is already known in the development community as a major analyst.

Sanjaya Lall
Oxford University
13 May 2004

1. Introduction

Rajah Rasiah

1.1 INTRODUCTION

Latecomer economies typically access technology through learning – via a combination of imports and domestic development. The cumulative dimension of technology offers firms the opportunity to learn from already developed technologies. While superior national innovation systems in developed economies support firms at the technology frontier so that the transnationalisation of economic activities by giant corporations is *inter alia* aimed at tapping knowledge appropriated globally,[1] developing economies – especially those emerging at the bottom of the technology ladder – generally attract them only on the basis of large low-wage labour, natural resources and domestic and regional markets. Nevertheless, whatever the reasons for relocation, the participation of foreign firms offers host sites the potential for knowledge spillovers. Some developing economies seek knowledge from abroad through imports, training of personnel overseas, licensing and subcontract deals. Transnational corporations (TNCs) still play a major role involving this channel, albeit indirectly as imitation and arm's-length transactions figure prominently. Countries such as Japan, South Korea and Taiwan generally absorbed foreign technology through imitation and licensing from TNCs. Others such as Singapore and Ireland have relied extensively on TNCs' foreign direct investment (FDI) to stimulate learning and innovation. Clearly, both strategies – learning and innovating to compete, using TNCs both directly and indirectly – are embedded in national economic policy. Hence discussions relating to the role of FDI on technology cannot be detached from the conditions prevailing and economic policies pursued at host sites.

The term foreign firm was preferred over TNCs[2] and multinational corporations (MNCs) here owing to significant participation of firms with no distinct production, marketing or R&D-based foreign parents or subsidiaries in a number of African economies. Both terms – TNCs and MNCs – essentially exclude stand-alone foreign firms. Most stand-alone foreign firms have foreign bank accounts, but so do a number of local firms. Given the relatively small size of most stand-alone foreign firms, they often compete with local firms on the basis of superior intangible assets involving owner-managers or owner-picked foreign human capital endowed with tacit knowledge or entrepreneurship. Interviews in Kenya and Uganda showed several firms owned by foreigners who had relocated either with entrepreneurial skills to take advantage of small business opportunities but willing to take big political risks or who have come to utilise the tacit knowledge gained working abroad.[3] Friendship and kinship relationships constitute a major source of social and political support to compensate risks associated with purely market-driven relationships. Given the technological backwardness and low income levels associated with these countries, both the participation and the relevance of these firms for technological capability building should not be overlooked. While the technological capabilities of these firms can be expected to be inferior to typical TNCs, the smaller size and a lack of inter-country production links reduce problems of power asymmetries with local firms.

While the role of foreign firms in the appropriation of knowledge, learning and innovation is growing in significance, little consensus exists on their impact on local firms. Scattered works – both anecdotal and analytical – detail spillovers of tacit and experiential knowledge embodied in human capital in the creation of local firms (e.g. Allen and Donnithorne, 1957; Rasiah, 1994, 2002a). Foreign-firm-driven technological capability development does not evolve in a vacuum. Domestic institutions through policy instruments and intermediation with markets and firms, and firms and institutions have been critical in stimulating learning and innovation (see Rasiah, 1999; Doner, 2001; Aoki, 2001). Network strength and cohesion has been shown to be critical to raise the fluidity of interactions and systems synergies (see Rasiah, 2002b).

This chapter attempts to examine the literature expounding the role of FDI in the development of exports, productivity and technological capabilities in developing economies with a view to formulating a conceptual and methodological approach to evaluating the empirical evidence from selected economies in Africa, Asia and Latin America. It is organised as follows. Sections 1.2 and 1.3 present the analytic and methodological frameworks to examine the nexus between exports and firm-level and systemic capabilities. Section 1.2 examines the main theories and findings on foreign firms and technology in developing economies. Section 1.3 discusses an alternative framework developed. Section 1.4 discusses the criteria used to select the economies examined in the study. Section 1.5 presents the conclusions.

1.2 PAST APPROACHES

Written works dealing with the nexus between technical change and markets have a long history. Smith (1776) had established the famous dictum that the 'division of labour is determined by the size of the market'. What is less discussed is Smith's other concurrent dictum, 'the size of the market is also determined by the division of labour', which was lucidly articulated by Young (1928). The scale effects of specialisation based on static comparative advantage and trade was discussed extensively by Ricardo (1830) – which was modelled robustly later by Sraffa (1960) using the standard system. Given the different approaches used by authors working on foreign firms and technology, their arguments are examined using three broad classifications: Marxist, structural and institutional, and neoclassical. This classification is used as a convenient means of discussing the issues and is not intended to define the leaning of the authors concerned.

Marxist

Marx (1965) expounded that competition forces firms to replace old modes of technology with new ones, which Schumpeter (1987) referred to as 'gales of creative destruction'. Marx (1964, 1965 and 1967), and later Luxemburg (1963) had argued that the creative destructive effects of early integration with capitalism through colonialism in most developing economies, despite the pain it causes, was necessary to initiate and engender the dynamic productive forces that characterise industrial capitalism.[4] Technical change constitutes the engine of productive forces, in which Marx had argued reach its zenith of capabilities under industrial capitalism and hence argued for capitalist expansion, which became the basis of Kalecki's (1976: 24) investment model for development. Subsequent Marxist works took two divergent approaches.

The first focused on exchange relations – the circuits of money and commodity – deriving from Lenin's (1965) claim that capitalism had reached a monopoly stage and hence offered little opportunities for an extension of surplus accumulation in new regions. Baran (1957, 1973) extended this thesis to contend that capitalist integration will set into motion the development of underdevelopment (see also Frank, 1973). Frobel et al. (1980) offered a TNC-specific analysis for the application of this argument: the creation of an international division of labour that is based on the Babbage–Taylorist decomposition of production so that low wage (including levels below reproduction costs) in host sites endowed with large industrial reserve army help extend development in the core and underdevelopment in the periphery. A more sophisticated analysis of this strand was offered by Wallerstein (1974,

1979), who introduced the concept of semi-periphery to allow the progression of some countries to achieve accumulation, but marginalisation would ensure that they remain behind the core economies. TNCs were viewed as a major instrument of capitalism exploiting developing economies to expand accumulation in the developed world. Brazil and Indonesia are some of the countries often quoted to make this point (e.g. Frank, 1973; Muto, 1977). Increased penetration of TNCs are also considered to de-skill workers as low-wage employment is claimed to be the basis of incorporation in developing economies (Frobel et al., 1980). While making the same point, Amin (1976) in addition argued that foreign firms bring inappropriate capital-intensive technology – thereby raising the costs of diffusion and distorting technology development in host sites. These arguments obviously departed from Marx's original explication of industrial capitalism and implied that increased participation of TNCs will sap developing economies of the potential to develop their technological capabilities.

Closer to Marx's and Luxemburg's original works, Warren (1973, 1980) led the argument on how competition between firms has transformed the global environment for the extension of accumulation to developing economies. Although Murray (1973) had contended that state power had declined to pressure foreign firms to engender, *inter alia*, technology transfer, Warren appeared convinced that competition between firms had risen far more and was opening opportunities for developing economies to learn and develop. The relocation of production sites in developing economies and the market access foreign firms enjoy offered the conduit for quickening learning and upgrading. Governments of developing countries were encouraged to launch policies to extract maximum gains from the operations of foreign firms. The successful development of Singapore and Ireland using foreign firms as the spearhead of learning and innovation through invitation and leveraging lends support to Warren.

Structural and Institutional

Like the Marxists, structural economists have produced mixed arguments and findings on the topic of foreign firms and technology diffusion in developing economies. Hirschman (1958, 1977) argued pervasively that export-oriented foreign firms tend initially to create severe imbalances in host economies but provide the catalyst for supply responses leading to the development of backward linkages.[5] The role of government to attract foreign firms and subsequent stimulation of backward linkages are viewed as critical for learning and eventually innovations to take place in developing economies. Akamatsu (1962) had argued, *inter alia*, that foreign investment was one of the instruments that would generate inter-country regional growth synergies.

Lall and Streeten (1977) discuss circumstances when such spillovers from the operations of foreign firms can occur, but raise doubts about their viability on the grounds of power asymmetries and the inherent problems posed by non-autonomous and corrupt host governments representing developing economies. Dunning (1958, 224–5) had examined American investment in British manufacturing using case studies to show technology transfer from American to local suppliers, customers and competitors. Allen and Donnithorne (1957) and Rasiah (1988, 1995: chs 6 and 7) offer empirical evidence of the development and movement of skilled human capital and entrepreneurial capabilities from foreign firms to start or support local firms in developing economies. Rasiah (2003b, 2003c) provided statistical evidence to demonstrate the importance of foreign ownership in the development of export (directly) and technological capabilities (indirectly) in the electronics industry in Indonesia, Malaysia, the Philippines and Thailand.

Singer (1950) contended otherwise, arguing that foreign investment is economically part of the investing country; with its monopoly over technology, it may weaken the recipient by diverting investment and resources away from local industry that might have otherwise developed. This is part of the 'crowding-out' thesis, which seriously affects developing economies. Newfarmer (1985: 185–6), Newfarmer and Mueller (1975), Agarwal (1976), and Lim and Pang (1979) provide anecdotal and statistical evidence to suggest that foreign firms produce few linkages in developing economies. Capannelli (1999) produced empirical evidence to show that Japanese consumer electronics firms in Malaysia generally retain all the key input supplies involving higher value added activities, leaving sourcing of only low value added inputs to local firms. In addition, Capannelli (1999: 208) also observed that the production technology used by Japanese subsidiaries in Malaysia involved in maintenance, inventory control, testing and inspection was inferior to that used in parent firms in Japan, but product technology involving some standardised products was superior. Lall (1978) and Moxon (1975) also questioned the relevance of TNC technology for diffusion in developing economies. The evidence amassed on this issue is still inconclusive owing to the problems associated with defining what is relevant, especially when economies integrated in the world economy have developed on the basis of catching up in industries where learning in path-dependent technologies dominates global exports. Learning in some industries has involved the pursuit of upgrading either through FDI or licensing and imitation. Some economies, e.g. Singapore and Malaysia, targeted technology-creating information technology to stimulate growth in fast-expanding industries. Upgrading in technology-using industries, e.g. garments and leather, offered the springboard to nurture learning and the foreign exchange to support higher-value-added industries. Korea, Taiwan and Singapore enjoyed completely different structures when active promotion of industrial policy started in the 1960s (see Amsden, 1989; Wade, 1990; Lall, 2001). It is difficult to extract experiential and tacit knowledge on the basis of specific experiences, as cross-diffusion of skills from one department to another in the same firm and from one industry to another constitutes the very essence of dynamism in industrial districts (see Saxenian, 1994; Best, 2001; Rasiah, 1994, 2002b). In addition, problems of infrastructure and absortive capacity have required foreign firms sometimes to introduce technologies that reflect little the influence of relative factor endowments. For example, Emmanuel (1989) argued that foreign firms are often forced to adopt capital-intensive technologies owing to infrastructure and labour control problems in Africa.

While disputes exist on the diffusion of skills and process technologies, the controversy involving foreign firms' role in engendering R&D activities in developing economies is even stronger. Vernon (1966, 1971) had argued using the product cycle argument that TNCs would relocate only standard-ised low-value stages of production at host sites. In addition to the need for strong institutional support and higher incomes to provide market demand, Vernon argued that governments in home countries also offered greater pro-prietary protection of such activities than host economies. Increased mobility of R&D scientists and engineers from developing economies such as India and China to major industrial clusters – e.g. Silicone Valley, Route 128, Ireland and Germany – has perpetuated the concentration of R&D activities at parent sites (see Rasiah, 2004). Some developing economies have managed to reverse some of these tendencies: e.g. Singapore attracts scientists and engineers from abroad and continues to build its institutional support facili-ties to stimulate R&D operations by TNCs. Nevertheless, the influence of agglomeration economies for R&D activities to be retained at parent sites has remained pervasive. Lall (1979, 1980), Mansfield et al. (1979), Creamer (1976), Ronstadt (1977), Behrman and Fischer (1980), Dunning (1994a, 1994b), Cantwell (1995) and Rasiah (1996) offered statistical evidence show-ing little R&D activities in TNC subsidiaries in developing economies. Cantwell (1995) and OECD (1998) make the same observation involving TNCs' R&D activities in developed economies. Mathews (1996)[6] and Dun-ning (1997)[7] introduced different variants of the stage-based notion of FDI articulated by Akamatsu (1962) and Vernon (1966) involving technological activities as countries develop. Much of the foreign R&D operations of TNCs tend to be focused on developmental aspects – including the adaptation of machinery and equipment. Using a framework to distinguish different types of activities involving R&D, Amsden et al. (2001) show that TNCs' involve-ment in R&D operations in developing economies is generally confined to simple activities, though Singapore was reported to have effected a transition in FDI from production-based to applied R&D activities through government policy. Sunkel (1989), Furtado (1973) and Cardoso (1977) have argued that

TNCs stimulate manufacturing in Latin American economies, but the nature of their operations tends to confine technological capabilities to low value-added activities.

Neoclassical

The effects of trade under neoclassical models – drawing from Ricardo (1830) and Marshall (1927) – led to the formulation of the Heckscher–Ohlin model where it was demonstrated that the static benefits of perfect competition and trade under conditions of factor (labour and capital) immobility would rise as specialisation based on relative factor endowments would maximise inter-country welfare. Bhagwati (1979: 96–8) relaxed the capital immobility condition to show how capital exports from a capital-surplus labour-scarce economy to capital-scarce labour-surplus economy can benefit both countries as the flows leads to equalisation of interest rates and wages. Technical change is not addressed directly and dynamically in this model. Subsequent works involving technical change have evolved truncatedly. The most influential technique showing technical change (assumed to be exogenous) that evolved from such analyses owes its existence to Solow's (1956) estimation of total factor productivity using the production function approach.[8]

Reuber et al. (1973) provided empirical evidence using simple discrete statistics to show that foreign firms operating in developing economies use 73 per cent of their process technology and 83 per cent of their quality control systems without any change. However, this study did not examine if the technological dimensions changed over time, and did not control for industrial specificities. This study and Hughes and You (1969: 193–4) explained that the most important reason for adaptations was to fit small-scale operations in developing economies. Rasiah (1988, 1994, 1995) offered empirical evidence from case studies in the semiconductor TNCs in Malaysia to show frontier process technology is critical especially in competitive industries characterised by rapid technological obsolescence – caused by shortening product cycles and efficiency-improving machinery and equipment change. Rasiah's (2003b) statistical analysis involving a larger sample of electronics firms – both foreign and local – from Indonesia, Malaysia, the Philippines and Thailand corroborated this finding.

Different postulations of technology, trade and FDI using general equilibrium models have also been advanced. Kojima (1975) developed a model to show that FDI in export-substituting rather than in import-competing industries in home countries will reduce trade with consequent negative implications for technology development. However, the static model used offered little explication of how technology development will be stunted as a result. A more sophisticated general equilibrium model was advanced by Krugman

(1979) showing how technology transfer will lower resource utilisation costs in developing economies and hence will stimulate FDI inflows. An empirical examination of this model will be useful, though it should be confined to specific industries where FDI flows are driven by resource endowments (including labour) and located alongside institutional and systemic developments at host sites. The development of the information hardware industry in Singapore and Taiwan relied extensively on technology transferred from TNCs, but the conditions and consequences were different. FDI inflows were sustained with greater technology transfer (which was also facilitated strongly by domestic institutional development in Singapore). The transfer of tacit and experiential knowledge embodied in human capital relocating from consumer electronics firms in Taiwan in the 1970s helped stimulate the initial growth of local firms in the industry. Using arm's-length licensing transactions, subcontract orders and Taiwanese human capital hired from TNCs in Taiwan and from the United States, and strong government support to promote R&D operations,[9] local firms subsequently expanded sharply to engage extensively in original equipment manufacturing (OEM), original design manufacturing (ODM) and original brand manufacturing (OBM) operations (see Lin and Rasiah, 2003).

Neoclassical statistical estimations of technology flows involving foreign firms to developing economies focus largely on production function estimations of spillovers. Caves (1974a, 1974b) presented arguably the first systematic production function estimation of spillovers, which led to a plethora of works extending the framework (e.g. Blomström and Persson, 1983; Blomström and Wolffe, 1994). Urata (2001) examined the nexus between investment and exports in Asia. Sjoholm (1999) and Blomström and Sjoholm (1999) showed that foreign firms in Indonesia enjoyed higher productivity than local firms, and also generated positive spillovers. Haddad and Harrison (1993) and Aitken et al. (1999), *inter alia*, took this approach to a new dimension by refining the methodology to address locational, industry-type, scale and demonstration effect variables. These works helped to improve the original instruments that Caves had used to extend the understanding of spillovers. However, there has been growing debate over whether the relationships traced through such methodologies can be equated with actual spillovers. Given that technological external economies are often difficult to picture exhaustively,[10] it is not wrong to contend that spillovers cannot be measured completely.

It can be seen that all three approaches offer considerable insights on foreign firms and technology in developing economies. While some approaches are inherently static, the main features of contention go beyond mere techniques. Removing static articulations, foreign firms' operations have correlated positively with technology development in some locations, industries and time periods but not in others. Some case studies offered rich analysis of dynamic relationships between firms and technology – *vis-à-vis* export intensity, firm-level capabilities (e.g. human resource, process and product technology), linkages and systemic influences. Large surveys have offered more representative measurement of discrete influences, though at the expense of excluding some dynamic relationships.

1.3 ALTERNATIVE APPROACH

Although the disjuncture between theory and empirical evidence and attempts to bridge the gap remains elusive, important insights on foreign firms, technology, exports and productivity have evolved over time. Many of these developments appear to have come from contributions in evolutionary economics. First is the local, national and regional innovation system within which foreign firms are embedded, which includes the significance of absorptive capacity. Second is the technology trajectory of host sites and regions – i.e. the technological position of foreign firms and local firms. While higher technological gaps offer greater room for learning and absorption, government instruments defined to stimulate capability building may fail if local firms have not reached the threshold levels necessary to participate in higher-value-added activities. For example, incentives to promote R&D would enjoy few takers if firms merely perform simple low-value-added activities. Third is the public goods characteristics of institutional development and systemic links that help resolve collective action problems. Knowledge flows and appropriation are clearly public goods, which are effectively diffused across firms and institutions in smoothly coordinated networks or clusters. Table 1.1 presents a taxonomy of capabilities and performance with influences from the environment firms embed, structure that define their operations and their own conduct. This framework is articulated alongside a model shown in Figure 1.1 for understanding foreign firms in the context of their operations in individual economies by their position in the development ladder and the role and impact of government policies on their conduct and impact (see Figure 1.1).

The approach adopted in this book takes the implicit argument from Smith (1776) and Young (1928) that market size and capabilities stimulate each other. Smith made the observation – which was lucidly articulated later by Young – that causation involving the division of labour and the size of the market runs both ways. Put simply, the scale and 'gales of creative destruction' effects of external markets and competition respectively influence capability building, while improvements in the latter help sustain exports. This argument is also consistent with Hirschman's (1958) dynamic analysis

Table 1.1 Taxonomy of capabilities and performance

Environment systemic	Structure	Conduct	Firm-level capabilities	Performance
Basic infrastructure, labour supply, socio-political and economic environment, high-tech support and network cohesion	Organisational structure of firms – vertically or horizontally integrated, domestic-oriented or internationalised, ownership and firm size	Human resource development and process and product technologies, and financial strategies	Human resource, process technology, process technology R&D, product technology, product technology R&D, financial capability	Export, value added, labour productivity, return on investment

Note: The NIS viewed from the lenses of firms – adapted with contributions from IO, IP and BS.

Source: Adapted from Rasiah (2003b).

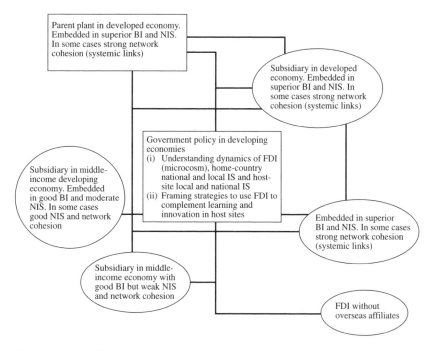

Source: Compiled by the author.

Figure 1.1   Towards a model of foreign firms, technological capabilities and NIS

calling for export orientation as the basis for promoting backward linkages. Although this chapter does not deal with backward linkages extensively as measurement is confined to firm-level capabilities, it captures a significant part of its potential. Technological capabilities rise with the location of firms on the technology ladder (see Dosi, 1982; Pavitt, 1984). High-tech infrastructure is essential to stimulate firms' participation in product and process technology development (e.g. R&D support).

A number of critical variables influence the development of technological capabilities, exports and labour productivity, the last two being indicators of competitiveness. The nature of foreign enterprise – defined by home-country origin, the industry, type (vertical, horizontal, conglomerate or stand-alone) with scale and scope ramifications – often strongly influence the conduct, technological capability and economic performance of individual firms. Chandler (1961, 1977) and Dunning (1997) articulated a similar, but with distinct business, perspective to the origin and growth of MNCs that is important in understanding the role of foreign firms in developing economies. The eclectic framework of Dunning (1997) sought to explain the economic rationale behind MNCs' efforts to internationalise operations addressing the advantages of ownership, location and internalisation (OLI), which helped the investigation of technological impact through understanding the motives of relocation. Hence any effort to understand the technological impact of foreign firms on host sites requires at least some knowledge of the motives and characteristics of the foreign firms involved. Natural resources (e.g. Angola, Chile and Liberia), large reserves of literate labour (e.g. China, the Philippines and Bangladesh), domestic markets (e.g. Brazil, China and Mexico), special trading spheres (e.g. Mexico under the North Atlantic Free Trade Area and Cambodia under the ASEAN Free Trade Area), the strength of the local and national innovation systems, including government policy instruments (e.g. Singapore, Israel, Taiwan and Korea), have been important in attracting foreign firms – especially when accompanied by political stability and bureaucratic efficiency (see Dunning and Narula, 2000; Rasiah, 2002a).

Apart from olipolistic advantages driving the expansion of firms to transnationals (see Hymer, 1960, 1972), the growth in the number of cross-border subsidiaries is also driven by efforts to internalise intangible assets – embodied and disembodied knowledge – and to appropriate the relative benefits offered by host sites. The social dimension used in the business school in the activities of MNCs was advanced by Dunning (2003: 1–21), who introduced the concept of relational assets, which are intangible assets that are either internalised directly or indirectly through alliances. Relational assets are human-intensive – though they may be embedded or articulated by individuals or organisations (ibid.: 4). Subsumed in this concept are the elements of economic transactions influenced by social relationships, which are referred to as social capital. Relational assets are internalised or appropriated directly or indirectly through participation in business networks – a two-way process of fostering intra-network and inter-firm relational capital (ibid.: 9). These relationships also help enrich human capital, but the diffusion of codified and tacit and experiential knowledge from foreign firms to the local economy is likely to be strong only when the systemic conditions – institutions, density of firms and systemic links (including elements of trust) – are strong.

Since a firm's performance is influenced by its own endowments and conduct, and the nature and degree of coordination with other economic agents, it can be examined according to the taxonomy shown in Table 1.1. Industrial organisation typically states that firms' performance is determined by the structure (or environment, including other economic agents in factor and final markets) in which the firm is located and its conduct (see Bain, 1968; Scherer, 1973, 1980; Greer, 1992). Four related and overlapping literatures – national innovation system (NIS), industrial policy (IP), industrial organisation and the

Business School (BS) – discuss the policy and institutional environment necessary to stimulate learning, innovation and firm-level performance. BS exponents such as Prahalad and Doz (1987), Bartlett and Ghoshal (1989), Birkinshaw et al. (1998), Cantwell and Mudambi (2001) and Andersson et al. (2002) discussed local integration, embeddedness and differentiated subsidiaries on the basis of competence-creating and competence-exploiting conduct of multinational firms. The earliest IP argument in economic literature can be traced to Smith (1776), Hamilton (1791), Mill (1848) and List (1885).[11] NIS examines knowledge production, flows and diffusion involving learning and innovation, which provides a systemic dimension to firms' conduct and performance (Freeman, 1989; Lundvall, 1992; Nelson, 1993; Nelson and Winter, 1982a, 1982b; Dosi, 1982; Pavitt, 1984). IP typically prescribes the trade and technology policy environment to nurture infant firms to competitive status (see Lewis, 1955; Myrdal, 1957; Kaldor, 1957). The institutional embeddedness of learning, innovation and knowledge flows can be viewed better by integrating the value chains approach (Gerrefi, 1994, 2003) and NIS. BS offers a broader exposition of the environment – socio-political and cultural, conduct of affiliates, and the importance of social capital to explain the operations of firms (see Dunning, 1997). The taxonomy used here assumes causation to run both ways.

Institutional and systemic influences can be examined using the proxies of basic infrastructure and high-tech infrastructure and network cohesion. The first and last are particularly important for firms to keep costs and defects low and meet tight delivery times. High-tech infrastructure becomes essential for firms to participate in higher-value-added activities. The NIS and IP literature actively supports government intervention to overcome market failures associated with firms' participation in R&D activities in particular, and the range of related activities such as human resource training beyond schooling, and process technology acquisition and development. Hence the NIS and IP literature advocates interventions for building the high-tech infrastructure necessary to stimulate innovations in firms.

The importance of clusters in creating competitive advantages was noted by Porter (1990, 1998). In addition, Putman (1993) and Enwright (2000) discussed important benefits of spatial clustering of related activities. Guerrieri and Pietrobelli (2003) articulated three specific forms of clusters contending that post-Marshallian clusters will be less locally driven and vertically disintegrated with increasing integration into global production networks. The Marshallian cluster – symptomatic of Emilia Romagna – is characterised by strong inter-firm links and cooperation between numerous small firms of similar size. The mother-firm-driven cluster is defined by the role of one or more of large firms that drive the expansion and participation of firms in the value chain located geographically. Although this development was arguably made famous by the Japanese firms – especially Toyota and subsequently other firms such as Nissan – Markusen (1996) also identified similar developments involving Boeing (in Seattle), Ford, Chrysler and General Motors (the last four in the Detroit cluster). The large hub firms also enjoy strong connections with firms located outside the geographically defined clusters. However, cooperation between competitors in such clusters is generally low. Guerrieri and Pietrobelli (2003: 4) identified a similar cluster around Fiat in Piedmont in Italy. Markusen (1996) defined a third type of cluster, which is driven by subsidiaries of MNCs in offshore locations. The latter may be the most important type of cluster that relates to technological spillover issues involving foreign firms in developing economies. Initial conditions at incorporation, the nature of host-institutional responses and the composition of firms and industries have produced significantly different cluster synergies in the developing economies. Rasiah (2002b) observed the influence of these features within just one country, i.e. Malaysia. Ernst (2003) attempted to examine the differential impact of foreign firms' global production networks in East Asia.

Best (2001) offered a dynamic explication of the concept of clusters when introducing his business model, i.e. the productivity triad. Arguing that dynamic clusters generate techno-diversity, thereby stimulating differentiation and division of labour, which in turn ensures growth and expansion of regions. While a cluster may have considerable density of firms and the requisite institutions, it may not enjoy strong connecting bonds between them. The role of systemic instruments in driving cluster cohesion has been important in the development of dynamic industrial districts. Inter-firm pecuniary relations through sales and purchases is only one channel of inter-firm interactions (Rasiah, 1995). Knowledge flows – rubbing-off effects from the interaction of workers and the movement of tacit and experiential skills embodied in human capital – raise systems synergies (Marshall, 1890; Polanyi, 1997; Penrose, 1959; Dunning, 2003). Open dynamic clusters encourage inter-firm movement of tacit and experiential knowledge embodied in human capital, which, *inter alia*, distinguishes dynamic from truncated clusters (see Best 2001; Rasiah, 2002b). New firms benefited from gaining managerial and technical personnel from older firms in the Silicon Valley irrespective of national ownership. American and Japanese firms hired technical and managerial personnel from old firms in Silicon Valley. Mature firms gain new ideas and processes to ensure continuous organisational change as some old employees are replaced to make way for fresh ones with new ideas, while new firms benefit from the entrepreneurial and technical – tacit and experiential – knowledge to start new firms (Rasiah, 2002b). Saxenian (1994, 1999) offered an impressive documentation of inter-firm movement of human capital, which helped support new firm creation capabilities in Silicon Valley. Rasiah (1994) traced, using detailed case studies, the creation of new local firms through the movement of personnel from foreign electronics firms to local firms in Penang. Despite the relative insignificance of FDI, Mathews (1997), and Guerrieri and Pietrobelli (2003) documented evidence of Taiwanese electronics firms started by former local employees of foreign multinationals. Rasiah (1999), Doner (2000) and Aoki (2001) had argued for the important role of intermediary organisations in strengthening network cohesion – including coordinating demand–supply relations between government, firms and institutions.

The role of government is only received positively by neoclassical frameworks generally when involving the provision of basic infrastructure (e.g. primary schooling, health and sanitation, road and telecommunications and basic utilities). IP and NIS exponents are quick to emphasise the public goods characteristics of high-tech infrastructure such as R&D, training and information communication technology (ICT) and hence argue that government support is necessary to stimulate learning and innovation. Institutions associated with human resource development and R&D often face collective action problems. Private agents are unlikely to participate in market-driven activities when the risks involved are not matched by returns. Moreover, private agents will never be able to appropriate fully gains from new innovations (Mansfield, 1985). Schumpeter (1934), Abramovitz (1956), Kaldor (1957) and Arrow (1962) had argued that interventions in markets are necessary to stimulate participation in welfare-enhancing public goods activities.[12] Training and R&D institutions involve considerable acquisition and diffusion of knowledge, which is a public good in that its consumption by one does not exclude that by others, which was lucidly captured using historical examples involving the development of new technologies in the United States by Wessner (2003). Hence knowledge-appropriating institutions such as universities, R&D labs and technical schools come under the category of public goods. It is well recognised that strong government support initiated technological progress in the Western economies and Japan (see Gerschenkron, 1962; Kaldor, 1967; Johnson, 1982).

Given the public good characteristics of training and R&D, it can be argued that government participation is essential to stimulate firms to engage extensively in human resource training and R&D activities. Government support can take the form of financial incentives or subsidies, launching of training and R&D organisations, and special programmes to build firm–university and firm–public training and R&D relationships. However, as advanced by Dosi (1984) and Pavitt (1984), firms at the bottom of the technology ladder hardly participate in R&D activities. Most developing economies – e.g. Bangladesh, Indonesia, Tanzania – are entrenched at the foot of the technology ladder in manufacturing. Only a few developing economies have developed sufficiently the high-tech institutions – e.g. Korea, Taiwan and

Singapore – to support firms' participation in R&D activities. Hence this book takes the view that product R&D capability will be low in most developing economies. Also, given the eclectic nature of government intervention in these countries, apart from laying the groundwork to attract FDI, government support is unlikely to be strongly correlated with even human resource and process technology capabilities. Nevertheless, network cohesion – often through concentration of basic infrastructure support in export-processing zones – is essential to facilitate firms' efforts to internalise much of the related transactions and coordinate their operations competitively.

The measurement of institutional and systemic influences on exports, productivity and technological capabilities is extremely difficult. Given that firms are likely to relate cohesion to the inherent properties of institutions and other firms rather than separately, it is more appropriate to just introduce one institutional and systemic variable – integrate the overlapping features with systems, cluster or network strength. This would help reduce if not eliminate the problem of double counting and the use of highly related variables. Given that this book seeks to go beyond the market–government dichotomy, network strength arises as a novel means of demonstrating institutional and systemic influences on firms to capture market–government interactions.

Labour market conditions often influence export competitiveness, productivity and technological capabilities, including the relocation of labour-intensive low-value-added activities. Hence the framework of analysis used examines wages and union affiliation. Given the problems associated with the reliability of firm-level data on labour market conditions and the conditioning domestic environment on the limited room enjoyed, trade unions are not necessarily effective instruments for ensuring strong labour conditions. Nevertheless, union incidence does reflect a certain minimum floor for labour welfare in the selected economies. Sabel (1989), Piore and Sabel (1984), Sengenberger and Zeitlin (1991), Sengenberger and Pyke (1991) and Wilkinson and You (1995) offered lucid accounts of the high road to industrialisation where good labour conditions were instrumental in stimulating long-term competitiveness and the converse involving the low road to industrialisation. Ghose (2003) produced statistical evidence involving a study commissioned by the International Labour Organization (ILO) showing positive effects on labour market conditions from outward export orientation. The difference can also be presented as flexible casualisation involving poor labour conditions (see Deyo, 1987) and flexible specialisation involving good labour market conditions (Piore and Sabel, 1984). It is for these reasons wage was preferred over unions as the labour market variable in the statistical regressions. However, given the low incidence of union affiliation in some industries globally (e.g. electronics), and high reserves of surplus labour in several developing economies – including supply of labour with at least secondary school education –

wages may show a mixed relationship with exports and technological capability. Given the high levels of literacy and technical knowledge required of electronics workers – especially in semiconductor assembly – exports are likely to show positive correlation with wages. The same may not hold for technological capability variables since firms may be required to have similar levels of capabilities in related stages and types of production to compete in industries where technology evolves quickly – e.g. electronics. For example, the Philippines offers low wages and yet enjoys a high share of literacy among secondary students among developing economies (see Rasiah, 2002b: Table 2, 2003b). Nonetheless, export market pressures in leather and garments and high-skilled and knowledge-intensive labour in auto parts may produce a positive relationship between exports, technological capabilities and wage. R&D capability may provide an exception as the main focus on process R&D in these countries could have influenced greater involvement of workers in creative decision making.

There is a standing debate on the importance of size on firms' export competitiveness, productivity and technological capabilities. Typical industrial organisation arguments posit that firms achieve competitiveness with a certain minimum efficiency scale (MES), which varies with industries (see Scherer, 1973, 1991; Pratten, 1971). Industries engaged in the manufacture of steel, automobiles and tankers are considered to enjoy scale economies and hence require higher MSE unit production numbers to achieve low unit costs. Where scale is not important – e.g. small-batch machine tools and plastic components – scope rather than scale is considered important (Piore and Sabel, 1984; Rasiah, 1995). Audretsch and Zoltan (1991) and Audretsch (2002) offered pervasive analysis of US data to dispel arguments related to the significance of large size in efficiency and innovative activities. The increasing decomposition and dispersal of production involving information technology industries has made small size very efficient. Given the controversy over the role of size in economic performance and the claims of industrial organisation exponents over MES differences across industries, size is considered to offer a neutral relationship with productivity and export competitiveness.

Industrial specificity has a strong bearing on exports, productivity and technological capabilities. Gerrefi (2002, 2003) offered a useful framework to map industrial influences through producer–buyer-driven value chains. Garments tend to be characterised by buyer-driven chains, while automobiles tend to be defined by producer-driven chains. In addition to the control features involving the main drivers in the value chains, industries also enjoy several other characteristics that often change with time. Increased liberalisation and the removal of the multi-fibre agreement by the end of 2004 have already triggered the closure or relocation of garment firms involving a number of developing economies. Auto parts is closely related to machinery and engineering industries, electronics assembly and test has transformed from being labour-intensive to knowledge-intensive particularly since the 1980s (see Rasiah, 1988; Hobday, 1995; Ernst, 2000a, 2000b, 2000c; Kraemer and Dedrick, 2003) and garments have become strong technology users. The nature of liberalisation seems to be increasingly reducing the number of specialised suppliers involving auto parts in host economies where such capabilities in the past evolved through import-substitution policies with emphasis on local capability development (Veloso and Kumar, 2003). South Africa, Brazil, Mexico, the Philippines and Taiwan are examples (Ofreneo, 2003; Barnes and Lorentzen, 2003; Quadros, 2003). Pharmaceuticals remains R&D-intensive – relying on pockets of R&D capabilities and raw materials in host economies – and its production technology is highly process-driven. Food processing varies with products – from high-volume, resource-dependent fruit packing by foreign firms (e.g. Del Monte and Chiquita) to small-scale bakeries. Even in fruit packing and wholesaling tensions have broken out between the packaging and distributing firms and supermarkets dealing with final sales (see Dolan and Humphrey, 2000). Mytelka (1999) and Mytelka and Farinelli (2000) offered greater focus on the elements and relationships that differentiate and define innovation networks, arguing persuasively that the so-called sunset or traditional industries such as garment and wine pro-ducing have become knowledge-intensive. Hence the empirical chapters in the book will either examine the relationships between exports, productivity and technological capability by ownership within industries, or use industry dummies as control variables in statistical analysis.

In light of the problems associated with measuring spillovers, two alterna-tive but related methodologies are advanced here. The first draws from past works and is the most simple and straightforward, albeit it does not help statistical estimations given the costs of amassing large data sets. The case studies, while proving costly if representative samples are pursued, are rich and help unravel dynamic relationships that do not often appear in large surveys. Although such an approach is often considered not representative of wider populations, its efficacy on the chosen firms cannot be rivalled. Case studies of course range from the simple examples – but with broader cover-age – used by Allen and Donnithorne (1957) and Dunning (1958), to the detailed ones used by Rasiah (1994), Best (2001), Ernst et al. (1998). Al-though all the chapters used case studies at least as the starting point in understanding industry dynamics in the related countries, only Chapter 8 uses this methodology exclusively as its mode of data collection and analysis.

The second methodology uses the technology capability framework, which relies on indexes and statistical methods; its antecedents can be traced to Lall (1992), Lall and Wignaraja (1995), Bell and Pavitt (1995), Westphal et al.

(1990), Ernst et al. (1998), Wignaraja (2002), Figuiredo (2002), Ariffin and Bell (1999); Ariffin and Figuiredo (2003). However, unlike these rich and dynamic frameworks, the methodology used here had to be adapted and simplified to run cross-industry regressions. Common proxies without an overlap between variables had to be computed for the statistical analysis. Hence the statistical methodology used in the empirical chapters required some departure from the rich explorations undertaken in the framework. The adapted framework has its limitations, as some capabilities may have been acquired above the socially optimal opportunity costs. The normalising formula used does not attach particular weights to a given set of proxies and hence may introduce biases. In addition, the cluster, systems or network strength variable requires subjective assessments by companies. Nevertheless, since the measurements use estimations of data drawn wholly from firms, these biases are outside the control of analysts and hence can be subsumed under the usual problem associated with data collection in general. Importantly, the approach allows to some extent the estimation of latent spillovers, the extent of realisation of which will depend, *inter alia*, on the absorptive capacity of the domestic environment.

Using the two methodologies introduced above, the empirical chapters in the book seek to test the hypothesis that FDI originating from superior NIS are generally endowed with higher export and technological capabilities than local firms, and hence offer developing economies strong latent capacity to stimulate technology transfer. Because participation in product R&D activities requires superior domestic institutions R&D support infrastructure, foreign firms typically retain such activities at home sites, and hence might demonstrate inferior product R&D capabilities than local firms. Nevertheless, foreign firms are expected to utilise host-site personnel to participate strongly in process R&D activities, and some levels of product diversification and proliferation activities where at least a minimal amount of R&D infrastructure exists – e.g. Brazil, South Africa and Malaysia. The case study approach allows an assessment of technology transfer and spillovers in Costa Rica, which is not possible in the statistical analysis using the survey data.

1.4 THE SETTING

Selection of economies was made on the basis of high FDI participation in manufacturing and varying levels of network, cluster or systems strength (NIS) to support learning and innovation in firms. While the former was easy to observe, the latter was not possible beyond the measurement of institutional proxies at the outset of the study. Hence the proxies of basic and high-tech infrastructure became the initial basis for locating the economies

Table 1.2   Economic and institutional position of economics selected for study, 1999

	Continent	Per capita income (US$)	BI	HI	FDI in manufacturing
Brazil	L. America	7037	0.375	0.101	Moderate
Costa Rica	L. America	8860	0.391	NA	High
Indonesia	Asia	2857	0.117	NA	Moderate
Kenya	Africa	1022	0.003	NA	High
Malaysia	Asia	8209	0.342	0.041	High
South Africa	Africa	8908	0.309	0.230	High
Uganda	Africa	1167	0.003	0.003	High

Notes: BI and HI refer to basic and high-tech infrastructure indexes computed using proxies (see Rasiah, 2003c for the proxies and the formula used to compute BI and HI). BI and HI vary between 0 and 1 with Italy and Japan holding the highest score of 1 in 1999; NA – not available.

Source: Computed from World Bank (2002).

on the institutional technology ladder (see Table 1.2). The adoption of the first criterion is obvious and extensively discussed in past literature. The second criterion of selection took cognisance of the contributions of evolutionary and institutional economics. The strength and embeddedness of local and national innovation systems have an important influence on the conduct of both foreign and local firms, and hence will have a bearing on exports, productivity and technological capability development. Interviews by the authors involving industry associations, three firms from each industry, officials from relevant government institutions – basic, high-tech (including R&D) institutions – was used to define the questions to capture network strength (connections and coordination between firms and institutions) (see also Table 1.3).

Given the focus on examining technological capabilities across a set of developing economies against varying degrees of strength of national innovation systems with specific focus on individual clusters, the countries were selected on the basis of strong participation of FDI (especially in manufacturing), the strength of high-tech infrastructure and per capita income levels. Malaysia, Brazil, South Africa and Costa Rica were selected on the basis of reasonable national innovation support strength (see Table 1.3) and fairly high FDI levels in GFCF (gross fixed capital formation – see Table 1.4). Indonesia, Kenya and Uganda were selected on the basis of missing institutions and poor systems strength. Peru was considered in this category but had

Table 1.3   Taxonomy of national (and local) innovation strength of selected economies, 2003

Missing and weak institutions	Weak institutions	Fairly strong institutions but relatively weak links with firms	Selected strong institutions
Uganda and Kenya	Indonesia	Kelang Valley (Malaysia)	Penang (Malaysia) and São Paulo (Brazil), Costa Rica and South Africa
Import of products, equipment and machinery, learning by doing and using	Adaptation and modification of existing technology	Production-related R&D operations. Local firms benefiting from government instruments to undertake R&D	Proliferation, diversification and re-engineering of process and product technology. Isolated applied research and development
Very few firms undertake any kind of R&D	Low levels of R&D participation	Truncated presence of R&D operations in some firms	Rising importance of production-related and re-engineering R&D

Source: Compiled by author (2003).

Table 1.4 Share of net FDI in GFCF, 1990–2000 (%)

	1990	1991	1992	1993	1994	1995	1996	1997	1998	1999	2000
Uganda	0.0	0.2	0.7	11.2	15.0	12.8	12.5	17.3	20.7	21.1	19.6
South Africa	NA	NA	NA	NA	1.8	4.5	3.4	16.1	2.7	7.9	5.1
Malaysia	16.4	22.8	24.4	19.5	14.7	10.9	12.0	12.0	11.2	8.9	7.2
Kenya	3.4	1.2	0.6	0.2	0.3	2.0	0.8	1.2	0.6	0.9	8.4
Costa Rica	10.4	13.9	13.0	12.3	14.1	15.8	22.6	17.6	21.3	25.0	15.1
Brazil	1.1	1.4	2.8	1.4	2.5	3.1	7.0	11.3	19.1	26.5	26.9
Indonesia	3.1	3.7	4.2	4.3	3.8	6.7	8.9	6.8	–2.2	–15.9	–16.6

Source: Compiled from World Bank (2002).

to be dropped owing to logistics problems. Singapore was excluded only because of logistics problems.[13] Among the countries involved, Indonesia and Kenya enjoyed low levels of overall FDI in GFCF in 1999, but their share in manufacturing fixed capital formation was high. FDI accounted for 63 per cent of ownership of manufacturing fixed assets in Kenya in 1999 (Gachino and Rasiah, 2003) and 20 per cent of manufactured exports in Indonesia in 2000.

FDI levels in the period 1990–2000 fluctuated strongly among the sampled economies (see Table 1.4). Uganda had extremely low levels of FDI until 1993 owing to severe macroeconomic failure that gripped the country (see Kasekende, 2000a, 2000b). Institutional failure and political uncertainty in Kenya and improved government–business coordination along with the liberalisation of FDI inflows attracted strong FDI inflows since 1993. In Kenya, after a barren period between 1991 and 1999 when FDI levels fell sharply and stagnated FDI levels rose considerably in 2000 following the introduction of the American-led African Growth Opportunity Act (AGOA) that stimulated FDI inflows into export-processing zones. FDI levels in GFCF rose to a peak in 1997 in South Africa before falling to 5.1 per cent in 2000. Nevertheless, FDI remained a key contributor to manufacturing value added and exports in 2000.

The selection of manufacturing subsectors from the countries was based on the importance of FDI and the contribution of the subsector to manufacturing value added in the economies selected (see Tables 1.5 and 1.6). As with social theory on systems, each industry enjoys its own unique properties to such an extent that it is difficult for policy makers to select one over the other purely on the merits of the internal dynamics of particular industries. Nevertheless, some industries enjoy synergising or clustering properties that help industrial expansion faster than others – e.g. complements such as engineering and electronics and enablers such as information communication technology and new materials. Some industries enjoy natural insulation owing to distance and host sites' natural resource support and cultural dimensions – e.g. agricultural processing and food and beverages. Some industries experienced a decentralisation of production as transnational corporations sought to internationalise operations to take advantage of the low-wage literate labour – e.g. electronics and garments (Frobel et al., 1980). Some industries emerged in particular countries largely as a consequence of deliberate government efforts to promote them – e.g. cars, steel and ships in Korea (see Amsden, 1989). Large domestic markets were important in attracting FDI automobile and parts assemblies into Brazil, Mexico and South Africa.

Table 1.7 shows the industries chosen in the seven countries selected. The dynamics of each of the industries in each country was screened through a profound study of the process flow charts, organisation of machinery and

Table 1.5 Share of manufacturing value added in GDP, 1990–2000 (%)

	1990	1991	1992	1993	1994	1995	1996	1997	1998	1999	2000
Uganda	5.7	5.8	6.2	6.0	6.5	6.8	7.9	8.6	8.9	8.7	9.1
South Africa	23.6	22.9	21.8	21.1	20.9	21.2	20.2	19.9	19.3	18.8	18.8
Malaysia	24.2	25.6	25.8	25.9	26.6	26.4	27.8	28.4	27.4	29.3	32.8
Kenya	11.8	12.2	11.1	10.0	10.7	9.9	10.6	10.2	11.1	12.3	13.1
Costa Rica	21.9	22.8	23.3	22.2	21.7	21.8	22.1	22.4	23.0	28.8	24.4
Brazil	NA	25.3	24.7	25.0	23.7	23.6	22.7	22.8	22.3	23.1	24.0
Indonesia	18.3	14.2	19.1	22.3	23.3	24.1	25.6	26.8	25.0	25.9	26.0

Source: Compiled from World Bank (2002).

Table 1.6 Share of manufactured exports in total exports, 1990–2000 (%)

	1990	1991	1992	1993	1994	1995	1996	1997	1998	1999	2000
Uganda	NA	NA	NA	NA	2.4	4.4	13.0	17.4	5.0	3.4	6.0
South Africa	21.9	24.8	36.4	38.7	39.2	43.5	55.3	57.8	53.7	55.0	54.3
Malaysia	53.8	60.6	64.4	69.7	73.6	74.7	75.7	76.6	78.8	80.4	80.4
Kenya	29.2	20.5	36.4	28.3	28.8	27.6	26.4	25.3	23.6	22.2	20.8
Costa Rica	26.8	24.0	25.2	26.9	26.8	25.1	25.4	42.9	52.9	68.0	65.6
Brazil	51.9	54.9	57.0	58.9	55.1	53.5	53.8	53.7	54.7	54.1	58.5
Indonesia	35.5	40.8	47.5	53.1	51.8	50.6	51.4	42.3	45.0	54.4	57.1

Source: Compiled from World Bank (2002).

25

Table 1.7 Industries selected for study by country, 2001

Country	Sector 1	Sector 2	Sector 3	Sector 4	Sector 5
Uganda	Food and beverages	Machinery and engineering	Textiles and garments	Plastics	Others
South Africa	Auto parts	Electronics	Pharmaceuticals	Food and beverages	Textiles and garments
Malaysia	Auto parts	Electronics	Textiles and garments		
Kenya	Food and beverages	Machinery and engineering	Textiles and garments		
Costa Rica	Electronics	Suppliers			
Brazil	Auto parts	Electronics	Pharmaceuticals	Textiles and garments	
Indonesia	Auto parts	Electronics	Textiles and garments		

Source: Rasiah (2004).

equipment, technical division of labour across the process layout, organisational structure of the firms, and nature of product and market integration, if any, in the global value chain. Case studies involving three firms in each industry in each of the countries constituted the basis for the definition of proxies related to human resource, process and product technology in these industries. Simplifications were unavoidable given the contrast in production and product technology involving the industries – especially food and beverages, auto parts and machinery and engineering. The limited amount of responses from Costa Rica led to the eventual selection of only Intel (electronics) and its suppliers. The focus on only one firm and its suppliers in Costa Rica enabled a more detailed examination of technological capability building involving foreign firms.

1.5   SUMMARY

This book examines exports, productivity and technological capabilities by comparing foreign and local firms. Since inflows of foreign investment directed at technology development are essentially born out of national economic development policy frameworks, efforts to evaluate the role of foreign firms in technology development cannot overlook economic policies. The theoretical basis underlying the analytic framework adopted goes beyond the government versus markets discourse – taking cognisance of the view that the interaction of both is vital for driving change in local and national systems to stimulate learning and innovation in firms. Given the problems associated with measuring spillovers involving large data sets, the empirical chapters attempt to examine the potential rather than the actual spillovers that are likely to occur. It is neither possible nor proper to subject foreign firms to actual spillover assessments since the embedding institutional and systemic structures set limits on their appropriation by local economic agents. Hence the empirical chapters will either map detailed case studies to establish dynamic relationships and the potential technological synergies foreign firms offer in relation to local firms, or estimate and compare technological capabilities developed in foreign and local firms. Chapters 2–7 go further to estimate statistically the determinants of export, productivity and technological capabilities.

The selection of economies was based on both relatively high levels of participation of FDI in manufacturing and differences in basic and high-tech infrastructure. The strength of network cohesion was subsequently added in the location of the clusters on the national innovation ladder (see Table 1.3). While the first is obvious, the latter offers a range of examples to test the proposition that the extent of development of technological capabilities in foreign and local firms in developing economies depends considerably on the strength of the local and national innovation system they embed (absorptive capacity).

Using the two methodologies introduced above, the empirical chapters in the book examine the hypothesis that FDI originating from superior NIS are generally endowed with higher export and technological capabilities than local firms, and hence offer developing economies strong latent capacity to stimulate technological capability building. Because participation in product R&D activities requires superior domestic institutions and R&D support infrastructure, foreign firms typically retain such activities at home sites, and hence might demonstrate inferior product R&D capabilities to local firms. Nevertheless, foreign firms are expected to utilise host-site personnel to participate strongly in process R&D activities, and some levels of product diversification and proliferation activities where at least a minimal amount of R&D infrastructure exists – e.g. Brazil, South Africa, Malaysia and Costa Rica.

The rest of the book is organised as follows. Chapters 2, 3 and 4 use empirical evidence and statistical analysis to examine the importance of foreign ownership on labour productivity, export intensity and technological capability in Kenya, South Africa and Uganda respectively. In addition, the chapter on South Africa analyses local sourcing intensities between foreign and local firms. Chapter 5 evaluates differences in technological capabilities between foreign and local firms in Indonesia. Chapter 6 discusses productivity and technological, export and local sourcing intensities between foreign and local firms in Malaysia. Chapter 7 examines the statistical differences and relationships between foreign and local firms in Brazil. Chapter 8 discusses the role of Intel in the creation of small and medium suppliers in Costa Rica.

The empirical chapters offer policy conclusions for the countries involved specifically and developing economies in general. The book is expected to offer a further refining of existing theory and methodology involving foreign firms' role in stimulating learning and innovation in developing economies. In addition to providing new information on the selected countries, the empirical chapters also offer industry-specific dynamics of technology, export, productivity and local sourcing, and the relationships between them that have not been examined in sufficient depth in the past.

NOTES

1. This book takes the view that path-dependent scientific knowledge exists in nature and that human discoveries only quicken its appropriation. This is different from works of art such as music and paintings where similar path-dependence cannot be guaranteed.
2. The term transnational corporation was used by the United Nations Centre for Transnational

Corporations in 1974 at the insistence of Latin American and Caribbean economies who wanted to distinguish foreign-owned transnationals and joint ventures of two or more participating countries established as part of regional integration schemes. The term was earlier advanced by the United Nations Economic and Social Council, which described all enterprises that control assets – factories, mines, sales offices and the like in two or more countries (UNCTC, 1978: 158). In doing so, the book attempts to avert any ideological debate over the selection. Nevertheless, the terms foreign firms and multinationals are used interchangeably in the text.

3. Interviews carried out by the author with 21 foreign entrepreneurs in Kenya and six foreign entrepreneurs in Uganda in the period 4–27 April 2002.
4. See also Kitching (1982: 160).
5. This argument is very similar to Marx (1965) and Luxemburg's (1963) original explication, though exports and backward linkages were not explicitly elucidated by them.
6. Mathews (1996) introduced the accelerator model with strong focus on institutional dynamics which help stimulate faster catch-up through a 'pulling effect' and leapfrogging once a threshold level of capabilities is achieved.
7. Dunning (1997) developed a five-stage investment development path to offer an explanation for relocation and operation strategies of MNCs as economies evolve from the first to the fifth stage of development.
8. See Romer (1986) and Vaitsos (2003) for a critique of the model as a means of demonstrating technical change.
9. The Industrial Technical Research Institute (ITRI), the Science and Technology Programme and the Hsinchu Science Park are three major initiatives the Taiwan government financed to promote R&D (see Lin and Rasiah, 2003).
10. Scitovsky (1964: 72–5) and Rosenstein-Rodan (1984: 214–16) differentiated technical and pecuniary external economies. However, their explication of technical external economies is vague (see Rasiah, 1995: 40).
11. It is believed that Henry VII was the first to introduce industrial policy instruments, which he did to promote manufacturing growth in England in 1485.
12. New growth economists such as Romer (1986) and Lucas (1988) demonstrated these ideas using elegant models.
13. The national consultant engaged became too busy to undertake the survey.

2. Productivity, export and technological differences in Kenya

Rajah Rasiah and Geoffrey Gachino

2.1 INTRODUCTION

Typical of many developing economies, Kenya pursued import-substitution industrialisation since independence in 1963 (Nyong'o, 1988). Although GDP on average grew at over 7.0 per cent per annum in the 'golden economic period' of 1965–72, extensive participation of the public sector behind infant-industry protection instruments in final consumer goods without a focus on capability building to face external competition undermined the country's resources (Coughlin and Ikiara, 1988; Nyong'o, 1988). A number of development finance and industrial training institutions were built to support small and large firms: e.g. Kenya Industrial Training Institute; Kenya Industrial Estates; Industrial and Commercial Development Corporation; Kenya Bureau of Standards; National Council for Science and Technology; and recently Kenya Industrial Property Office (KIPO) (Ikiara, 1988; Enos, 1995).

Liberal instruments were introduced to attract foreign direct investment (FDI): e.g. the Foreign Investment Protection Act of 1964 guaranteed foreign investors the right to transfer profits, dividends and capital out of the country. Inward-oriented policies, low wages, raw materials and politically unstable neighbouring economies (e.g. Uganda) helped attract FDI particularly in the 1960s and 1970s (Kaplinsky, 1978). Textiles and garments, and agro-industries became important recipients of FDI in this period (Leys, 1975, 1996; Langdon, 1978; Kaplinsky, 1978), with food processing and beverages becoming most important since the 1980s.

In contrast to the 1960s and 1970s, in the 1980s the Kenyan economy slowed down substantially: annual GDP and manufacturing output growth rates dipped from 6.2 per cent and 10.3 per cent respectively in 1977–80 to 3.6 per cent and 3.8 per cent respectively in 1981–85 (Gachino, 2003: Table 1). A number of instruments were introduced in the 1990s to stimulate investment to revive GDP growth and employment creation. FDI became a major target as the government introduced the Investment Promotion Council, export schemes that included the enactment of the Export Processing Zones

(EPZ)[1] Act in 1990, the Export Promotion Centre (EPC) and the Export Programmes Office in 1992 (Glenday and Ndii, 2000; Bigsten and Kimuyu, 2002). Glenday and Ndii (2000) argue that these programmes helped raise manufacturing value added from 13 per cent in 1992 to over 20 per cent of GDP in 1996. Hence, although overall FDI levels in gross capital formation (GCF) in Kenya hovered between 0.3 per cent in 1994 and 1.0 per cent in 2000,[2] its commensurate shares in manufacturing were 69.1 per cent in 1994 and 63.0 per cent in 2001.[3]

Apart from anecdotal descriptions of policy instruments and FDI trends in the economy, little work exists comparing technological capabilities of foreign and local firms in Kenya. Gachino and Rasiah (2003) and Gachino (2003) are two exceptions. This chapter seeks to add to this literature and offers an empirical example of a low-income African economy endowed with weak and missing institutions located at the bottom of the development trajectory. Kenya is a low-income economy with relatively strong FDI participation in manufacturing. This chapter examines productivity, export intensity, skills intensity and technological differences between foreign and local firms in the Kenyan food and beverages, metal engineering and textile and garment industries. The three industries were selected on the basis of their high levels of value added. In 1995, the three industries accounted for over 63 per cent of manufacturing value added in Kenya (Kimuyu, 1999). The rest of the chapter is organised as follows. Section 2.2 compares foreign and local firms in Kenyan manufacturing. Section 2.3 introduces the data and methodology used. Section 2.4 examines statistical differences in productivity, export intensity, skills intensity and technological levels between foreign and local firms, and the statistical relationships involving these variables. Section 2.5 concludes.

2.2   ECONOMIC BACKGROUND

Economic stagnation in the mid-1980s and 1990s affected Kenyan industrialisation with consequent effects on labour productivity (see Gachino and Rasiah, 2003). Political and macroeconomic stabilisation in neighbouring economies (especially Uganda) also drew markets and investment away from Kenya. Macroeconomic constraints arising from a collapse in the IMF's structural adjustment package (SAP) introduced in 1986, massive destruction to physical infrastructure from the El Niño rains and weakening of institutions had severely damaged the economy by 1997–98 (Kenya, 1998; Phillips and Obwana, 2000; Todaro, 2000).

The restructuring enforced following liberalisation also meant that since the mid-1980s but especially from the 1990s prevailing firms were restructuring to face external competition. FDI's focus on manufacturing in most African economies shifted from inward orientation to particularly regional markets. MNCs targeting domestic markets in the past typically geared little production towards export markets beyond neighbouring economies (see Narula and Dunning, 2000). Kenya had in the past benefited from relative political stability to dominate exports to the Common Market of East and Central Africa (COMESA) and African exports to the European Union.[4] Kenya still accounted for 42 per cent of COMESA trade and 30 per cent of COMESA exports to the European Union. While the new environment that has emerged since 1995 – a combination of globally driven deregulation following the opening of WTO – is conducive to greater regional market penetration, two major factors have restricted extensive participation by Kenyan firms. First, the emergence of imports – especially from South Africa (after the end of the apartheid regime) – has intensified competition. Second, institutional failure has severely restricted Kenyan firms' capacity to generate efficient exports.[5] Hence, although Kenya introduced a number of instruments to promote FDI and export-oriented industrialisation, manufacturing has stagnated. Among the instruments introduced to promote exports included manufacturing under bond (MUB) in 1986, which was administered by the Investment Promotion Council (IPC) and exempted firms from duties and value added tax, export-processing zones (EPZs) in 1990, Export Promotion Centre and the Export Programme Office (EPO) in 1992 (Kimuyu, 1999; Glenday and Ndii, 2000). Exports from Kenya declined in the period 1994–2001. Interviews suggest that institutional failure in Kenya is so severe that several foreign firms have relocated to neighbouring economies.[6]

Although overall FDI in Kenya was extremely small – accounting for 1 per cent of GFCF in 2000, its participation in manufacturing has been high. Foreign firms continued to enjoy over 60 per cent of fixed capital ownership in the sector between 1994 and 2001 (see Figure 2.1). Despite economic stagnation, foreign firms accounted for over 50 per cent of manufactured exports in the period 1994–2001 (see Figure 2.2).[7]

2.3   METHODOLOGY AND DATA

This chapter uses the technology capability framework advanced in Chapter 1. The national sampling frame was used as the initial basis of the interview survey, which had the support of the Kenyan Bureau of Statistics. However, the poor response rate prevented a strict adherence to the procedure. Hence, although data collection was still carried out randomly, it did not adhere strictly to the original sampling procedure used. The proxies used in section 2.4 were measured and defined as follows.

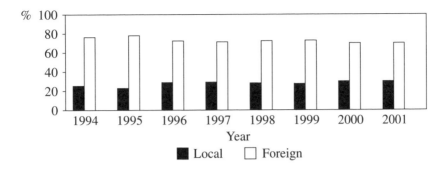

Source: Computed from data compiled from the Ministry of Trade and Industry, Kenya, 2001.

Figure 2.1 Fixed capital by ownership, Kenya, 1994–2001

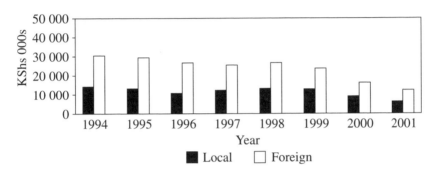

Source: Computed from data compiled from the Ministry of Trade and Industry, Kenya, 2002.

Figure 2.2 Manufactured exports by ownership, Kenya, 1994–2001

2.3.1 Productivity and Export Performance

The proxies of labour productivity and export intensities were used to denote productivity and export performance respectively. Both variables have problems but they do allow useful assessments.

$$\text{Labour productivity} = VA_i/L_i,$$

where *VA* and *L* refer to value added, total employees respectively of firm *i* in 2001.

$$\text{Export intensity} = X_i/Y_i,$$

where X and Y refer to exports and gross output respectively of firm i in 2001. Local firms (64.8 per cent) on average enjoyed higher export incidence than foreign firms (35.2 per cent): the breakdown by industry was 68.6 per cent local and 31.4 per cent foreign in textiles and garments; 47.8 per cent local and 52.2 per cent foreign in metal engineering; and 70.2 per cent local and 29.8 per cent foreign in food and beverages (see Table 2.1).

2.3.2   Technological Capabilities

Firm-level dynamics include minor improvements to machinery and equipment, improved inventory control systems and training methods and R&D strategies. Since a number of characteristics and strategies have overlapping objectives and effects, it is methodologically better to integrate related proxies into a composition of indexes, which will not only help minimise double counting, but also avert multi-collinearity problems in statistical analysis. In addition, adjusting firms' responses involving specific variables, e.g. R&D, will offer a better approximation of its intensity than just any one proxy – e.g. R&D sales as a percentage of overall sales and R&D staff in workforce. Including all the proxies as separate variables can cause multi-collinearity problems. Because there are no *a priori* reasons to attach greater significance to any of the proxies used, the normalisation procedure was not weighted. However, the indirect effects of these proxies would still remain, as the hiring of key R&D scientists or engineers by one firm from another would inevitably have a bearing on its R&D capability. The following broad capabilities and related composition of proxies were used.

Human resource
Two alternative proxies were used to represent human resource. However, human resource capability was used separately to measure human resource practices that denote development in firms, and hence it excluded intensity, technical, professional and skilled human resource endowments in the workforce. The exclusion allows the measurement of human resource capability that is developed by each firm – rather than those that are acquired or poached from other firms.

Human resource practices
Human resource (*HR*) practice is expected to have a positive relationship to process technology and skills intensity. Given the dominance of exports to neighbouring countries, a strong and positive relationship is not expected between *HR* and *X/Y*.

Human resource capability (*HR*) was measured as:

Table 2.1 Distribution of sampled firms by ownership, size and export incidence, Kenyan firms, 2001

	N	Ownership		Size		Export experience	
		FO = 1	FO = 0	S = 1	S = 0	X = 1	X = 0
Textiles and garments	35	11 (31.4)	24 (65.6)	8 (22.9)	27 (77.1)	11 (31.4)	24 (68.6)
Metal engineering	23	12 (52.2)	11 (47.8)	13 (56.5)	10 (43.5)	12 (52.2)	11 (47.8)
Food and beverages	47	14 (29.8)	33 (70.2)	22 (46.8)	25 (53.2)	14 (29.8)	33 (70.2)
Total	105	37 (35.2)	68 (64.8)	43 (41.0)	62 (59.0)	37 (35.2)	68 (64.8)

Note: X refers to export incidence

Source: Tabulated from UNU–INTECH Survey (2002) using Stata Package 7.0.

$$HR_i = 1/3[TM_i, TE_i, CHR_i] \tag{2.1}$$

where *TM*, *TE* and *CHR* refer to training mode and training expense as a share of payroll and cutting-edge human resource practices used. *TM* was measured as a multinomial logistic variable of 1 when staff are sent out to external organisations for training, 2 when external staff are used to train employees, 3 when staff with training responsibilities are on payroll, 4 when a training department is used, 5 when a separate training centre is used and 0 when no formal training is undertaken. *CHR* was measured by a score of 1 for each of the practices and totalled. The firms were asked if it was their policy to encourage team-working, small group activities to improve company performance, multi-skilling, interaction with marketing, customer service and R&D department, lifelong learning and upward mobility. The *HR* score was divided by three, which is the number of proxies used. The proxies were normalised using the formula below:

$$\text{Normalisation score} = (X_i - X_{min})/(X_{max} - X_{min}), \tag{2.2}$$

where X_i, X_{min} and X_{max} refer to the minimum and maximum values respectively of the related proxy of firm *i*.

Skills intensity
Skills intensity (*SI*) was used separately to capture the effects of different shares of managerial, professional, engineering, technical and supervisory personnel in the workforce. *SI* was measured as:

$$SI = H_i/L_i,$$

where *H* and *L* refer to managers, professionals, engineers, technicians and supervisors, and total employees respectively in 2001 of firm *i*.

Process technology capability
Process technology (*PT*) – being central to participation in export markets even in low-value-added operations – can be expected to show a positive relationship with exports and *HR*. The same can also be expected with R&D since process improvements dominate early participation in R&D activities.

Data on four proxies facilitated the computation of *PT*, which was calculated using the formula:

$$PT_i = 1/4[EM_i, PTE_i, ITC_i, QC_i] \tag{2.3}$$

where *EM*, *PTE*, *ITC* and *QC* refer to equipment and machinery, process technology expenditure as a share of sales, information technology components and quality control instruments respectively of firm *i*. *EM* was computed as multinomial logistic variable with average age of over five years = 0, three to five years = 1, two to less than three years = 2 and less than two years = 3. Likert scale scores ranging from 1 to 5 (least to most) were used to measure *ITC*. *QC* was measured as a dummy variable (*QC* = 1 if cutting-edge methods were used, *QC* = 0 otherwise). *PT* was divided by four, which is the number of proxies used.

R&D capability

The learning process leads firms to participate eventually in new product development. While beginners only learn and absorb, firms typically hire R&D personnel to learn and develop new products as they get closer to the technology frontier (Pavitt, 1984; Dosi, 1982). With the exception of funding of public labs and universities, firms seldom participate in basic research. Hence, firm-level R&D is largely focused on process technology and product development – especially diversification of use and proliferation. Given Kenya's underdeveloped institutional and systemic facilities and the preponderance of labour-intensive assembly and processing operations, R&D is unlikely to produce statistically meaningful results involving export intensity. The R&D focus on process technology changes in low-value-added food and beverages, metal engineering, textiles and garments and other manufacturing, is expected to produce a positive relationship between *RD* and *PT*.

The data collected enabled the computation of two R&D proxies, i.e. R&D expenditure as a percentage of sales and R&D personnel as a share of employment. It was not possible from the sample data to disentangle investment advanced between process and product R&D, and hence this proxy was measured to relate to both product and process R&D as:

$$RD_i = 1/2[RD_{\text{exp}i}, RD_{\text{emp}i}], \tag{2.4}$$

where RD_{exp} and RD_{emp} refer to R&D expenditure as a share of sales and R&D personnel in the workforce respectively of firm *i*. RD was divided by two, which is the number of proxies used.

Other technology variables

Three additional technological variables were computed when examining the statistical relationships involving *HR*, *PT* and *RD* to avert problems of multicollinearity between them (see Appendix 2.1).

$$HRT_i = [HR_i + PT_i]. \tag{2.5}$$

HRT refers to technological influences of human and process technology resources of firm *i*.

$$HRD_i = [HR_i + RD_i]. \tag{2.6}$$

HRD refers to technological influences of human and R&D technology resources of firm *i*.

$$PRDi = [PT_i + RD_i]. \tag{2.7}$$

PRD refers to technological influences of process and R&D technology resources of firm *i*.

Wages
Wages was used to represent labour market conditions. Union was dropped owing to reasons advanced in Chapter 1. Moreover, there were only nine firms that had unionized workers in 2001 (see Table 2.1).

Overall technological intensity
Overall technological intensity (*TI*) was estimated by simply adding the components *HR*, *PT* and *RD*, and was measured as:

$$TI_i = HR_i + PT_i + RD_i$$

It is now clear why *HR*, *PT* and *RD* were divided by the number of proxies used, which is to facilitate the computation of *TI* by giving equal weight to all three components.

Given the premium involving skilled and knowledge workers, a positive relationship can be expected between productivity and wages. Average monthly wages were used. Since it is difficult to obtain wages of workers on their own, it was measured by dividing total salaries and remuneration by the workforce. Average wages in million Kenyan shillings per year was used in all the regressions and was measured as:

$$W_i = S_i/L_i,$$

where *W* and *S* refer to wages per worker and total monthly salary bill respectively of firm *i*.

Other critical firm-level variables

Four other important firm-level structural variables were included in the analysis, i.e. ownership, size, management type and age. Merger and acquisition was dropped because it involved only seven firms. Export-processing zone (EPZ) was also dropped owing to the few firms involved.

Ownership There were only five joint-venture firms in the sample and all of them had 50 per cent foreign equity. The classifications of whether any foreign equity or at least 50 per cent foreign was involved would not matter as a consequence. Ownership was measured as:

$$FO_i = 1 \text{ if foreign equity ownership of firm } i \text{ was 50 per cent or more;}$$
$$FO = 0 \text{ otherwise,}$$

where FO refers to status of ownership of firm i. Using this classification, there were 37 (35.2 per cent) foreign and 68 (64.8 per cent) local firms: the breakdown by industry was 11 (31.4 per cent) foreign and 24 (68.6 per cent) local in textiles and garments; 12 (52.2 per cent) foreign and 11 (47.8 per cent) local in metal engineering; and 14 (29.8 per cent) foreign and 33 (70.2 per cent) local in food and beverages (see Table 2. 1).

Size There were only three firms with employment size exceeding 500, which is understandable given the low capacity utilisation rates caused by economic stagnation in Kenya. Hence medium firms with employment size exceeding 100 were added to large firms, and hence the variable S representing this category. Size was measured as:

$$S_i = 1 \text{ if employment size exceeded 100; } S_i = 0 \text{ otherwise,}$$

where S refers to size of firm i. Using this definition, small firms (59.0 per cent) still exceeded the number of large firms (41.0 per cent): the breakdown by industry was 77.1 per cent small and 22.9 per cent large and medium in textiles and garments; 43.5 per cent small and 56.5 per cent large and medium in metal engineering; and 53.2 per cent small and 46.8 per cent large and medium in food and beverages (see Table 2.1).

The variables of management type and age were dropped owing to a lack of any statistical influence, and the stepwise regressions were used to drop them.

Specific industry-level questionnaires were designed, pilot tested and mailed to all firms listed in official government statistics records in Kenya. In addition, the authors distributed and collected some questionnaires personally. Case studies of at least three firms in each industry were undertaken by the authors to help extract industry-type characteristics. The survey and the case studies constitute the basis for the results and analysis in the chapter.

The data collected are presented in Table 2.1. A total of 150 questionnaires was distributed personally by the authors. The response rate was high (around 80 per cent) owing to the support from the Central Bureau of Statistics. The analysis here used 105, which contained complete responses. The breakdown by industry was 35 textile and garment, 23 metal engineering and 47 food and beverage firms. The breakdown by ownership and size was 37 foreign and 68 local firms, and 43 large and medium, and 62 small firms respectively. Of the total, 37 enjoyed export experience, while the remaining 68 only sold in the domestic market.

2.3.3   Statistical Analysis

Two-tail t-tests were used to examine if statistically significant differences involving *VA/L*, *X/Y* and *SI*, and the technology variables of *TI*, *HR*, *PT* and *RD* existed between foreign and local firms. Two-tail tests were preferred over one-tail tests owing to the possibility of the means of foreign firms (H_0) being less or more than that of local firms (H_1) (see Kmenta, 1971; Gujarati, 1988).

The following models were specified to estimate the statistical relationships involving labour productivity, and export and technological intensities. OLS regressions were used when the dependent variable was value added per worker. Tobit regressions were preferred when export intensity, skills intensity and the technological variables were used because they are censored both on the right and the left sides of the data sets. The models were run with industry dummies:

$$\text{OLS: } VA/L = \alpha + \beta_1 X/Y + \beta_2 TI + \beta_3 FO + \beta_4 W + \beta_5 S + \mu \qquad (2.8)$$

$$\text{Tobit: } X/Y = \alpha + \beta_1 TI + \beta_2 FO + \beta_3 W + \beta_4 S + \mu \qquad (2.9)$$

$$\text{Tobit: } TI = \alpha + \beta_1 X/Y + \beta_2 SI + \beta_3 FO + \beta_4 W + \beta_5 S + \mu \qquad (2.10)$$

$$\text{Tobit: } HR = \alpha + \beta_1 X/Y + \beta_2 SI + \beta_3 PRD + \beta_4 FO + \beta_5 W + \beta_6 S + \mu \qquad (2.11)$$

$$\text{Tobit: } PT = \alpha + \beta_1 X/Y + \beta_2 HRD + \beta_3 FO + \beta_4 W + \beta_5 S + \mu \qquad (2.12)$$

$$\text{Tobit: } RD = \alpha + \beta_1 X/Y + \beta_2 HRT + \beta_3 FO + \beta_4 W + \beta_5 S + \mu \qquad (2.13)$$

Regressions (2.8)–(2.13) were repeated using foreign and local firm samples separately. All independent variables that showed problems of multi-collinearity

– either statistically or through overlapping composition with other independent variables – were dropped (see Appendix 2.1).

2.4   STATISTICAL RESULTS

The methodology employed produced interesting results. Significant differences existed between foreign and local firms especially involving overall technology and human resource index variables, and foreign ownership was also an important determinant of labour productivity and technology and human resource intensity. The lack of convergence prevented an assessment of the sample by foreign and local firms. All tests easily passed the White test of heteroscedacity.

2.4.1   Statistical Differences

The two-tail *t*-test results are shown in Table 2.2. It can be seen that foreign firms enjoyed statistically very significantly higher labour productivity means than local firms in textile and garment manufacturing. The differences were not statistically significant in the metal engineering and food and beverage industries. Foreign firms enjoyed statistically significant higher export intensity means than local firms in the textile and garment, and metal engineering industries. The results show that foreign firms were more productive and export-intensive than local firms in textile and garment manufacturing. Foreign firms were more export-intensive than local firms in metal engineering. Foreign firms enjoyed statistically significant higher skills intensity only in food and beverages. There was no statistically meaningful difference between foreign and local firms in the remaining industries.

The results involving *TI* were statistically significant, with foreign firms enjoying higher means than local firms in all industries, though the margin was not very high in metal engineering. Decomposing *TI* into *HR*, *PT* and *RD* produced interesting results too. Foreign firms enjoyed statistically significant higher human resource intensities in metal engineering and food and beverages. Given that skilled labour was not used as a component, it demonstrates clearly higher HR practices in foreign firms than in local firms in these industries. Foreign firms enjoyed statistically significant and higher process technology intensity means than local firms only in textile and garment manufacturing. Foreign firms enjoyed statistically significant and higher RD means than local firms in textile and garment, and food and beverage industries.

Interestingly, foreign firms enjoyed higher means in all the statistically significant results involving labour productivity, export intensity, skills intensity and technological intensity. Despite the presence of stand-alone firms,

Table 2.2 *Two-tail t-test results comparing foreign and local firms, Kenya sample, 2001*

	Foreign	Local	t		Foreign	Local	t
VA/L				**TI**			
Textiles and garments	3.248	0.688	3.76*	Textiles and garments	1.198	0.732	3.44*
Metal engineering	0.314	0.404	–0.67	Metal engineering	0.878	0.625	1.88***
Food and beverages	1.599	0.907	1.51	Food and beverages	1.097	0.709	2.79*
X/Y				**HR**			
Textiles and garments	0.284	0.112	2.17**	Textiles and garments	0.381	0.351	0.43
Metal engineering	0.476	0.177	2.07**	Metal engineering	0.331	0.176	2.77*
Food and beverages	0.237	0.131	1.21	Food and beverages	0.461	0.245	3.23*
W				**PT**			
Textiles and garments	0.073	0.136	1.30	Textiles and garments	0.456	0.203	4.00*
Metal engineering	0.058	0.174	–1.30	Metal engineering	0.275	0.278	–0.06
Food and beverages	0.124	0.094	0.49	Food and beverages	0.399	0.315	1.55
SI				**RD**			
Textiles and garments	0.715	0.685	0.38	Textiles and garments	0.363	0.175	2.55*
Metal engineering	0.597	0.651	–0.66	Metal engineering	0.275	0.172	1.12
Food and beverages	0.568	0.418	2.14**	Food and beverages	0.236	0.150	1.70***

Notes: *, ** and *** – significant at 1%, 5% and 10% levels respectively.

Source: Computed from UNU–INTECH Survey (2002) using Stata Package 7.0.

the results tend to conform to expectations. Local firms in underdeveloped locations generally lack the technological capabilities to match the technologies foreign firms have access to from foreign locations.

2.4.2   Statistical Relationships

This section presents the statistical relationships involving the critical explanatory variables. The results presented in Tables 2.3 and 2.4 easily passed the White test for heteroscedasticity. The results involving the Tobit regressions on *TI*, *HR*, *PT* and *RD* by ownership samples are not reported since all of them did not converge. The industry dummies used were also not reported in the tables.

Labour productivity and export intensity
TI enjoyed a statistically strong and positive relationship with *VA/L* in all three regressions, its coefficient well exceeding 1 (see Table 2.3). Clearly technology intensity is highly correlated with labour productivity. The coefficient is much stronger with foreign firms than with local firms, suggesting more productive utilisation of technology in the former than the latter. Export intensity was statistically insignificant in both the overall and foreign firms' sample, but was inversely correlated with labour productivity in the local firms' sample. The inverse relationship could be a result of external markets offering lower margins than domestic markets. The control variable of age was statistically significant only in the overall sample and its coefficient negative but small, suggesting a marginal influence over labour productivity. Size was inversely correlated with labour productivity in the overall and foreign firms' sample. The high coefficient of *S* showed that large and medium firms were less productive than small firms. Whereas small firms are lean and often flexible enough to switch production from one product to another, medium and large firms lack these features, especially under circumstances of economic stagnation, which affected capacity utilisation rates in Kenya.

The results were somewhat different for export intensity. Regressions involving the local firms' sample did not converge. *TI* did not enjoy a statistically significant relationship with *X/Y*, owing to export specialisation in sub-Saharan regional markets where both competition and technological demand are relatively low. Size was positively correlated with export intensity in the overall sample, and though statistically insignificant, its coefficient in the foreign firms' sample was also positive. Medium and large firms tend to enjoy higher export intensity than small firms. *FO* was positively correlated with export intensity, showing that foreign firms were more export-intensive than local firms.

Table 2.3   Labour productivity and export intensity, Kenya sample, 2001

	VA/L			X/Y		
	All	Foreign	Local	All	Foreign	Local
X/Y	−0.226	0.397	−0.850			
	(−0.50)	(0.44)	(−2.10)**			
TI	2.525	2.822	1.737	0.116	0.071	0.121
	(7.87)*	(4.60)*	(5.58)*	(0.66)	(0.31)	(0.42)
S	−0.647	−0.816	−0.096	0.376	0.565	0.313
	(−2.32)**	(−1.18)	(−0.41)	(2.39)**	(2.02)**	(1.44)
FO	0.403			0.223		
	(1.39)			(1.45)		
W	0.374	1.449	0.475	−0.174	−4.672	0.239
	(0.56)	(0.79)	(0.96)	(−0.44)	(−1.77)***	(0.54)
μ	−0.710	−0.128	−0.534	−0.404	0.100	−0.457
	(−2.12)**	(−0.14)	(−2.04)**	(−2.00)**	(0.27)	(−1.69)***
N	105	37	68	105	37	68
F, χ^2	13.50*	6.50*	7.80*	24.81*	13.24**	5.62**
R^2	0.494	0.565	0.434			
Adj. R^2	0.457	0.479	0.379			

Notes: *, ** and *** – significant at 1%, 5% and 10% levels respectively; figures in parentheses refer to *t* ratios.

Source: Computed from UNU–INTECH Survey (2002) using Stata Package 7.0.

Technological intensity

Tobit regressions involving technological variables produced interesting results (see Table 2.4). The results of the industry dummy variables were not reported in the tables. Regressions involving the disaggregated samples by ownership did not converge and hence the results are not reported here. The lack of correlation between *TI* and *X/Y* is confirmed with the reversed equation. *FO* was positively correlated and statistically highly significant, showing that foreign firms enjoy higher technological intensity than local firms, which is consistent with the *t*-test results reported earlier in the chapter. *TI* was positively correlated with *SI*, but its influence was marginal. Higher shares of human capital are necessary to drive technical change. Size was positively correlated with *TI*, suggesting that large and medium firms enjoyed higher technological intensity than small firms.

X/Y was inversely correlated with *HR*, which is likely to be spurious given that much of the limited exports generated actually go to neighbouring markets where demand patterns are similar to Kenya. *FO* enjoyed a statistically highly significant and positive relationship with *HR*, showing that foreign

Table 2.4 Technological intensity, Kenya sample, 2001

	TI	HR			PT			RD		
		All	Foreign	Local	All	Foreign	Local	All	Foreign	Local
X/Y	0.026 (0.19)	-0.109 (-1.69)***	-0.208 (-2.02)**	-0.022 (-0.28)	0.055 (1.02)	0.133 (1.67)***	-0.047 (-0.70)	0.143 (1.60)	0.102 (1.35)	0.177 (1.35)
SI	0.004 (2.04)**	0.003 (4.00)*	0.003 (1.43)	0.003 (4.21)						
PTD		0.135 (2.27)**	0.339 (3.31)*	0.041 (0.54)						
HRD					0.296 (5.6)*	0.345 (4.55)*	0.252 (3.63)*			
HPT	0.218 (2.66)*	0.038 (0.96)	-0.057 (-0.71)	0.074 (1.63)	0.023 (0.69)	0.062 (1.01)	0.057 (1.51)	0.280 (3.27)*	0.276 (2.58)*	0.213 (1.58)
S	0.295 (3.54)*	0.107 (2.65)*	0.176 (0.84)	0.163 (1.67)***	0.027 (0.77)	0.015 (0.10)	0.096 (1.19)	0.070 (1.26)	-0.026 (-0.28)	0.152 (2.12)**
FO	0.090 (0.44)	0.154 (1.67)***			0.049 (0.61)			0.033 (0.57)		
W	0.476 (3.44)*	0.023 (0.33)	-0.039 (-0.24)	0.064 (0.91)	0.076 (1.95)***	0.150 (1.91)***	0.048 (1.11)	-0.241 (-1.58)	-0.387 (-1.21)	-0.153 (-0.85)
U								-0.002 (-0.04)	0.137 (1.14)	-0.026 (-0.30)
N	105	105	37	68	105	37	68	105	37	68
χ^2	33.23*	40.47**	15.91**	29.54*	46.34*	24.37*	30.90*	28.97*	11.88***	13.70**

Notes: *, ** and *** – significant at 1%, 5% and 10% levels respectively; figures in parentheses refer to t ratios. The TI regressions by foreign and local firms' samples were statistically insignificant for interpretation (χ^2 was statistically insignificant).

Source: Computed from UNU–INTECH Survey (2002) using Stata Package 7.0.

firms are better endowed with *HR* practices than local firms. Size and wages were positively correlated with *HR*, demonstrating that medium and large firms and firms paying higher wages were better endowed with *HR* practices. *PTD* was positively correlated with *HR*, which is expected given the close relationship between choice of techniques and R&D focus and the requisite *HR* practices. Age was positively correlated but its influence was marginal.

Age and *HRD* enjoyed statistically significant results with *PT*. Foreign ownership was not statistically significant here. Age was inversely correlated but its influence was marginal. *HRD* was statistically highly significant, which is expected given that the choice of process technology employed is strongly related to *HR* practices and R&D activities. *HR* in particular is the prime influence here since firms in Kenya are little engaged in R&D activities

Only *HRT* enjoyed a statistically significant relationship with *RD*. The weakly developed R&D capabilities in Kenyan firms obviously meant that it enjoyed little statistically meaningful relationship with the explanatory variables. *RD* intensity as expected enjoyed strong relationship with *HR* expenses and practices, and process technology.

Taken together, foreign firms were more productive, and export- and technology-intensive than local firms. Foreign firms enjoyed substantially higher labour productivity and were more export-oriented in textiles and garments than local firms. Foreign firms were also more export-oriented in metal engineering. Foreign firms enjoyed higher *TI* in all three industries. Foreign firms had higher *HR* means than local firms in metal engineering and food and beverages, *PT* means in textiles and garments, and *RD* means in textiles and garments, and food and beverages. The econometric exercise showed that foreign ownership was positively correlated with *TI* and *HR*. The higher coefficient of *TI* in the foreign firms' sample compared to the local firms' sample showed that foreign firms' technology influenced labour productivity more than local firms. Local firms enjoyed higher value added in domestic markets rather than export markets. Export intensity enjoyed a positive relationship in the *PT* regressions, but an inverse one in the *HR* regressions in the foreign firms' sample.

2.5   CONCLUSIONS

Kenya presented an interesting case of an underdeveloped economy with high amounts of FDI in manufacturing. Despite its poor infrastructure, low overall FDI levels in GCF and macroeconomic weaknesses since 1986, ownership in the manufacturing sector is still dominated by foreign ownership. However, economic stagnation and weak institutions forced firms to face poor market – factor and final demand – conditions. Despite these problems, the analysis in the chapter produced interesting results that can serve as assessment material for Kenya and other economies with similar endowments.

The statistically significant *t*-test results showed that foreign firms were more productive, export-intensive and technology-intensive than local firms. Foreign firms enjoyed substantially higher labour productivity, and were also more export-oriented in textiles and garments than local firms. Foreign firms were also more export-oriented in metal engineering. Foreign firms clearly enjoyed higher overall technology intensity in all three industries. Foreign firms had higher *HR* means than local firms in metal engineering and food and beverages, *PT* means in textiles and garments, and *RD* means in textiles and garments, and food and beverages.

Foreign ownership enjoyed a statistically significant and positive relationship with *TI* and *HR*. The regressions by ownership showed that firms' reliance on firm-level technology is higher in the foreign firms' sample as its coefficient was much higher than in the local firms' sample. Local firms enjoyed higher value added in domestic than in export markets. Export intensity enjoyed a positive relationship in the process technology regressions, but an inverse one in the human resource regressions in the foreign firms' sample. Overall, the significant Kenyan results suggest that foreign firms' technology, productivity and export intensity levels in economies with weak institutions tend to be superior to those of local firms.

It is still early to draw policy conclusions from Kenya's experience, given that much of sub-Saharan Africa remains politically uncertain. However, the Kenyan experience shows that foreign firms' technology, productivity and export intensity levels in economies with very low development tend to be superior to those of local firms. Although a panel study is necessary to confirm the results, the results of this study do show that foreign firms' productive, export intensity and technological superiority can be harnessed by governments to stimulate spillovers. The careful promotion of entrepreneurs with affordable loans and access to infrastructure as well as stepping up of the supply of human capital and high-tech infrastructure may offer local firms the fillip to benefit from demonstration effect, competition and markets arising from the participation of foreign firms.

NOTES

1. A detailed analysis of EPZ in Kenya is provided in Ikiara and Odhiambo (2001).
2. Computed from the World Bank (2002).
3. Computed from data supplied by the Ministry of Trade and Industry, Nairobi.
4. COMESA was formed in 1994 to promote regional integration. It had a membership of 20 countries in 2003.

5. Kenyan firms also faced a nominal interest rate of 20 per cent and severe failures afflicting power supply, road infrastructure and telecommunication in 2002 (interviews by Rasiah and Gachino, 4–16 April 2002).
6. Interviews conducted by Rasiah and Gachino in Nairobi and Kampala, 4–16 April 2002.
7. Computed from data supplied by the Ministry of Trade and Industry, Nairobi.

APPENDIX 2.1

Table 2A.1 Correlation matrix of independent variables, Kenya sample, 2001

	HR	RD	PT	X/Y	A	S	SI	PTD	HRD	HRT	TI	FO	W
HR	1.000												
RD	0.175	1.000											
PT	0.356	0.466*	1.000										
X/Y	-0.037	0.239	0.164	1.000									
A	0.075	0.017	-0.210	-0.165	1.000								
S	0.179	0.165	0.166	0.273	-0.271	1.000							
SI	0.359#	0.132	-0.039	0.082	0.049	0.045	1.000						
PTD	0.304	0.873*#	0.839*#	0.239	-0.104	0.190	0.062	1.000					
HRD	0.779*#	0.754*#	0.533*	0.125	0.062	0.221	0.324#	0.758*#	1.000				
HRT	0.851*#	0.376	0.794*#	0.069	-0.068	0.208	0.213	0.669	0.806*#	1.000			
TI	0.704*#	0.733*#	0.785*#	0.158	-0.043	0.227	0.217#	0.890	0.937*#	0.906*#	1.000		
FO	0.291	0.304	0.289	0.324	-0.014	-0.035	0.144	0.347	0.386	0.351	0.396	1.000	
W	0.098	-0.146	0.005	-0.093	-0.042	-0.083	-0.007	-0.086	-0.028	0.068	-0.017	-0.092	1.000

Note: * high correlation; # overlapping composition.

Source: Computed from UNU–INTECH Survey (2002) using Stata Package 7.0.

49

3. Technology, local sourcing and economic performance in South Africa

Rajah Rasiah and Thabo Gopane

3.1 INTRODUCTION

South Africa is the largest and richest economy in sub-Saharan Africa. It has enjoyed a long history of inward-oriented industrialisation where firms were forced to manufacture a number of critical goods during the apartheid regime following the imposition of economic sanctions. In addition, unlike most parts of Africa, South Africa enjoys fairly strong effective demand, and basic and science and technology (S&T) infrastructure. Since intensified liberalisation from the 1990s a number of firms have rationalised to orient manufacturing to global markets.

Increasing liberalisation had forced considerable rationalisation in South Africa's manufacturing industry. The auto parts industry has seen the closure of inefficient firms but strong efficiency improvements in the surviving firms from external competition and the widening of markets from exports (Black, 2001). Wood (2003) argued that the liberalisation trend on balance has worked favourably for the textile and garment, auto parts and steel industries in South Africa, but that incoherent policy signals have reduced the potential for attracting FDI into the country. Gelb (2002) provided evidence of positive contributions from the operations of foreign firms. Barnes and Lorentzen (2003) discussed the significance of foreign firms in automobile value chains.

This chapter attempts to add to the above literature and offer an African example of a middle-income economy with fairly developed high-tech infrastructure by examining technology, local sourcing and performance of foreign and local firms in the auto parts, electronics, textile and garment, pharmaceutical and food industries in South Africa. The rest of the chapter is organised as follows. Section 3.2 discusses the growing importance of FDI and export manufacturing in South Africa. Section 3.3 presents the methodology and data. Section 3.4 examines technological characteristics of the firms in the sample and compares the productivity, exports, skills and technological and local sourcing intensities of foreign and local firms, and the statistical relationships involving them. Section 3.5 concludes.

3.2   FDI TRENDS AND EXPORT MANUFACTURING

FDI played a leading role in the development of manufacturing in South Africa in the first half of the twentieth century. However, by the 1980s FDI levels had fallen sharply following international pressures exerted owing to its apartheid policies. Two major developments helped revive FDI inflows to South Africa, i.e., constitutional discussions in 1990 that led to the abolition of the apartheid regime, and a shift in trade policy regime following the 1994 elections towards greater liberalisation and outward orientation.

However, official statistics still showed relatively low levels of FDI in gross capital formation (GCF) in South Africa. Between 1994 and 2000, FDI levels rose to a peak of 16.1 per cent in 1997 before falling to 5.1 per cent in 2000 (see Figure 3.1). Although the overall shares are relatively low, FDI operates strongly in manufacturing. Foreign companies have considerable participation especially in the automobile, pharmaceuticals, electronics, textile and garment and food-processing industries – the four industries chosen for examination in this chapter.

The share of manufacturing value added in GDP has fluctuated slightly since 1960, reaching a peak of 23.9 per cent in 1984 before gradually falling to 18.8 per cent in 2000 (see Figure 3.1). The export share of manufacturing

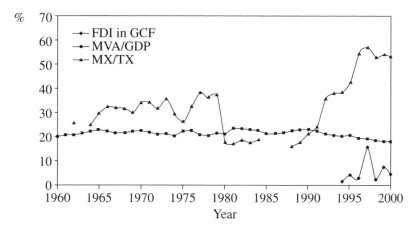

Notes: FDI – foreign direct investment; GCF – gross capital formation; MVA – manufacturing value added; MX – manufactured exports; TX – total exports.

Source: Computed from World Bank (2002).

Figure 3.1   FDI, and manufacturing value added and exports, South Africa, 1960–2000

rose gradually from the 1960s until 1979, falling sharply thereafter before rising strongly from 1984 to reach a peak of 55.0 per cent in 1999. Markets still dominate foreign firms' choice of South Africa as a location (including regional markets in the African continent) (see Gelb, 2002), though natural resources and the relatively high human capital endowments have been instrumental in stimulating R&D activities (e.g. pharmaceuticals and food processing). South Africa obviously enjoys an institutional structure that is far superior to that of the poorer economies of Africa such as Kenya, Uganda, Tanzania and Congo to support stronger learning and innovation activities. It is against this economic background that the chapter will examine differences in productivity, and export, technological and local sourcing intensities between foreign and local firms in South Africa.

3.3   METHODOLOGY AND DATA

This chapter uses the technological capability framework advanced in Chapter 1. Overall, 179 firms responded to the interview survey, but 31 responses were dropped owing to incomplete information for analysis. Although the national sampling frame was not used, data collection was carried out randomly. The proxies used in section 3.4 were measured and defined as follows.

3.3.1   Productivity and Export Performance

The proxies of labour productivity and export intensities were used to denote productivity and export performance respectively. Both variables have problems but they do allow useful assessments.

$$\text{Labour productivity} = VA_i/L_i$$

where *VA* and *L* refer to value added and total employees respectively of firm *i* in 2001.

$$\text{Export intensity} = X_i/Y_i,$$

where *X* and *Y* refer to exports and gross output respectively of firm *i* in 2001.

3.3.2   Technological Capabilities

Firm-level technology include efficiency and age of machinery and equipment, inventory and quality control systems and training methods and R&D strategies. Since a number of characteristics and strategies have common effects, related proxies were integrated into technological indexes which will not only help minimise double counting, but also avert collinearity problems in statistical analysis. The following broad capabilities and related composition of proxies were used.

Human resource

Two alternative proxies were used to represent human resource. However, human resource capability was used separately to measure human resource practices that denote development in firms, and hence it excluded the share of technical, professional and skilled human resource in workforce. The exclusion allows the measurement of human resource capability that is developed by each firm – rather than those that are acquired or "poached" from other firms.

Human resource capability

Human resource (HR) is expected to have a positive relationship to skills intensity.

Human resource practices (HR) was measured as:

$$HR_i = 1/3[TM_i, TE_i, CHR_i] \qquad (3.1)$$

where TM, TE and CHR refer to training mode and training expense as a share of payroll and cutting-edge human resource practices used. TM was measured as a multinomial logistic variable of 1 when staff are sent out to external organisations for training, 2 when external staff are used to train employees, 3 when staff with training responsibilities are on payroll, 4 when a separate training department is used, 5 when a separate training centre is used and 0 when no formal training is undertaken. CHR was measured by a score of 1 for each of the practices. The firms were asked if it was their policy to encourage team-working, small group activities to improve company performance, multi-skilling, interaction with marketing, customer service and R&D department, lifelong learning and upward mobility. HR was divided by three, which is the number of proxies used. The proxies were normalised using the formula below:

$$\text{Normalisation score} = (X_i - X_{min})/(X_{max} - X_{min}), \qquad (3.2)$$

where X_i, X_{min} and X_{max} refer to the ith, minimum and maximum values respectively of the proxy X.

Skills intensity

Skills intensity (*SI*) was used separately to capture the effects of different shares of managerial, professional, engineering, technical and supervisory personnel in the workforce. *SI* was measured as:

$$SI = H_i/L_i,$$

where *H* and *L* refer to managers, professionals, engineers, technicians and supervisers, and total employees respectively in 2001 of firm *i*.

Process technology capability

Process technology (*PT*) – being central to participation in export markets even in low-value-added operations – can be expected to show a positive relationship with exports and *SI*.

Four proxies facilitated the computation of *PT*, which was calculated using the formula:

$$PT_i = 1/4[EM_i, PTE_i, ITC_i, QC_i] \tag{3.3}$$

where *EM*, *PTE*, *ITC* and *QC* refer to equipment and machinery, process technology expenditure in sales, information technology components and quality control instruments respectively of firm *i*. *EM* was computed as multinomial logistic variable with average age of over five years = 0, three to five years = 1, two to less than three years = 2 and less than two years = 3. Likert scale scores ranging from 1 to 5 (least to most) was used to measure *ITC*. *QC* was measured as a dummy variable (*QC* = 1 if cutting-edge methods were used, *QC* = 0 otherwise). *PT* was divided by four, which refers to the number of proxies used.

R&D capability

In contrast to Kenya, the relatively stronger high-tech institutions in South Africa can be expected to support more R&D activities, albeit much of it is likely to be confined to improvements in process technology and product enhancement activities.

The data collected enabled the computation of two R&D proxies, i.e. R&D expenditure as a percentage of sales and R&D personnel as a share of employment. It was not possible from the sample data to disentangle investment advanced between process and product R&D, and hence this proxy was measured to relate to both product and process R&D and was measured as:

$$RD_i = 1/2[RD_{expi}, RD_{empi}], \tag{3.4}$$

where RD_{exp} and RD_{emp} refer to R&D expenditure as a share of sales and R&D personnel in workforce respectively of firm i. RD was divided by two owing to the use of the two proxies.

Overall technological intensity

Overall technological intensity (*TI*) was estimated by simply adding the components *HR*, *PT* and *RD*, and was measured as:

$$TI_i = HR_i + PT_i + RD_i$$

As noted in chapter 2, *HR*, *PT* and *RD* were divided by the number of proxies used to facilitate the computation of *TI* by giving equal weight to all three components.

Other technology variables

Three additional technological variables were computed when examining the determinants of *HR*, *PT* and *RD* to avert problems of collinearity between them but were dropped owing to collinearity problems (see Appendix 3.1). Independent variables were dropped on the basis of compositional overlaps and when correlations were high (R 0.4).

$$HRT_i = [HR_i + PT_i] \tag{3.5}$$

HRT refers to technological influences of human and process technology resources of firm i.

$$HRD_i = [HR_i + RD_i] \tag{3.6}$$

HRD refers to technological influences of human and R&D technology resources of firm i.

$$PRD_i = [PT_i + RD_i] \tag{3.7}$$

PRD refers to technological influences of process and R&D technology resources of firm i.

Wages

Wages was used to represent labour market conditions. Union was dropped owing to reasons advanced in Chapter 1. Moreover, interviews showed that union density in firms with unionised workers in South Africa varied significantly. Given the premium involving skilled and knowledge workers, a positive relationship can be expected between productivity and wages (see Ghose,

2003). Average monthly wages were used. Since it is difficult to obtain wages of workers on their own, it was measured by dividing total salaries and remuneration by the workforce. Average wages in thousand rand per month was used in all the regressions and was measured as:

$$W_i = S_i/L_i,$$

where W and S refer to wages per worker and total monthly salary bill respectively of firm i.

Local sourcing

There is a long-standing debate on the role of local sourcing in foreign exchange implications, backward linkages and the diffusion of knowledge in the domestic economy. Several studies have attempted to examine the impact of foreign firms on local sourcing with mixed results (e.g. Hirschman, 1958; Lall and Streeten, 1977). The nature of data used here does not provide a time trend and its impact on the diffusion of knowledge involving the domestic economy as examined by Rasiah (1995). Nevertheless, it provides the usual measure of local share in inputs purchased. Local sourcing is measured as:

$$LS_i = DI_i/TI_i,$$

where LS, DI and TI refer to local sourcing, domestic inputs and total inputs respectively of firm i.

Because foreign firms – especially with transnational operations – are thought to enjoy superior connections to best-practice suppliers abroad, their relative import shares are considered higher than those involving local firms. Export-oriented firms – especially when targeted to developed economies – generally require higher-quality supplies. Hence export intensities in developing economies such as South Africa may be inversely correlated with local sourcing. With the exception of auto parts, among the four industries examined in the chapter, small and medium firms tend to enjoy less access in export markets and hence are likely to be positively correlated with local sourcing.

Other critical firm-level variables

Four other important firm-level structural variables were included in the analysis, i.e. ownership, size, age and management type.

Ownership Foreign ownership was defined using equity share of 50 per cent or more. Using this criterion, foreign ownership in the sample was highest in the electronics industry (75.0 per cent of 16 firms), followed by pharmaceuticals (56.3 per cent of 16 firms), auto parts (41.9 per cent of 31 firms) and textiles and garments (23.1 per cent of 26 firms) (see Table 3.1). Ownership was measured as:

$$FO_i = 1 \text{ if foreign equity ownership of firm } i \text{ was 50 per cent or more;}$$
$$FO = 0 \text{ otherwise,}$$

where *FO* refers to status of ownership of firm *i*.

Size   A neutral hypothesis was framed linking size with productivity, and export and technological intensities. The theoretical justification for this un- clear relationship was advanced in chapter 1. This hypothesis is also useful for the analysis here since most firms have employment size of fewer than 500 employees. Also, given that the industries chosen in this chapter are broad, firm specialisation – which varies with the type of products made – is difficult to separate by scale and scope.

Owing to most firms having relatively small employment levels, the fol- lowing two categories of size were chosen, i.e. small and medium, and large, and was measured as a dummy variable:

$$S_i = i \text{ when employment size was 300 or more; } S_i = 0 \text{ otherwise,}$$

where *S* refers to size of firm *i*. In spite of using 300 employees as the cut-off point, small and medium firms still dominated the auto parts, electronics, food and beverages and pharmaceutical samples (see Table 3.1). Large firms accounted for more than half the firms only in textile and garments.

Age   Given that firms with longer experience are considered to enjoy greater experiential and tacit knowledge, age is considered to provide a positive relationship with exports and technological capabilities. The absolute age of the firm is used as an independent variable. The statistical relationship may not be positive if foreign firms using superior technology from abroad and enjoying strong access to global markets began establishing or relocating operations recently. Age was measured as:

$$A_i = \text{years in operation of firm } i,$$

where *A* refers to age of operation of firm *i*.

Owner-managed firms   It is often argued that owner-managers impact both positively and negatively on firms' performance. On the one hand, owners are

Table 3.1 Breakdown of firms, South Africa sample, 2001

	Foreign	Local	Large size		Export experience		Owner-managed firms		Patents		Total firms
			Foreign	Local	Foreign	Local	Foreign	Local	Foreign	Local	
Auto parts	35	20	6 (17.1)	8 (40.0)	17 (48.6)	17 (85.0)	17 (48.6)	8 (40.0)	33 (94.3)	15 (75.0)	55
Electronics	29	4	0 (0.0)	0 (0.0)	7 (24.1)	4 (100.0)	17 (58.6)	4 (100.0)	17 (58.6)	3 (75.0)	33
Food and beverages	4	11	0 (0.0)	1 (9.1)	4 (100.0)	7 (63.6)	4 (100.0)	11 (100.0)	4 (100.0)	9 (81.8)	15
Pharmaceuticals	18	4	0 (0.0)	0 (0.0)	6 (33.3)	0 (0.0)	15 (83.3)	0 (0.0)	16 (88.9)	0 (0.0)	22
Textiles and garments	29	4	18 (62.1)	4 (100.0)	14 (48.3)	0 (0.0)	26 (89.7)	4 (100.0)	26 (89.7)	4 (100.0)	33
Total	105	43	24 (22.9)	13 (30.2)	46 (43.8)	28 (65.1)	79 (75.2)	27 (75.2)	96 (91.4)	31 (72.1)	148

Note: Figures in parentheses refer to incidence.

Source: Tabulated from UNU–INTECH Survey (2002) using Stata 7.0 package.

considered to show greater drive to succeed owing to lower agency costs, and can make quicker decisions. On the other hand, owner-managers are considered to be less professional, especially when involving big businesses, and hence may lack the instruments to succeed in export markets. Hence a neutral hypothesis with either a positive or a negative sign is expected. There were more local firms with owner-management compared to foreign firms: 17 local (34.7 per cent of 49 firms) and four foreign (10.0 per cent of 40 firms) (see Table 3.1). *OM* is measured using a dummy variable as follows:

$$OM_i = 1 \text{ if firm is managed either partly or fully by the owner;}$$
$$OM = 0 \text{ otherwise,}$$

where *OM* refers to status of management of firm *i*.

3.3.3 Statistical Analysis

The following models were specified to estimate the statistical relationships involving labour productivity, and export intensity. OLS regressions were used when the dependent variable was value added per worker. Tobit regressions were preferred when export, skills, local sourcing and technological intensities were used because they are censored both on the right and the left sides of the data sets. The models were run with industry dummies:

OLS: $VA/L = \alpha + \beta_1 X/Y + \beta_2 TI + \beta_3 S + \beta_4 FO + \beta_5 W + \beta_6 OM$
$$+ \beta_7 A + \mu \tag{3.8}$$

Tobit: $X/Y = \alpha + \beta_1 TI + \beta_2 S + \beta_3 FO + \beta_4 W + \beta_5 OM + \beta_6 A + \mu \tag{3.9}$

Tobit: $SI = \alpha + \beta_1 X/Y + \beta_2 TI + \beta_3 S + \beta_4 FO + \beta_5 W + \beta_6 OM$
$$+ \beta_7 A + \mu \tag{3.10}$$

Tobit: $LS = \alpha + \beta_1 X/Y + \beta_2 TI + \beta_3 S + \beta_4 FO + \beta_5 W + \beta_6 OM$
$$+ \beta_7 A + \mu \tag{3.11}$$

Tobit: $TI = \alpha + \beta_1 X/Y + \beta_2 SI + \beta_3 S + \beta_4 FO + \beta_5 OM + \beta_6 A + \mu \tag{3.12}$

Tobit: $HR = \alpha + \beta_1 X/Y + \beta_2 SI + \beta_3 S + \beta_4 PRD + \beta_5 FO + \beta_6 W$
$$+ \beta_7 OM + \beta_8 A + \mu \tag{3.13}$$

Tobit: $PT = \alpha + \beta_1 X/Y + \beta_2 HRD + \beta_3 S + \beta_4 FO + \beta_5 W + \beta_6 OM$
$$+ \beta_7 A + \beta_8 SI + \mu \tag{3.14}$$

Tobit: $RD = \alpha + \beta_1 X/Y + \beta_2 HRT + \beta_3 S + \beta_4 FO + \beta_5 W + \beta_6 OM$
$$+ \beta_7 A + \beta_8 SI + \mu \tag{3.15}$$

Regressions (3.8)–(3.15) were repeated using foreign and local firm samples separately.

Questionnaires were both mailed and supplied directly to manufacturers by McRade, which is a South African consultant company located in Johannesburg. A total of 148 filled questionnaires was obtained through both channels. Case studies of at least three firms in each industry were undertaken by the authors to help extract industry-type characteristics. The survey and the case studies constitute the basis for the results and analysis in the chapter. Industry dummies were included in all the regressions but the results are not reported here.

3.4   DATA AND RESULTS

The survey netted 105 foreign and 43 local firms with a fairly high incidence of export experience: 46 (43.8 per cent) foreign firms and 28 (65.1 per cent) local firms (see Table 3.1). Foreign firms enjoyed greater export experience than local firms in food and beverages, pharmaceuticals and textiles and garments. Local firms enjoyed higher export experience in auto parts and electronics. Interestingly, the incidence of owner-managed firms in the sample was very high. Owner-managed firms were high in the foreign food and beverage (100.0 per cent), textile and garment (89.7 per cent), pharmaceuticals (83.3 per cent) and electronics (58.6 per cent) firms. Owner-managed firms were also high in local food and beverage (100.0 per cent), electronics (100.0 per cent) and textile and garment (100.0 per cent) firms.

The strong human capital and resource endowments of South Africa seem to have influenced a high incidence of patent take-up among both foreign and local firms. The percentages were high for all industries except for pharmaceuticals, where local firms reported no new-approved patents (see Table 3.1). Local pharmaceuticals firms reported producing drugs using licences from foreign companies, and that all their sales go to the domestic market. In addition to the patents reported in the sample, foreign firms reported first applying for their initial patents abroad owing to a highly cumbersome mechanism used in South Africa. It is interesting to note that foreign firms use local universities (e.g. Stellenbosch, Cape Town and Witwatersrand) to undertake R&D on a number of drugs.[1]

3.4.1 Statistical Differences

This section examines if there are statistically significant differences between foreign and local firms in labour productivity, export-intensity, skills-intensity and technological capabilities. Differences in technological capabilities are examined using *TI*, and its components *HR*, *PT* and *RD*. As mentioned earlier, South Africa is likely to produce results unique to a middle-income economy. In addition to its developed infrastructure and fairly large domestic market, South Africa is likely to attract significant levels of foreign high-tech operations owing to its fairly strong human capital endowments.

The *t*-tests on labour productivity, wages, and export, skills, local sourcing and technological intensities produced interesting results (see Table 3.2). Labour productivity differences were only statistically significant involving pharmaceuticals firms and only at the 10 per cent level: foreign firms enjoyed a higher productivity level than local firms. Although the mean of foreign firms was slightly higher for all the industries examined, with the exception of pharmaceuticals firms, there were no obvious productivity differences by ownership. Export intensity differences were statistically significant involving auto parts (5 per cent level) and pharmaceuticals (10 per cent level): local firms enjoyed higher intensity in auto parts but lower intensity in pharmaceuticals. None of the local pharmaceutical firms in the sample exported, but the export intensity of foreign firms was also extremely low.

Differences in skills intensity levels were only statistically significant involving the electronics, food and beverages and pharmaceutical firms. Local firms enjoyed a statistically significant higher mean than foreign firms in electronics (at the 1 per cent level) and food and beverages (at the 5 per cent level). Foreign firms enjoyed a statistically significant higher mean than local firms in pharmaceuticals (at the 10 per cent level).

Differences in the mean wage levels between foreign and local firms were statistically significant in the electronics (at the 5 per cent level) and textile and garment (at the 10 per cent level) industries. Local firms enjoyed higher wages than foreign firms in electronics, while the reverse held with textile and garment firms. Foreign firms enjoyed a slightly higher mean than local firms in pharmaceuticals (at the 1 per cent level) and textiles and garments (at the 10 per cent level).

The overall technological intensity (*TI*) of pharmaceuticals firms was statistically significant at the 5 per cent level, with foreign firms showing higher intensity than local firms. The main sources of foreign firms' lead over local firms in pharmaceuticals were in *PT* and *RD* capabilities. Foreign firms enjoyed a statistically significant higher mean in R&D capabilities and a statistically significant lower mean in *HR* capabilities than local firms in textile and garments. Local firms enjoyed a statistically significant higher *PT*

Table 3.2   Two-tail t-tests of productivity, export intensity and technology intensity, South Africa sample, 2001

	Foreign	Local	t		Foreign	Local	t		Foreign	Local	t
VA/L#				**TI**				**TE**			
Auto parts	17.328	14.130	1.01	Auto parts	1.417	1.556	−1.42	Auto parts	0.389	0.540	−2.50**
Electronics	15.062	13.430	0.48	Electronics	1.593	1.340	1.00	Electronics	0.558	0.500	0.64
Food & beverages	14.493	13.435	0.40	Food & beverages	1.533	1.580	−0.34	Food & beverages	0.575	0.545	0.25
Pharmaceuticals	14.383	11.548	1.71***	Pharmaceuticals	1.401	1.103	2.42**	Pharmaceuticals	0.583	0.650	−0.63
Textiles & garments	15.401	14.000	0.32	Textiles & garments	1.461	1.340	0.93	Textiles & garments	0.534	0.700	−1.54
X/Y				**HR**				**PTE**			
Auto parts	0.117	0.202	−2.35**	Auto parts	0.458	0.465	−0.12	Auto parts	0.567	0.716	1.80***
Electronics	0.099	0.170	0.97	Electronics	0.642	0.529	1.38	Electronics	0.518	0.331	1.27
Food & beverages	0.350	0.182	1.28	Food & beverages	0.696	0.662	−0.59	Food & beverages	0.472	0.466	0.04
Pharmaceuticals	0.065	0.000	1.23	Pharmaceuticals	0.626	0.770	−1.49	Pharmaceuticals	0.593	0.171	3.26*
Textiles & garments	0.121	0.000	1.69***	Textiles & garments	0.638	0.888	−3.27*	Textiles & garments	0.447	0.260	1.27
W+				**PT**				**RDE**			
Auto parts	3.735	5.344	−1.33	Auto parts	0.514	0.632	−2.46**	Auto parts	0.100	0.110	−0.78
Electronics	4.045	6.887	−2.31	Electronics	0.449	0.381	0.54	Electronics	0.109	0.110	−0.04
Food & beverages	4.473	4.248	0.17	Food & beverages	0.452	0.449	0.04	Food & beverages	0.093	0.101	−0.32
Pharmaceuticals	2.653	1.046	2.98*	Pharmaceuticals	0.358	0.101	2.53**	Pharmaceuticals	0.111	0.025	3.62*
Textiles & garments	1.755	0.821	1.75***	Textiles & garments	0.440	0.346	1.27	Textiles & garments	0.116	0.050	3.02*
SI				**RD**				**LS**			
Auto parts	0.349	0.347	0.07	Auto parts	0.446	0.464	−0.30	Auto parts	0.611	0.666	−0.80
Electronics	0.372	0.538	−2.92*	Electronics	0.502	0.430	0.69	Electronics	0.385	0.460	−0.79
Food & beverages	0.215	0.374	−2.43**	Food & beverages	0.383	0.467	0.83	Food & beverages	0.378	0.385	−0.07
Pharmaceuticals	0.414	0.325	1.71***	Pharmaceuticals	0.418	0.230	3.21*	Pharmaceuticals	0.445	0.843	−3.78*
Textiles & garments	0.343	0.355	−0.22	Textiles & garments	0.383	0.100	3.39*	Textiles & garments	0.395	0.510	−1.30

Note: *, ** and *** refer to 1, 5 and 10% levels of significance, respectively; # in 10 000 rand per month; + 1000 rand per month.

Source: Computed from UNU-INTECH Survey (2002) data using State 7.0 Package.

mean than foreign firms in auto parts. A further decomposition of the technology variables was also undertaken given the significance attached to expenditures on training (*TE*), process technology (*PTE*) and R&D (*RDE*). Local firms enjoyed a statistically significant higher mean in *TE* (at the 5 per cent level) and *PTE* (at the 10 per cent level) expenditures as a share of sales than foreign firms in auto parts. Foreign firms enjoyed a statistically significant higher mean than local firms in pharmaceuticals in *PTE* and *RDE* (at the 1 per cent level). Foreign firms also enjoyed a statistically highly significant mean than local firms in textiles and garments in *RDE* (at the 1 per cent level).

Although local firms enjoyed a higher mean than foreign firms, local sourcing intensity was only statistically significant in pharmaceuticals (at the 1 per cent level). Interviews[2] show that this is partly accounted for by the purchase of older machinery and equipment by local firms from foreign firms. The higher overall means achieved by local firms is also largely a consequence of foreign firms accessing inputs and components from their global supply chains and from their own subsidiaries.

Overall, the statistically significant results were mixed. Only in pharmaceuticals did foreign firms enjoy a slightly higher labour productivity mean than local firms. Local firms generally enjoyed a higher export intensity mean than foreign firms in auto parts, but it was the reverse in pharmaceuticals. Local firms enjoyed a higher skills intensity mean than foreign firms in electronics and food processing. Local firms generally paid higher wages than foreign firms in the electronics industry, but it was the opposite in pharmaceuticals, and in textiles and garments. Foreign firms enjoyed a higher overall technological intensity mean than local firms only in pharmaceuticals. Local firms generally enjoyed higher local sourcing intensities than foreign firms across all four industries, but this was statistically significant only in pharmaceuticals. Foreign firms enjoyed a higher process technology and R&D mean than local firms in pharmaceuticals, and textiles and garments. Foreign pharmaceutical firms use South Africa both as a resource base as well as a centre to harness the R&D capabilities developed in local universities. Foreign textile and garment firms are engaged in buyer-driven chains, where product and process development has increasingly become centralised among manufacturers rather than brand holders (see Gerrefi, 2002). Local firms enjoyed a higher *HR* mean than foreign firms in textiles and garments, and *PT* mean in auto parts. Local firms have responded to competition and rationalisation by investing more in training and process technology to compete with foreign firms and imports in auto parts.

3.4.2   Statistical Relationships

Having identified statistical differences involving the sample data by owner-ship in the previous section, this section evaluates the relationship involving labour productivity, export and skills, technological and local sourcing intensities controlling for wages, age, management type, size and ownership.

Productivity, exports, skills and local sourcing
Table 3.3 presents the econometric results establishing the statistical relation-ships involving labour productivity, export intensity and skills intensity by models (3.8), (3.9), (3.10) and (3.11) formulated in section 3.3. These re-gressions were also run using ownership samples. With the exception of the foreign sample involving model (3.10) above, not only were the overall model fits (*F*-stats) of the remaining models statistically significant; all the regressions also easily passed the Cook–Weisberg tests for heteroscedascity.

Against labour productivity as the dependent variable, *TI* was statistically highly significant (at the 1 per cent level) and its coefficient was positive and strong, demonstrating a strong link between technology and productivity (see Table 3.3). *FO* was statistically insignificant. While the link between *TI* and *VA/L* were also statistically highly significant (at the 1 per cent level) and positive involving both sets of firms, the relationship was stronger involving local firms demonstrating a higher technology-productivity propensity in-volving local firms. Wages was also statistically highly significant in the overall and local firms' samples, and their coefficients strong and positive. Wages was statistically insignificant in the foreign firms' sample. Size was inversely correlated and statistically significant in the overall and foreign firms' samples, demonstrating that smaller firms were more productive than larger firms.

Skills intensity produced similar relationships involving *TI* and wages, suggesting that productivity levels in local firms are driven by employees paid higher wages for their higher skills intensity levels. However, the coeffi-cient of *TI* in the foreign firms' sample was marginal and wages was also statistically insignificant. *FO* was statistically insignificant. Size was statisti-cally significant in the overall and local firms' samples, but the coefficient was positive, demonstrating that larger firms enjoyed higher skills intensities than smaller firms.

The explanatory variable of *TI* was statistically insignificant when involv-ing export intensity, though the coefficients were positive. The foreign firm sample also did not converge to provide a statistically significant model fit (χ^2). Only wages among the independent variables was statistically signifi-cant. Its coefficient was positive and significant at the 5 per cent level, showing a positive link between wages and export orientation in local firms.

Table 3.3 *Statistical relationship involving productivity, skills, export and local sourcing intensities, South Africa sample, 2001*

	Labour productivity			Skills intensity			Export intensity			Local sourcing		
	All	Foreign	Local	All	Foreign	Local	All	Foreign	Local	All	Foreign	Local
X/Y	−0.612 (−0.15)	−0.3116 (−0.53)	−1.174 (−0.35)	0.058 (0.89)	0.073 (0.94)	−0.126 (−1.34)				0.059 (0.48)	0.168 (1.08)	0.122 (0.65)
TI	7.876 (3.88)*	7.870 (2.90)*	9.095 (5.56)*	0.078 (2.45)**	0.066 (1.85)**	0.382 (2.58)**	0.047 (0.62)	0.102 (0.86)	0.017 (0.16)	−0.046 (−0.77)	0.048 (0.67)	−0.404 (−4.39)
S	−7.212 (−3.86)*	−10.667 (−4.39)*	−1.489 (−0.42)	0.064 (2.17)**	0.010 (0.30)	0.312 (3.12)*	0.047 (0.67)	−0.055 (−0.55)	0.328 (1.36)	−0.107 (−1.95)**	−0.020 (−0.31)	−0.412 (−2.05)**
FO	1.058 (0.71)			−0.013 (−0.57)			0.009 (0.16)			−0.118 (−2.73)*		
OM	0.315 (0.18)	−1.552 (−0.69)	4.985 (1.31)	0.035 (1.29)	−0.021 (−0.72)	0.085 (0.90)	0.108 (1.58)	−0.012 (−0.12)	0.108 (0.45)	0.015 (0.29)	0.067 (1.12)	0.116 (0.54)
A	0.085 (1.91)***	0.099 (1.86)***	0.032 (0.34)	0.000 (1.29)	0.000 (0.28)	−0.006 (−2.43)**	−0.002 (−1.11)	−0.002 (−0.92)	−0.016 (−2.50)**	−0.002 (−1.56)	−0.002 (−1.59)	0.011 (2.05)**
W	2.596 (2.48)*	0.152 (0.32)	1.179 (6.54)*	0.008 (2.10)**	−0.002 (−0.34)	0.019 (2.43)**	0.020 (2.35)**	0.002 (0.09)	0.049 (3.56)*	−0.006 (−0.88)	−0.015 (−1.20)	−0.018 (−1.65)
μ	1.978 (0.61)	6.985 (1.60)	−7.920 (−3.44)*	0.161 (3.14)*	0.260 (4.49)**	−0.370 (−1.87)***	−0.118 (−0.93)	−0.095 (−0.50)	−0.086 (−0.50)	0.842 (8.86)*	0.588 (5.09)*	1.354 (10.05)*
N	148	105	43	148	105	43	148	105	43	148	105	43
F, χ²	7.14*	4.36*	28.90*	31.57*	18.66***	79.76*	24.11*	12.29**	39.44*	48.18*	30.62*	47.75*
R²	0.366	0.317	0.900									
Adj. R²	0.315	0.244	0.869									

Notes: *, ** and *** refer to 1, 5 and 10% levels of significance respectively. Industry dummies were used but their results are not reported here.

Source: Computed from data compiled from UNU–INTECH (2002) Survey using Stata 7.0 Package.

Age was the only other variable statistically significant but only in the local firms' sample and its influence was negative and marginal.

Against *LS*, *FO* was statistically highly significant and its negative coefficient shows that foreign firms sourced at significantly lower levels than local firms. Interestingly, *TI* was statistically highly significant in the local firms' sample, but its negative coefficient shows that local sourcing is much higher in firms with lower technology-intensity levels. It is likely that local firms lack high-technology supplies domestically and hence rely more on imports involving such items. In addition, the statistically significant and inverse relationship involving size in the overall but especially in the local firms' sample obviously shows that smaller local firms source more locally than larger local firms.

Technological intensities

Table 3.4 presents the econometric results establishing the statistical relationships involving *TI*, *HR*, *PT* and *RD* using models (3.12)–(3.15) formulated in section 3.3. These regressions were also run using ownership samples. Apart from the *PT* regressions involving the foreign sample, not only was the overall model fit (χ^2-stats) statistically significant; all the regressions also easily passed the Cook–Weisberg as well as the White tests for heteroscedascity. The results involving the *PT* regressions failed the chi-square statistics owing to a lack of convergence.

Against *TI*, the explanatory variable of *X/Y* was statistically insignificant, though its coefficient was positive in all three samples. The variables of *SI*, *S*, *OM* and *W* were statistically significant. *FO* was statistically insignificant in the overall sample. *SI* was statistically significant in all three samples, and its coefficients were positive. *SI* exerted a far stronger influence on *TI* in the local firms' sample than in the other samples, demonstrating that skills intensity levels have a strong impact on the overall technology levels in local firms. Size enjoyed an inverse relationship, with far stronger influence in the local firms' sample than in the foreign firms sample. Smaller firms enjoyed higher technological intensities in all the samples. Owner-managed firms enjoyed higher technological intensities in the overall and foreign firms' samples. Wages enjoyed a statistically significant positive relationship (at the 5 per cent level) in the overall sample, but was negative and highly significant (at the 1 per cent level) in the local firms' sample. In addition, age was highly significant in the local firms' sample.

FO was statistically highly significant at the 1 per cent level in the *HR* regressions. Its negative coefficient shows that local firms enjoy higher human resource practices than foreign firms. The negative relationship between *X/Y* and *HR* in the overall sample is likely to be spurious owing to foreign firms' reliance on domestic markets rather than exports. The coefficient of

Table 3.4 *Statistical relationship involving technological intensities, South Africa sample, 2001*

	TI			HR			PT			RD		
	All	Foreign	Local	All	Foreign	Local	All	Foreign	Local	All	Foreign	Local
X/Y	-0.056	0.086	0.471	-0.131	-0.110	0.053	0.066	0.074	0.228	0.127	0.120	0.088
	(0.33)	(0.41)	(1.59)	(-1.78)***	(-1.40)	(0.43)	(0.62)	(0.56)	(1.50)	(1.34)	(0.97)	(0.59)
SI	0.538	0.495	2.463	0.031	0.018	0.706	0.352	0.334	1.280	0.143	0.105	0.104
	(2.52)*	(1.87)***	(5.37)*	(0.33)	(0.18)	(3.09)*	(2.63)*	(2.03)**	(5.50)*	(1.20)	(0.68)	(0.46)
S	-0.215	-0.205	-1.129	-0.023	-0.031	0.157	-0.014	0.008	-0.567	-0.162	-0.176	-0.457
	(-2.90)*	(-2.41)**	(-3.68)*	(-0.70)	(-0.95)	(1.02)	(-0.31)	(0.15)	(-3.94)*	(-3.93)*	(-3.57)*	(-3.20)*
FO	-0.033			-0.079			-0.006			0.024		
	(-0.56)			(-3.01)*			(-0.16)			(0.72)		
OM	0.343	0.389	0.342	0.309	0.356	-0.083	0.010	0.010	0.070	0.034	0.025	0.381
	(5.28)*	(5.39)*	(1.07)	(10.93)*	(13.38)*	(-0.58)	(0.24)	(0.23)	(0.43)	(0.93)	(0.61)	(2.31)**
A	-0.000	-0.001	0.027	-0.003	-0.002	-0.007	0.001	-0.000	0.017	0.002	0.001	0.011
	(-0.10)	(-0.61)	(3.50)*	(-3.60)*	(-2.31)**	(-1.60)	(0.64)	(-0.27)	(4.30)*	(1.86)**	(0.63)	(2.76)*
W	0.020	0.015	-0.059	-0.003	0.001	-0.014	0.003	0.003	-0.047	0.023	0.011	0.017
	(2.18)**	(0.90)	(-3.05)*	(-0.83)	(0.19)	(-1.59)	(0.55)	(0.25)	(-4.76)*	(4.23)*	(1.12)	(1.71)***
μ	1.108	1.041	0.829	0.412	0.257	0.230	0.408	0.377	0.371	0.276	0.363	0.225
	(11.06)*	(7.57)*	(6.77)*	(7.92)*	(4.34)*	(2.85)*	(6.51)*	(4.43)*	(5.93)*	(4.92)*	(4.55)*	(3.61)*
N	148	105	43	148	105	43	148	105	43	148	105	43
χ^2	50.14*	38.35*	43.58*	147.73*	132.22*	81.58*	40.46*	13.83**	64.36*	70.72*	24.31*	74.76*

Notes: *, ** and *** refer to 1, 5 and 10% levels of significance respectively. Industry dummies were used but their results are not reported here.

Source: Computed from data compiled from UNU–INTECH (2002) Survey using Stata 7.0 Package.

X/Y in the foreign firms' sample was also negative, although it was statistically insignificant. The *X/Y* coefficient was positive in the local firms' sample, but it was not statistically significant. *SI* was only statistically significant in the local firms' sample and its coefficient was strong and positive, suggesting that skills-intensity levels were important in driving higher *HR* practices only in local firms. Age was statistically significant in the overall and foreign firms' samples; its negative coefficient suggests that newer foreign firms train and expose workers more to cutting-edge *HR* practices than older firms.

FO was statistically insignificant in the *PT* regressions. The *PT* regressions involving the foreign firms' sample failed the chi-square statistics of model fit. Although *X/Y* coefficients were positive in the samples, the results were not statistically significant. *SI* was statistically significant and its coefficients positive in the overall and local firms' samples, suggesting that South African firms are likely to have higher process technology levels when the requisite human capital is there to run them. However, *SI* in the local firms' sample was not only much more significant statistically, but its coefficient was also much higher than the overall sample. *S* was only statistically highly significant (at the 1 per cent level) in the local firms' sample, and its coefficient was negative and strong, showing that smaller firms enjoyed higher *PT* levels than the more labour-intensive larger firms. Age and wages were also statistically highly significant (at the 1 per cent level) in the local firms' sample. Age was positively correlated but wages was negatively correlated.

FO was also statistically insignificant in the *RD* regressions. The explanatory variables of *X/Y* and *SI* were statistically insignificant in all three samples, though their coefficients were positive. Size was statistically highly significant in all three samples, and its negative coefficients suggest that smaller firms engage more in R&D activities than larger firms. *OM* was also significant and its coefficient positive in the local firms' sample, suggesting that owner-managed local firms in South Africa are driven more by innovation than otherwise. The positive coefficient involving wages means that R&D-intensive firms pay higher wages than other firms. The coefficient of *W* was positive in all three samples though it was statistically significant only in the overall and local firms' samples. Age was also highly significant in the local firms' sample.

Taken together, *TI* had a strong influence on labour productivity and skills intensity levels, with higher coefficients in the local firms' sample than in the foreign firms' sample. However, *TI* enjoyed no statistically significant relationship with *X/Y*. Export intensity also produced generally statistically insignificant results when the relationship was reversed against *TI*, *HR*, *PT* and *RD*. The general lack of statistical significance between the technology and export intensity variables is likely to be a consequence of specialisation in domestic and regional markets. Foreign ownership was inversely correlated with *HR*, suggesting that local firms enjoy higher *HR* practices than foreign firms. Foreign ownership was statistically insignificant in the *PT* and *RD* regressions. *SI* was statistically significant in all the *TI* and *PT* regressions, but only in the local firms' sample of the *HR* regression. Its coefficient was also much stronger in the local firms' sample than in the foreign firms' sample, suggesting that human capital is more critical in driving technical change in the former than in the latter. Also, as noted earlier, local firms seem to have responded productively to competition by investing more in training and process technology whereas foreign firms spent smaller amounts owing to access to superior *HR* and *PT* technology from their parent locations. The lack of a statistically strong relationship between *SI* and *RD* suggests that R&D is still not an overriding feature of employee hiring in the firms.

3.5   CONCLUSIONS

South Africa presented an interesting case of a developing economy with fairly strong S&T endowments and a resurgence in importance of FDI participation in manufacturing activities. Despite relatively low levels of FDI in GCF, good infrastructure, human capital endowments and a large domestic market have kept significant operations by foreign firms in the country. Foreign firms also use South Africa as an important location to produce for the overall African market, though export intensity levels are relatively low.

The mixed results suggest that there were no clear technology and performance differences between foreign and local firms, though firms generally specialise in domestic and regional markets. Only in pharmaceuticals did foreign firms enjoy a slightly higher labour productivity mean than local firms. Local firms enjoyed a higher export intensity mean than foreign firms in auto parts, but it was the reverse in pharmaceuticals. Local firms enjoyed a higher skills intensity mean than foreign firms in electronics and food processing. Local firms generally paid higher wages than foreign firms in the electronics industry, but it was the opposite in pharmaceuticals, and in textiles and garments. Foreign firms enjoyed a higher *TI* mean than local firms only in pharmaceuticals. Local firms generally enjoyed higher local sourcing intensities than foreign firms across all four industries, but this was statistically significant only in pharmaceuticals. Foreign firms enjoyed a higher *PT* and *RD* mean that local firms in pharmaceuticals and in textiles and garments. Local firms enjoyed a higher *HR* mean than foreign firms in textiles and garments, and *PT* mean in auto parts. Local firms invested more in training and process technology to compete with foreign firms and imports in auto parts. The mixed but fairly close means suggest that local firms have acquired considerable learning and innovation potential to compete with foreign firms, though production is still geared primarily towards domestic and regional markets.

Technological intensity strongly influenced labour productivity and skills intensity levels, with higher coefficients in the local firms' sample, but without a significant impact on export intensity. Export intensity also produced generally statistically insignificant results when the relationship was reversed against *TI*, *HR*, *PT* and *RD*. The general lack of statistical significance between the technology and export intensity variables is likely to be a consequence of export focus on inferior regional markets. The positive relationship between *TI* and *SI* shows that human capital is essential to support technology-intensive activities, especially in local firms. Foreign ownership was inversely correlated with *HR*, suggesting that local firms enjoy higher *HR* practices than foreign firms. Foreign ownership was statistically insignificant in the *PT* and *RD* regressions. *SI* was statistically significant in all the *TI* and *PT* regressions, but only in local firms' sample of the *HR* regression. Its coefficient was also much stronger in the local firms' sample than in the foreign firms' sample, suggesting that human capital endowments are more instrumental in driving technical change in the former than the latter. With the exception of pharmaceuticals, the stronger relationships between *TI*, *HR* and *PT* in the local sample are also likely to be the result of foreign firms' focus on adapting technology from parent plants when local firms had to acquire or develop new *HR* practices and *PT*.

The results offer policy implications particularly for economies with good basic infrastructure and fairly developed S&T infrastructure, and where production is still driven mainly by domestic and regional markets. Strong technological capabilities in local firms, especially in auto parts, electronics and food processing, suggest that considerable learning has already taken place. Apart from pharmaceuticals firms, local firms show high incidence of patent take-up in the remaining industries. In addition, foreign pharmaceuticals firms use South Africa as an important site to undertake R&D activities. If only the problems of poverty and inequality can be resolved, South Africa looks a good base for firms – both foreign and local – to learn, innovate and compete in global markets.

NOTES

1. These findings were also confirmed by authors interviews conducted in 2002 in South Africa.
2. Author interviews conducted in May 2002 in Pretoria.

APPENDIX 3.1

Table 3A.1   *Correlation matrix of independent variables, South Africa sample, 2001*

	X/Y	FO	PT	RD	OM	S	HR	TI	SI	PTD	HRT	HRD	LS	W	A
X/Y	1.000														
FO	-0.161	1.000													
PT	0.124	-0.144	1.000												
RD	0.158	0.032	0.204	1.000											
OM	0.042	0.078	-0.170	-0.118	1.000										
S	-0.015	-0.099	0.002	-0.438*	0.212	1.000									
HR	-0.049	0.006	-0.126	-0.105	0.778*	0.168	1.000								
TI	0.133	-0.061	0.619*#	0.633*#	0.298	-0.151	0.464*#	1.000							
SI	0.062	-0.057	0.144	0.128	0.171	0.031	0.150	0.248	1.000						
PTD	0.180	-0.071	0.776*#	0.776*#	-0.184	-0.280	-0.148	0.808*#	0.174	1.000					
HRT	0.053	-0.102	0.645*#	0.067	0.472*	0.128	0.675*#	0.814*#	0.225	0.460*#	1.000				
HRD	0.077	0.031	0.049	0.654*#	0.506*	-0.196	0.684*#	0.815*#	0.209	0.454*#	0.560*#	1.000			
LS	0.065	-0.159	0.109	0.026	-0.228	-0.074	-0.213	-0.053	-0.161	0.085	-0.087	-0.144	1.000		
W	0.199	-0.217	0.183	0.472*	-0.320	-0.396	-0.300	0.201	0.132	0.422*	-0.093	0.117	0.065	1.000	
A	-0.141	0.220	-0.080	0.116	0.123	0.010	-0.019	0.011	0.111	0.024	-0.078	0.072	-0.212	0.041	1.000

Notes: # compositional overlap; * high correlation.

Source: Computed from UNU-INTECH (2002) Survey data using Stata 7.0 Package.

71

4. Technology and economic performance in Uganda

Rajah Rasiah and Henry Tamale

4.1 INTRODUCTION

Uganda is a land-locked country, which has a high comparative cost premium for location of industries for export processing compared to Kenya and Tanzania. Consequently Uganda's natural manufacturing base is by and large in the processing of its abundant primary raw materials. With a per capita income measured using purchasing power parity (PPP) of US$1167 in 2001, Uganda was one of the most underdeveloped economies in the world. Ugandan manufacturing declined or stagnated during the 1970s, 1980s and the first half of the 1990s owing to poor macroeconomic conditions. Macroeconomic stabilisation from the late 1980s and external developments in the 1990s offered Uganda the opportunity to promote industrialisation aggressively from the mid-1990s. A combination of severe economic failure in Kenya and slow transition in Tanzania, and the adoption of business-friendly policy instruments domestically has helped attract industries that would not normally relocate in Uganda. Hence, manufacturing has grown since 1997. The share of manufacturing value added in GDP rose from 5.7 per cent in 1990 to 8.7 per cent in 1999. Although the share still left Uganda as a typical non-industrial economy, manufacturing enjoyed its highest contribution of 9.1 per cent to GDP in 2000 (World Bank, 2002). Rapid manufacturing growth has coincided with strong foreign direct investment (FDI) inflows from the second half of the 1990s: FDI shares in gross capital formation (GCF) rose from 0.0 per cent in 1990 to 21.1 per cent in 1999. The rise in FDI in manufacturing has made Uganda an exciting case to examine for its potential impact on technological capability development and economic performance.

Little work exists examining the role of FDI in Ugandan manufacturing, which could be because much of the inflow into the sector occurred only from the late 1990s. Hence this chapter can offer useful insights into the state of technological capabilities developed in foreign and local firms. In addition, the weak basic and high-tech infrastructure of Uganda at the bottom of the development trajectory offers a good example of a poor African economy at the bottom of the technology trajectory for examining differences in technological capabilities and performance between foreign and local firms. The rest of the chapter is organised as follows. Section 4.2 discusses the macroeconomic and industrial setting of Uganda against which the firm-level data will be examined. Section 4.3 presents the methodology and data. Section 4.4 compares the productivity, exports and technological capabilities of foreign and local firms, and examines the strength of the statistical relationships involving productivity, export-intensity and technological capabilities. Section 4.5 finishes with the conclusions and policy implications.

4.2 MACROECONOMIC CONDITIONS AND INDUSTRIAL GROWTH

It is important to examine the macroeconomic situation in general and industrialisation in particular before productivity, exports and technological capability of foreign and local firms are compared and their determinants examined. Like most African economies, Uganda was gripped by political turmoil for several decades with severe economic consequences. Changing circumstances – both internally and externally – helped economic recovery from the late 1980s and spurred industrial growth from the late 1990s.

Uganda faced an inflation rate of around 240 per cent annually in the 1980s, with the average ratio of parallel exchange rates between 11 and 1 (Kasekende, 2000a). The economy, which was stagnating under President Milton Obote, deteriorated sharply under President Idi Amin. Economic restrictions further limited export and access to foreign exchange.[1] The government failed to meet IMF conditions, which led to the cancellation of the structural adjustment package (SAP) in 1983–84. Average capacity utilisation in the economy had fallen to 25 per cent by 1985. Heavy government subsidies to support industries further increased government debt. By 1991, Uganda was facing a severe foreign exchange constraint, which was exacerbated by growing current account deficits (Kasekende, 2000a). GDP growth either declined or stagnated in the mid-1980s: Uganda recorded an average annual growth rate of 0.6 per cent in the period 1982–86. Exports as a share of GDP fell from 19.4 per cent in 1980 to 8.4 per cent in 1982 (computed from World Bank, 2002).

From 1987 Uganda began to administer currency and tax reforms. While the reduction of the Ugandan shilling by 60 per cent was aimed to lower inflation, it was not until the 1990s that macroeconomic stability was achieved. Tax collection by an autonomous authority and the strengthening of financial instruments brought greater stability. The general improvement in the macroeconomic climate helped raise GDP growth, which grew on average by 6.7

per cent per annum in the period 1987–91. However, high interest rates – owing to IMF-imposed conditions on IMF-disbursed loans and the lack of domestic funds – restricted the growth of local firms.

The establishment of macroeconomic stability not only helped stimulate GDP growth; it also helped attract FDI. Between 1991 and 1999 Uganda's GDP grew on average by 7.0 per cent per annum. FDI in gross fixed capital formation (GFCF) rose from zero in 1990 to 11.2 per cent in 1993, 12.8 per cent in 1995 and 21.1 per cent in 1999 before falling slightly to 19.6 per cent in 2000 (World Bank, 2001). In fact Uganda enjoyed the highest share of FDI in GFCF among non-mineral-exporting countries in Africa in 1999.

As with the overall economy, manufacturing performed badly in the 1980s. Heavy government subsidies failed to spur growth so that the average capacity utilisation rate was around only 10 per cent in the 1980s (Kasekende, 2000a). While the economy picked up from the late 1980s, manufacturing began to follow from the 1990s following a surge in FDI inflows. The initial push offered by the government through subsidies was not sustainable as debts and the current account deficit mounted. Hence the government introduced reforms to stimulate FDI (Kasekende, 2000b). FDI in GFCF only reached double-digit percentage shares from 1994, with further expansion occurring from 1998.

Manufacturing stagnated in the 1980s: the average annual growth rate of manufacturing value added was only 0.8 per cent in the period 1983–87. The low starting base allowed manufacturing value added to grow on average by 10.5 per cent per annum in the period 1988–93 and subsequently to 15.2 per cent per annum in the period 1994–99.[2] As the manufacturing base expanded, value-added growth settled on average to 8.9 per cent per annum in the period 1998–2002 (see Table 4.1). The fastest average annual growth was recorded in metal products (20.9 per cent), bricks and cement (12.6 per cent) and apparel industries (12.3 per cent). Beverages and tobacco recorded the slowest growth (2.9 per cent). In addition to economic turmoil and infrastructure failure in the neighbouring economies – particularly in Kenya – business-friendly promotional instruments helped attract FDI into manufacturing in Uganda. Even industries traditionally favouring a sea-front owing to the need for importing iron and steel, such as metal engineering, have expanded operations in land-locked Uganda.

As with most East African economies, foreign firms' operations in Uganda's manufacturing sector have been dominated by activities where no significant foreign affiliate existed. Transnational corporations are typically dominated by at least one parent plant and one or more subsidiaries abroad. Only a few firms in East Africa (e.g. in beer brewing and tobacco) qualify as transnationals with superior operations abroad. Even beer firms in East Africa are largely African owned (e.g. Castle beer from South Africa in Tanzania)

Table 4.1   Industrial production index, Uganda, 1998–2002

	Food	Beverages & tobacco	Apparel	PPP	Chemical	Bricks & cement	Metal	Other	All
1998	100	100	100	100	100	100	100	100	100
1999	122	108	168	125	119	118	122	104	120
2000	118	113	192	153	125	127	140	101	125
2001	129	104	190	162	128	148	165	93	131
2002	128	112	159	151	144	161	213	137	140
Annual average growth (1998–2002)	6.3	2.9	12.3	10.8	9.5	12.6	20.9	8.2	8.9

Note: PPP refers to paper, printing and publishing.

Source: Computed from Bank of Uganda (2003).

75

(see Portelli and Narula, 2003). In addition, only a handful of foreign firms have used their superior process knowledge – but in technology-using industries (e.g. food and beverages and metal engineering) – to participate in engineering improvements. Nevertheless, it is interesting to note that manufacturing has grown rapidly in such a short period in the face of economic liberalisation.

It is against this macroeconomic and industrial background that the data involving foreign and local manufacturing firms in Uganda will be examined. Given the short experience of rapid manufacturing growth – particularly after 1998 – many of the implications may be useful for underdeveloped economies still experiencing nascent industrialisation.

4.3   METHODOLOGY AND DATA

This chapter uses the technological capability framework advanced in Chapter 1. Selection of industries in Uganda was extremely difficult owing to the lack of reliable official data, and hence the questionnaires were sent to all manufacturing firms where addresses were available. Overall, the response rate was 36.7 per cent, which is impressive given the lack of official records on several firms. The 'other' category comprises firms in industries where the responses were fewer than ten to undertake a meaningful statistical analysis. The proxies used in section 4.4 were measured and defined as follows.

4.3.1   Productivity and Export Performance

The proxies of labour productivity and export intensities were used to denote productivity and export performance respectively. Both variables have problems but they do allow useful assessments.

$$\text{Labour productivity} = VA_i/L_i$$

where VA and L refer to value added and total employees respectively of firm i in 2001.

$$\text{Export intensity} = X_i/Y_i,$$

where X and Y refer to exports and gross output respectively of firm i in 2001.

4.3.2   Technological Capabilities

This chapter uses the conceptualisation of technological capabilities as advanced in Chapter 1. It uses the rationale presented in Chapter 2 (see section 2.3.2) for the computation of human resource, process technology, R&D and overall technology indexes. The following broad capabilities and related composition of proxies were used.

Human resource

Two alternative proxies were used to represent human resource. However, human resource capability was used separately to measure human resource practices that denote development in firms, and therefore it excluded skills intensity. The exclusion allows the measurement of human resource capability that is developed by each firm, rather than those that are hired from other firms.

Human resource capability

Given the nascent manufacturing experience in Uganda, the statistical relationships are difficult to predict *ex ante*. Nevertheless, *HR* practices can be expected to be positively correlated with export intensity as firms compete with especially exports from Kenya and South Africa. *HR* is also expected to be positively correlated with wages.

Human resource capability (*HR*) was measured as:

$$HR_i = 1/3[TM_i, TE_i, CHR_i] \qquad (4.1)$$

where *TM*, *TE* and *CHR* refer to training mode, training expense as a share of payroll and cutting-edge human resource practices used respectively. *TM* was measured as a multinomial logistic variable of 1 when staff are sent out to external organisations for training, 2 when external staff are used to train employees, 3 when staff with training responsibilities are on payroll, 4 when a separate training department is used, 5 when a separate training centre is used and 0 when no formal training is undertaken. *CHR* was measured by a score of 1 for each of the practices and totalled. The firms were asked if it was their policy to encourage team-working, small-group activities to improve company performance, multi-skilling, interaction with marketing, customer service and R&D department, lifelong learning and upward mobility. *HR* was divided by the three proxies used. The proxies were normalised using the formula below:

$$\text{Normalisation score} = (X_i - X_{min})/(X_{max} - X_{min}), \qquad (4.2)$$

where X_i, X_{min} and X_{max} refer to the ith, minimum and maximum values respectively of the proxy X.

Skills intensity

Skills intensity (*SI*) was used separately to capture the effects of different shares of managerial, professional, engineering, technical and supervisory personnel in the workforce. *SI* was measured as:

$$SI = H_i/L_i,$$

where H and L refer to managers, professionals, engineers, technicians and supervisors, and total employees respectively in 2001 of firm i.

Process technology capability

Given Uganda's underdeveloped status, exporting firms are likely to be entrenched in low value added activities using older process technology. Hence, it can be hypothesized that there exists little or no statistical relationship between *PT* and *X/Y*. The higher *HR* and *SI* required to drive process technology is likely to produce a positive statistical relationship between *PT* and wages.

Four proxies were used to compute *PT*, which was calculated using the formula:

$$PT_i = 1/4[EM_i, PTE_i, ITC_i, QC_i] \tag{4.3}$$

where *E*, *M*, *PTE*, *ITC* and *QC* refer to equipment and machinery, process technology expenditure in sales, information technology components and quality control instruments respectively of firm i. *EM* was computed as a multinomial logistic variable with average age of over five years = 0, three to five years = 1, two to less than three years = 2 and less than two years = 3. Likert scale scores ranging from 1 to 5 (least to most) were used to measure *ITC*. *QC* was measured as a dummy variable (*QC* = 1 if cutting-edge methods were used, *QC* = 0 otherwise). *PT* was divided by the number of proxies used, which is four.

R&D capability

Given Uganda's underdeveloped NIS and systemic facilities and the preponderance of labour-intensive assembly and processing operations, R&D is unlikely to produce statistically meaningful results involving export intensity. Given the R&D focus on process technology changes in low-value-added food and beverages, metal engineering, textile and garment and other manufacturing, a positive relationship can be expected with process technology.

The data collected enabled the computation of two R&D proxies, i.e. R&D expenditure as a percentage of sales and R&D personnel as a share of employment. It was not possible from the sample data to disentangle investment advanced between process and product R&D, and hence this proxy was measured to relate to both product and process R&D as:

$$RD_i = 1/2[RD_{expi}, RD_{empi}], \tag{4.4}$$

where RD_{exp} and RD_{emp} refer to R&D expenditure as a share of sales and R&D personnel in workforce respectively of firm i. RD was divided by two to take account of the two proxies used.

Overall technological intensity

Overall technological intensity (TI) was estimated by simply adding the components HR, PT and RD, and was measured as:

$$TI_i = HR_i + PT_i + RD_i,$$

As noted in Chapters 2 and 3, HR, PT and RD were divided by the number of proxies used to facilitate the computation of TI by giving equal weight to all three components.

Other technology variables

Three additional technological variables were computed when examining the relationships involving HR, PT and RD to avoid problems of collinearity between them (see Appendix 4.1).

$$HRT_i = [HR_i + PT_i]. \tag{4.5}$$

HRT refers to technological influences of human and process technology resources of firm i.

$$HRD_i = [HR_i + RD_i]. \tag{4.6}$$

HRD refers to technological influences of human and R&D technology resources of firm i.

$$PRD_i = [PT_i + RD_i]. \tag{4.7}$$

PRD refers to technological influences of process and R&D technology resources of firm i.

Wages

Wages was used to represent labour market conditions. Unions was dropped owing to reasons advanced in Chapter 1. Moreover, only eight firms had unionised workers. (See Table 4.2.)

Given the premium involving skilled and knowledge workers, a positive relationship can be expected between productivity and wages. Average monthly wages was used. Since it is difficult to obtain wages of workers on their own, it was measured by dividing total salaries and remuneration by the workforce. Average wages in million Ugandan shillings per year was used in all the regressions and was measured as:

$$W_i = S_i / L_i,$$

where W and S refer to wages per worker and total monthly salary bill respectively of firm i.

Other critical firm-level variables

Three other important firm-level structural variables were included in the analysis, i.e. ownership, age and management type. Size was excluded owing to most firms having employment size less than 100 employees. Merger and acquisition was dropped because it involved only seven firms. Export-processing zone (EPZ) was also dropped owing to the few firms involved (see Table 4.1).

Ownership   There were only five joint-venture firms in the sample and all of them had 50 per cent foreign equity. The classifications of whether any foreign equity or at least 50 per cent foreign equity was involved would not matter as a consequence. Ownership was measured as:

$FO_i = 1$ if foreign equity ownership of firm i was 50 per cent or more;
$FO = 0$ otherwise,

where FO refers to status of ownership of firm i.

Age   Given that firms with longer experience are considered to enjoy greater experiential and tacit knowledge, age is considered to provide a positive relationship with exports and technological capabilities. The absolute age of the firm is used as an independent variable. The statistical relationship may not be positive if foreign firms using superior technology from abroad and enjoying strong access to global markets began establishing or relocating operations recently. Given the importance of investment from former Africans of Asian origin in Uganda and their involvement in small-scale activities without any significant overseas affiliates, age may provide atypical results. Age was measured as:

$$A_i = \text{years in operation of firm } i,$$

where A refers to age of operation of firm i.

Owner-managed firms   With 52 firms involved with owners being at least part of the management, management type may have a bearing on the statistical results. It is often argued that owner-managers impact both positively and negatively on firms' performance. On the one hand, owners are considered to show greater drive to succeed owing to lower agency costs, and their ability to make quick decisions. On the other hand, owner-managers are considered to be less professional, especially when involving big businesses, and hence may lack the instruments to succeed in export markets. Hence a neutral hypothesis with either a positive or negative sign is expected. *OM* is measured using a dummy variable as follows:

$$OM_i = 1 \text{ if the firm is managed either partly or fully by the owner;}$$
$$OM = 0 \text{ otherwise,}$$

where *OM* refers to status of management of firms i.

4.3.3   Statistical Analysis

The following models were specified to estimate the statistical relationships involving labour productivity and export intensity. OLS regressions were used when the dependent variable was value added per worker. Tobit regressions were preferred when export-intensity, skills intensity and the technological variables were used because they are censored both on the right and the left sides of the data sets. The models were run with industry dummies:

$$\text{OLS: } VA/L = \alpha + \beta_1 TI + \beta_2 FO + \beta_3 W + \beta_4 A + \beta_5 OM + \mu \qquad (4.8)$$

$$\text{Tobit: } X/Y = \alpha + \beta_1 TI + \beta_2 FO + \beta_3 W + \beta_4 A + \beta_5 OM + \mu \qquad (4.9)$$

$$\text{Tobit: } SI = \alpha + \beta_1 TI + \beta_2 FO + \beta_3 W + \beta_4 A + \beta_5 OM + \mu \qquad (4.10)$$

$$\text{Tobit: } TI = \alpha + \beta_1 SI + \beta_2 FO + \beta_3 W + \beta_4 A + \beta_5 OM + \mu \qquad (4.11)$$

$$\text{Tobit: } HR = \alpha + \beta_1 X/Y + \beta_2 PRD + \beta_3 FO + \beta_4 W + \beta_5 OM + \beta_6 A + \mu \qquad (4.12)$$

Tobit: $PT = \alpha + \beta_1 X/Y + \beta_2 HRD + \beta_3 FO + \beta_4 W + \beta_5 A + \mu$ \hfill (4.13)

Tobit: $RD = \alpha + \beta_1 X/Y + \beta_2 HRT + \beta_3 FO + \beta_4 W + \beta_5 A + \mu$ \hfill (4.14)

Regressions (4.8)–(4.14) were repeated using foreign and local firm samples separately.

Specific industry-level questionnaires were designed, pilot tested and mailed to all firms listed in official government statistics records in Uganda. In addition, the authors distributed and collected some questionnaires personally. Case studies of at least three firms in each industry were undertaken by the authors to help extract industry-type characteristics. The survey and the case studies constitute the basis for the results and analysis in the chapter.

4.4 STATISTICAL RESULTS

The data collected are shown in Table 4.2. The survey produced 48 foreign and 43 local firms with a fairly high incidence of export experience: 34 (70.8 per cent) of foreign firms and 27 (62.8 per cent) of local firms. Although the incidence of participation in R&D activities was fairly high for an under-developed economy – 26 (54.2 per cent) involving foreign firms and 19 (44.2 per cent) involving local firms, the levels were extremely low. The incidence of unionisation and location in export-processing zones (EPZs) was extremely low, and hence both these variables were removed from the econometric analysis undertaken in the chapter. Food and beverages, and plastics enjoyed the most respondents. Only seven of the 91 firms (all foreign-owned) had either a production or a distribution plant abroad.

4.4.1 Statistical Differences

This section examines if there are statistically significant differences between foreign and local firms in labour productivity, export intensity, skills intensity and technological capabilities. Differences in technological capabilities are examined using the overall aggregate *TI*, and its components *HR*, *PT* and *RD*. As mentioned earlier, Uganda is likely to produce results unique to Africa since most foreign firms operate as stand-alone firms without significant links to an internal knowledge base abroad. In addition to the underdeveloped infrastructure and small domestic market, Uganda is unlikely to attract significant levels of high-tech operations owing to its location in a politically insecure region. Hence foreign firms may not show vastly superior technological intensities over local firms – something that would normally be the case if transnational corporations were involved.

Table 4.2 *Sample breakdown, Uganda sample, 2001*

	Ownership		Export experience		Unions		Located in EPZs		R&D experience		Total
	Foreign	Local	Foreign	Local	Foreign	Local	Foreign	Local	Foreign	Local	
Textiles and garments	5	5	2	1	1	0	2	0	3	0	10
Metal engineering	8	4	7	4	0	0	2	0	5	0	12
Food and beverages	12	14	8	10	4	0	2	0	4	8	26
Plastics	13	12	11	7	0	1	2	0	8	5	25
Others	10	8	6	5	2	0	4	2	6	6	18
All	48	43	34	27	7	1	12	2	26	19	91

Source: Tabulated from UNU–INTECH (2002; 2003) using Stata 7.0 Package.

Table 4.3   T-tests by ownership, Uganda sample, 2001

	Foreign	Local	P > t		Foreign	Local	P > t
VA/L				*HR*			
Textiles & garments	35.282	4.548	0.154	Garments	0.516	0.257	0.137
Metal engineering	5.772	6.053	0.906	Metal engineering	0.322	0.136	0.024**
Food & beverages	42.713	9.138	0.077***	Food & beverages	0.498	0.354	0.254
Plastics	6.970	8.990	0.534	Plastics	0.356	0.339	0.743
Others	3.322	2.329	0.524	Others	0.280	0.427	0.026**
TI				*PT*			
Garments	1.052	0.472	0.171	Garments	0.319	0.214	0.383
Metal engineering	0.701	0.212	0.000*	Metal engineering	0.292	0.075	0.000*
Food & beverages	0.824	0.675	0.459	Food & beverages	0.252	0.205	0.591
Plastics	0.748	0.675	0.593	Plastics	0.264	0.271	0.900
Others	0.819	0.912	0.667	Others	0.293	0.298	0.914

X/Y

Garments	0.021	0.067	0.520
Metal engineering	0.135	0.521	0.004*
Food & beverages	0.329	0.344	0.909
Plastics	0.273	0.049	0.019**
Others	0.292	0.347	0.774

SI

Garments	0.084	0.198	0.104***
Metal engineering	0.245	0.184	0.623
Food & beverages	0.116	0.188	0.167
Plastics	0.156	0.240	0.123
Others	0.271	0.198	0.599

RD

Garments	0.217	0.000	0.137
Metal engineering	0.087	0.000	0.104***
Food & beverages	0.074	0.117	0.458
Plastics	0.121	0.072	0.356
Others	0.245	0.187	0.675

Wages

Textiles and garments	0.628	1.775	0.002*
Metal engineering	4.346	1.967	0.425
Food & beverages	8.961	2.657	0.052**
Plastics	2.806	3.102	0.791
Others	0.911	0.476	0.032

Note: *, ** and *** refer to statistical significance at 1, 5 and 10% levels respectively.

Source: Computed from UNU–INTECH (2002; 2003) using Stata 7.0 Package.

The *t*-tests conducted generally produced mixed results involving labour productivity, export intensity, skills intensity and wages (see Table 4.3). Labour productivity differences were only statistically significant involving food and beverages at the 10 per cent level: foreign firms enjoyed a higher productivity level than local firms. Export intensity differences were statistically significant involving metal engineering (at the 1 per cent level) and plastics (at the 5 per cent level): foreign firms enjoyed higher intensity in plastics but lower intensity in metal engineering. Only textiles and garments were significant involving skills intensity (at the 10 per cent level): foreign firms enjoyed a lower mean than local firms. Wage differences were significant involving textiles and garments, food and beverages, and others: foreign firms had a lower mean than local firms in textiles and garments, but a higher mean in food and beverages, and others. The higher skills intensity helps explain the higher wages in local textile and garment firms compared to foreign firms. The *t*-test results involving the skills intensity index also showed that there are no obvious differences between foreign and local firms, suggesting the lack of crowding-out tendencies. A more detailed assessment of the origin of human capital in the firms is necessary to confirm this.

All technological capabilities in metal engineering were statistically significant: foreign firms enjoyed higher *TI* (1 per cent level), *HR* (5 per cent level), *PT* (1 per cent level) and *RD* (10 per cent level) capabilities than local firms. Local firms only enjoyed an advantage in other industries (5 per cent level) involving human resource. However, excluding metal engineering the results did not show a significant advantage enjoyed by foreign firms. This could be a consequence of a fairly open regime enforced since the implementation of the structural adjustment package in the country, underdeveloped infrastructure, the dominance of small stand-alone foreign firms and the small and politically risky regional markets.

Overall, the statistical analysis produced mixed results. No clear statistically significant productivity, export intensity and skills intensity differences existed between foreign and local firms in most industries. Foreign firms in food and beverages enjoyed a substantially higher labour productivity, and were more export-oriented in plastics than local firms. Foreign firms also paid higher wages than local firms in food and beverages, and other industries than local firms. Local firms in textiles and garments enjoyed higher skills intensity and wages, and were more export-oriented in metal engineering than foreign firms. Foreign firms clearly enjoyed higher technology levels – *TI, HR, PT* and *RD* – in metal engineering than local firms. Local firms had an advantage over foreign firms in *HR* and in other industries.

4.4.2   Statistical Relationships

Having identified statistical differences in the sample data by ownership in the previous section, this section evaluates the relationship involving labour productivity, export intensity and skills intensity, and the technological variables controlling for wages, age, management type and ownership.

Productivity, exports and skills

Table 4.4 presents the econometric results establishing the statistical relationships involving labour productivity, export intensity and skills intensity using models (4.8)–(4.10) formulated in section 4.3. These regressions were also run using ownership samples. Not only was the overall model fit (*F*-statistics and chi-square statistics) statistically significant; all the regressions also easily passed the Cook–Weisberg as well as the White tests for heteroscedascity.

Against labour productivity as the dependent variable, *TI* was statistically highly significant (1 per cent level) and its coefficient was positive and strong, demonstrating an extremely strong link between technological intensity and productivity. While the results were also statistically highly significant (1 per cent level) and positive involving both sets of firms, the relationship was much stronger involving foreign firms, demonstrating that the relationship between productivity and technical change was more elastic involving foreign firms. Wages was also statistically highly significant and its coefficients positive, with foreign firms' higher coefficient demonstrating that wages in foreign firms are more responsive to productivity changes than local firms.

Using export intensity as the dependent variable, *TI* was only statistically significant when involving the foreign firms' sample. Its coefficient was positive and significant at the 5 per cent level, showing a positive link between technology and export orientation in foreign firms. Age was the only other variable statistically significant but only in the overall sample and foreign firms sample. The relationship is positive but its influence on export intensity was marginal.

The relationship between skills intensity and *TI* was statistically insignificant, suggesting that there is no statistical relationship between technological endowments and skills intensity. However, export intensity enjoyed a strong and positive statistical relationship (1 per cent level) with skills intensity irrespective of ownership. Firms seem to hire more skilled and professional employees to drive export-oriented activities. The elasticity is higher involving foreign firms. Age had an inverse statistical link with skills intensity, though its impact was marginal. Wages (positive but marginal) and management type (negative) were also statistically significant, but only in the local firms' sample.

Table 4.4 *Statistical relationships involving labour productivity, export and skills intensities, Uganda sample, 2001*

	VA/L			X/Y			SI		
	All	Foreign	Local	All	Foreign	Local	All	Foreign	Local
X/Y	2.826	−7.674	−1.816				0.286	0.445	0.284
	(0.46)	(−0.65)	(−0.45)				(4.02)*	(3.99)*	(2.89)*
TI	22.306	25.833	16.216	0.076	0.239	−0.190	0.012	−0.012	−0.009
	(4.95)*	(3.49)*	(4.13)*	(0.62)	(1.97)**	(−0.83)	(0.22)	(−0.17)	(−0.10)
FO	1.639			0.078			−0.034		
	(0.45)			(0.84)			(−0.79)		
A	0.015	0.265	0.120	0.012	0.015	0.010	−0.005	−0.011	−0.007
	(0.09)	(0.78)	(1.05)	(2.70)*	(3.05)*	(1.56)	(−2.50)*	(−3.15)*	(−2.35)**
W	3.535	3.858	1.312	0.009	0.008	−0.008	0.002	−0.001	0.023
	(9.04)*	(6.72)*	(2.89)*	(0.89)	(0.85)	(−0.32)	(0.42)	(−0.25)	(2.09)**
OM	−1.865	−5.515	−2.917	0.144	0.050	0.153	−0.068	0.004	−0.119
	(−0.52)	(−0.97)	(−1.09)	(1.59)	(0.52)	(0.94)	(−1.61)	(0.08)	(−1.82)***
μ	1.517	6.298	−5.672	−0.559	−0.575	−0.329	0.195	0.090	0.282
	(−0.21)	(0.47)	(−1.44)	(−2.68)*	(−2.64)*	(−1.17)	(2.32)**	(0.71)	(2.95)*
N	91	48	43	91	48	43	91	48	43
F, χ²	24.10*	18.61*	5.90*	20.16*	19.21*	16.38*	22.76*	27.44*	14.56***
R²	0.751	0.815	0.617						
Adj. R²	0.720	0.771	0.512						

Notes: *, ** and *** refer to statistical significance at the 1, 5 and 10% levels respectively; industry dummies used not reported here.

Source: Computed from UNU–INTECH (2002; 2003) using Stata 7.0 Package.

The explanatory variable of *TI* shows a stronger impact on productivity in foreign firms than in local firms. *TI* also showed a statistically positive link with *X/Y* only with the foreign firms' sample. The results for foreign firms show a higher propensity of *TI* to raise productivity improvements, a stronger link between export intensity and skills endowments and the only meaningful statistical link with export intensity. These results suggest that local firms obviously can learn through both demonstration effect as well as hiring tacit human capital from foreign firms to raise productivity levels and exports. Panel data are necessary to examine if these developments are already occurring.

Technological capabilities
Table 4.5 presents the econometric results establishing the statistical relationships involving *TI*, *HR*, *PT* and *RD* using models (4.11)–(4.14) formulated in section 4.3. These regressions were also run using ownership samples. Not only was the overall model fit (chi-square) statistically significant; all the regressions also easily passed the Cook–Weisberg as well as the White tests for heteroscedascity. However, the results involving the *RD* regressions using the local sample were dropped owing to a lack of convergence.

Against *TI*, wages was the only variable statistically significant (1 per cent level) in the overall sample and its coefficient was positive. Export intensity was statistically significant (10 per cent level) only in the foreign firms' sample, and its coefficient was positive. This demonstrates that technological intensity of foreign firms is higher involving export-oriented firms. Age was inversely correlated with *TI* in foreign firms but its impact was marginal.

Decomposing the technology index into *HR*, *PT* and *RD* produced some interesting results. Regressions using *SI* as an independent variable were dropped owing to a lack of statistical significance – suggesting that skills intensity did not enjoy a statistical relationship with the decomposed capability variables. Nevertheless, the individual capability variables enjoyed a strong statistical relationship with each other (see Section 4.2).

Wages and process and R&D technology taken together (*PRD*) enjoyed a strong statistical relationship with *HR*. *PRD* and wages were statistically highly significant (1 per cent level) in all three regressions and their coefficients were positive. Foreign firms enjoyed a stronger relationship between export intensities and *HR* than local firms. However, the *PRD* coefficient for local firms was slightly higher than for foreign firms, demonstrating that process and R&D technology in local firms are more elastic to *HR* levels than in foreign firms. Foreign firms also produced an inverse relationship between *HR* and *OM*, suggesting that owner-managed firms are less endowed with *HR*. Local firms show higher influence of firm-level technology on *HR* than foreign firms.

Regressed against *PT*, wages and human resource and R&D technology (*HRD*) were statistically highly significant (1 per cent level), and their

Table 4.5 Statistical relationships involving technological intensities, Uganda sample, 2001

	TI			HR			PT			RD#	
	All	Foreign	Local	All	Foreign	Local	All	Foreign	Local	All	Foreign
X/Y	0.013 (0.08)	0.484 (1.83)***	−0.260 (−1.49)	0.123 (2.20)**	0.165 (1.78)***	0.098 (1.97)**	−0.033 (−0.76)	−0.069 (−0.96)	0.056 (0.88)	−0.195 (−1.79)***	0.117 (0.72)
SI	0.151 (0.61)	0.108 (0.31)	−0.116 (−0.38)								
HRT										0.614 (5.05)*	0.574 (3.43)*
HRD							0.270 (6.56)*	0.262 (4.59)*	0.329 (3.79)*		
PRD				0.342 (5.74)*	0.264 (2.90)*	0.353 (5.40)*					
FO	0.062 (0.72)			−0.024 (−0.73)			0.015 (0.61)			0.126 (1.96)**	
A	−0.007 (−1.64)	−0.017 (−2.45)**	−0.005 (−0.96)	−0.001 (−0.36)	−0.002 (−0.57)	−0.000 (−0.05)	0.002 (1.53)	0.002 (1.03)	0.002 (1.32)	−0.006 (−1.85)***	−0.007 (−1.57)
W	0.040 (4.85)*	0.040 (4.01)*	0.042 (2.33)**	0.022 (6.56)*	0.025 (5.54)*	0.010 (1.89)***	0.011 (4.21)*	0.012 (3.77)*	0.017 (2.54)**	−0.031 (−3.82)*	−0.038 (−3.13)*
OM	0.002 (0.03)	−0.124 (−1.10)	0.151 (1.39)	−0.052 (−1.61)	−0.109 (−2.23)**	−0.033 (−1.02)	0.021 (0.85)	0.001 (0.03)	0.084 (2.08)**	0.125 (1.96)**	0.253 (1.89)***
μ	0.753 (4.67)*	1.297 (6.29)*	0.436 (2.66)*	0.273 (4.38)*	0.439 (4.25)*	0.171 (3.91)*	0.080 (1.62)	0.098 (1.26)	0.032 (0.52)	−0.541 (−2.95)*	−0.332 (−1.47)
N	91	48	43	91	48	43	91	48	43	91	48
χ²	34.50*	29.49*	29.77*	81.99*	52.11*	49.85*	71.63*	44.21*	32.45*	48.17*	24.15*

Notes: *, ** and *** refer to statistical significance at the 1, 5 and 10% levels respectively; # χ² result involving the local firms' sample was statistically insignificant; results of industry dummies not reported here.

Source: Computed from UNU–INTECH (2002; 2003) using Stata 7.0 Package.

coefficients were positive. Given that the contribution of R&D in the overall index is small, the similar coefficients of *HRD* and *PRD* obtained in the *HR* regressions suggest a fairly similar influence of *HR* (human resource training and practices) and *PT* (techniques, machinery and equipment) on each other. Local firms show a higher influence of firm-level technology on *PT* than foreign firms. However, export intensity was statistically insignificant, suggesting that firms irrespective of ownership did not specifically choose techniques, machinery and equipment on the basis of markets. This appears sensible since most firms only export to Tanzania, Rwanda, Burundi, Zambia and Kenya, where the demand conditions are similar.

The regression results involving *RD* using local firms were dropped owing to non-convergence. Over 50 per cent of the firms had no R&D at all and the levels among firms where it existed were very low. Nevertheless, the overall and foreign samples produced statistically meaningful results for interpretation. All the independent variables were statistically significant involving the overall sample. *HRT* was statistically highly significant (1 per cent level) and its coefficient was positive. The higher coefficients compared to those of *HRD* and *PRD* in the regressions involving *HR* and *PT* demonstrate that *RD* has much less influence on *HR* and *PT* than the converse. *FO* enjoyed a positive and statistically significant (5 per cent level) relationship with *RD*. Owner-managed firms also enjoyed a positive and statistically significant relationship (5 per cent level). Age (10 per cent) and wages (1 per cent) were inversely correlated but their influence was marginal. The latter is likely to be spurious.

Overall, foreign firms produced generally stronger statistical relationships involving the explanatory variables than local firms. Foreign firms enjoyed stronger relationship between *TI* and labour productivity, and export intensity and skills intensity than local firms. Only foreign firms had a statistically significant relationship between export intensities and *TI*, demonstrating that export markets have an influence over their choice of technology. Foreign firms also enjoyed higher export intensity coefficients against *TI* and *HR* than local firms. The foreign firms' dummy was statistically significant when regressed against *RD*.

4.5 CONCLUSIONS

Uganda presented an interesting case of an underdeveloped economy with high amounts of FDI in GCF – including in manufacturing. Despite its poor infrastructure, the economy has managed to attract significant amounts of FDI through both internal promotional policies and the external environment that constrained inflows to neighbouring economies – particularly Kenya.

Political stability and a business-friendly government helped stimulate FDI inflows from the mid-1990s. However, despite a steady inflow of foreign capital, its extremely weak infrastructure has set limits on the depth of its participation in Uganda. Despite these caveats, the analysis in the chapter produced some interesting results that can serve as assessment material for Uganda and other economies with similar endowments.

The *t*-tests to examine statistical differences between foreign and local firms produced mixed results. No clear statistically significant productivity, export intensity and skills intensity differences existed between foreign and local firms in most industries. Foreign firms in food and beverages enjoyed substantially higher labour productivity, and were more export-oriented in plastics than local firms. Foreign firms also paid higher wages than local firms in food and beverages, and other industries than local firms. Local firms in textiles and garments enjoyed higher skills intensity and wages, and were more export-oriented in metal engineering than foreign firms. Foreign firms clearly enjoyed higher overall technology, human resource, process technology and R&D capabilities in metal engineering than local firms. Local firms enjoyed higher human resource intensities than foreign firms in other industries.

Foreign firms produced generally stronger statistical relationships involving the explanatory variables than local firms. Foreign firms enjoyed a stronger relationship between *TI* and labour productivity, and export intensity and skills intensity than local firms. Export orientation has a statistical influence over the choice of technology only in foreign firms. Foreign firms also enjoyed higher export intensity coefficients with *TI* and *HR* than local firms.

Like the experience of Kenya, it is early to draw policy implications from Uganda's experience given that rapid manufacturing growth only occurred from the late 1980s and FDI inflows became important from the mid-1990s. Although Uganda has become quite stable since the mid-1990s, foreign firms may still prefer to keep their foundations shallow so that they can relocate if and when a crisis breaks out. In addition, Kenya enjoys better access to trade routes and resources to attract manufacturing activities and hence any improvement in infrastructure and political stability by the government may drive capital inflows away from Uganda. Nevertheless, if the present political circumstances hold or improve, strengthening its basic and high-tech infrastructure will help quicken learning, innovation and efficiency improvements in both foreign and local firms, and hence will act as a snowballing effect on manufacturing expansion. While the sophisticated technology associated with transnational foreign firms is not sufficiently present to diffuse locally, the current dominance of stand-alone owner-managed foreign firms may offer room for the growth of local firms.

NOTES

1. At the height of Idi Amin's dictatorship, Ugandan harvest of crops were exported through Kenya.
2. Computed using World Bank (2002) data.

APPENDIX 4.1

Table 4A.1 Correlation coefficient matrix of independent variables, Uganda sample, 2001

	X/Y	TI	HR	PT	RD	A	OM	FO	SI	W
X/Y	1.000									
TI	0.056	1.000								
HR	0.168	0.836*#	1.000							
PT	0.028	0.829*#	0.632*	1.000						
RD	-0.091	0.686*#	0.268	0.374	1.000					
A	0.229	-0.213	-0.152	-0.074	-0.265	1.000				
OM	0.134	0.020	-0.055	0.020	0.095	-0.166	1.000			
FO	-0.008	0.175	0.126	0.165	0.127	-0.207	-0.242	1.000		
SI	0.335	0.142	0.137	0.034	0.147	-0.080	-0.058	0.052	1.000	
W	0.153	0.421	0.601*	0.446	-0.090	-0.166	-0.019	0.171	0.077	1.000

Notes: # overlapping composition; * high correlation.

Source: Computed from Interview Survey (Authors, 2002) using Stata Package 7.0.

94

5. Technological intensity and export incidence in Indonesia

Rajah Rasiah

5.1 INTRODUCTION

Indonesia is a low-income economy, which until the financial and political crisis that erupted in 1997 was considered as one of the high-performing miracle economies by the World Bank (1993). Its per capita income and its manufacturing value added in real terms grew by more than 5.4 per cent and 9.9 per cent per annum respectively in the period 1989–96 (World Bank, 2002). For a country with a highly scattered landmass, and a population exceeding 210 million people in 1996, these figures were impressive by most measures. However, the severe downturn that accompanied the financial crisis of 1997 and its contagion politically undermined the macroeconomic environment so badly that the growth rates have still not reached pre-crisis levels. Nevertheless, Indonesia offers a good example of a country where foreign ownership conditions prevailed in most parts, although total equity ownership was allowed in Batam in the 1990s (Rasiah, 2003a). Foreign ownership was particularly important in manufacturing from the second half of the 1980s when both external (e.g. the Plaza Accord of 1985) and internal factors (domestic reforms) drove East Asian firms to relocate manufacturing primarily in Southeast Asia (see Pangestu, 1993; Thee and Pangestu, 1998; Hill, 1996). Although foreign ownership regulations were liberalised considerably in the 1990s, transaction costs were still substantially higher until the reforms that took place after the financial crisis.

Economic analyses of the role of foreign direct investment in Indonesia tend to show a positive effect on exports, productivity and employment (see Hill, 1988, 1995; Thee and Pangestu, 1998; Sjoholm, 1999, 2002; Okamoto and Sjoholm, 2003). Allen and Donnithorne (1957) had discussed specific cases of Western enterprises that offered the experiential knowledge for starting or working in local firms. These accounts offer a rich analysis of the contributions of foreign firms. However, there has been little work that deals directly with comparing technological capabilities of foreign and local firms, and the relationships between them and key explanatory variables. This chapter attempts to fill some of these gaps, but its focus is primarily on complementing the earlier works noted above.

Three important but related developments must be addressed when evaluating technology and exports of foreign and local firms in Indonesia. First, the financial crisis triggered a massive political upheaval, which has severely damaged macroeconomic conditions in the country. Second, investment – both local and foreign – fell sharply in the aftermath of the financial crisis as the ensuing political crisis worsened the economic situation in the country. As a share of GDP, gross domestic capital formation fell from 32 per cent in 1997 to 19 per cent in 1999. Foreign investment fell from US$6.5 billion in 1996–97 to US$1.6 billion in 1997–98 (Dhanani, 2000: 55). Third, liberalisation under IMF's structural adjustment package (SAP) ensured the formalisation of the deregulation of foreign ownership conditions in Indonesia since 1998, begun in 1986 and resumed with more reforms in mid-1994. Foreign ownership regulations in Indonesia had changed substantially over the years. From complete exclusion under the Sukarno regime, ownership was completely liberalised initially during the New Order (NO) regime, but was once again heavily regulated following the anti-Japanese riots of the mid-1970s. Through the 'one roof service', the Investment Coordination Board introduced a detailed plan to simplify, promote and improve coordination between investors, parliament and regional governments (UNCTAD, 2003: 48).

This chapter examines differences in technological intensities between foreign and local firms, and their statistical relationships in Indonesia. Unlike the other chapters, the data collected did not allow the computation of productivity and export intensity to undertake an analysis of economic performance. The chapter is organised as follows. Section 5.2 presents the methodology and data used. Section 5.3 compares export and technological capabilities recorded by foreign and local auto parts, electronics and garment firms. Section 5.4 evaluates the statistical relationships involving export incidence and technological capabilities. Section 5.5 presents the conclusions.

5.2   FDI AND DYNAMICS OF INDONESIAN INDUSTRIALISATION

Import substitution with complete exclusion of foreign capital constituted early industrial promotion in Indonesia, which was begun in 1945 under its founding president Sukarno. Apart from the opening of ownership to 100 per cent foreign equity in the period 1967–74,[1] Indonesia imposed controls on foreign capital until the 1990s. The liberal environment under the early phase of the Suharto regime was replaced with controls on foreign ownership following the anti-foreign riots that marked Japanese Prime Minister Tanaka's visit to Indonesia (Panglaykim, 1983; Robison, 1986). Severe balance of payments problems by the mid-1980s forced the government to seek export orientation as one element of a multi-strategy approach to revive economic growth (see Prawiro, 1998). Extensive promotion of import-dependent heavy industries without emphasis on building competitive technological capabilities drained the economy, and the macroeconomic environment was aggravated further by falling commodity prices in the early 1980s and a major slide in oil prices from 1982. Hill (1996), Pangestu (1993) and Thee (2000) argued extensively about the unproductive role of government intervention in Indonesia on manufacturing performance (see also Thee and Pangestu, 1998). In addition to the devaluation of the rupiah in 1983 and 1986 and subsequent 5 per cent devaluation annually, the government liberalised the economy and improved the macroeconomic environment[2] to attract export-oriented foreign firms. An exodus of Northeast Asian firms seeking offshore locations following the Plaza Accord of 1985 and the withdrawal of the generalised system of preferences (GSP) from the Asian newly industrialising economies (NIEs) in February 1988 attracted significant inflows of industrial FDI to Indonesia.[3] Nevertheless, despite being essentially light, garments and electronics initially evolved as inward-oriented industries, albeit growth was not very rapid.[4] Export orientation stimulated rapid growth in these industries from the late 1980s and early 1990s. Auto parts manufacturing became important initially under the IS regime and continued to enjoy protection rents until the collapse of the Suharto regime following the financial crisis of 1997. The aftermath of the political fallout after Suharto included the closure of the Timur–Kia deal to assemble Indonesian cars, and the national aeroplane manufacturing company.

From being inward-looking, garment and electronics became export-oriented by the 1990s. Export credits was introduced in January 1982. Bapeksta was formed in 1983 to spearhead export orientation, which initiated in Indonesia the opening of export-processing zones, duty drawbacks (on imported inputs against exports) and tax holidays to attract foreign direct investment (FDI). Firms exporting a minimum of 85 per cent were exempted from domestic content requirements from May 1986 (Balassa, 1991: 122). Tariffs were reduced sharply from the mid-1980s, the highest tariffs falling from 225 per cent to 60 per cent and the number of tariff lines dropping from 25 to 11 in March 1985 (Rasiah, 2003a). Trade reforms and increased emphasis on export orientation raised manufactured exports from only 2.3 per cent in 1980 to 50.6 per cent in 1992 (Rasiah, 2003a: Table 5). From negligible amounts in 1980, garments and electronics accounted for 25.1 per cent and 5.1 per cent of manufactured exports in 1998 (Thee, 2000: 446). Foreign ownership regulations remained unclear even after the mid-1994 reforms. Government

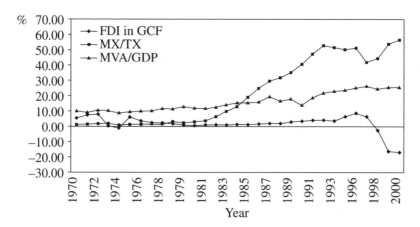

Notes: FDI – foreign direct investment; GCF – gross capital formation; MX – manufactured exports; TX – total exports; MVA – manufacturing value added; GDP – gross domestic product.

Source: Compiled from World Bank (2002).

Figure 5.1   FDI, manufactured exports and value added, Indonesia, 1970–2000

Regulation 20/1994 opened a number of sectors to 100 per cent equity ownership by foreign capital. Nevertheless, the uncertainty involving foreign ownership was removed following the imposition of the IMF-led SAP in 1998. All sectors other than wholesale and retail – where a 49 per cent ownership by companies registered in Indonesia was required – were open to 100 per cent foreign equity. Even in retail and wholesale activities, foreign firms can still own 100 per cent equity so long as at least 49 per cent of equity is registered in Indonesia.

Given the increasing emphasis on foreign firms – though FDI inflows have slowed down considerably since the financial crisis of 1997–98 and the political crisis that followed – it will be interesting to examine its role *vis-à-vis* local firms in generating exports and technological capabilities in Indonesia. It should be pointed out that the data represent firms under crisis conditions, though foreign ownership conditions at the time are arguably the most liberal in Indonesian manufacturing history. The industries of electronics and garments were chosen on the basis of fairly strong FDI levels and export shares in manufactured exports exceeding 5 per cent. Textiles and garments, and electronics accounted for 25.1 per cent and 5.1 per cent respectively of Indonesia's manufactured exports in 1998 (Thee, 2000: 446). Auto parts was added to the list owing to the impact of foreign automobile assemblies in

Indonesia that emerged largely under IS policies when domestic content legislation was used strongly until the enforcement of the Trade Related-Investment Measures Agreement of the World Trade Organization (WTO) in January 2000.

5.3   METHODOLOGY AND DATA

This chapter uses the same technological capability methodology advanced in Chapter 1, and hence only the specific variables and their measurement procedures are introduced here. Although the national sampling frame was not used, data collection was carried out randomly.

5.3.1   Specification of Variables

As explained earlier, the variables defined here for analysis are far less rich than those in the taxonomies advanced in Chapter 1, which was partly a consequence of the nature of the responses and partly a deliberate effort to enable cross-industry regressions. The variables used in the statistical analysis were measured and defined as follows.

Export incidence
In the absence of sufficient responses on value added, sales and export values, the chapter uses only the incidence of firms exporting as the proxy representing performance. It was measured as:

$$X_i = 1 \text{ if firm } i \text{ exports; } X_i = 0 \text{ otherwise,}$$

where X_i refers to export incidence of firm i. Using this criterion, foreign firms enjoyed higher export experience in all three industries: 66.7 per cent foreign against 35.0 per cent local in auto parts; 90.0 per cent foreign against 37.5 per cent local in electronics; and 100.0 per cent foreign against 67.4 per cent local in garments (see Table 5.1).

Firm-level technological capabilities
Using the methodology advanced in Chapter 1, three separate technological capability variables were estimated in this chapter. Human resource, process technology and R&D were the three component technologies computed, and subsequently added to define the overall technological intensity of firms. The estimation procedures used are described below.

Table 5.1 Ownership, export experience, size and management type by ownership, Indonesian sample, 2001

	Ownership		Export experience		Large size		Owner-managed		Total
	Foreign	Local	Foreign	Local	Foreign	Local	Foreign	Local	
Auto parts	12 (23.1)	40 (76.9)	8 (66.7)	14 (35.0)	4 (33.3)	8 (20.0)	0 (0.0)	18 (45.0)	52 (100.0)
Electronics	20 (45.5)	24 (54.5)	18 (90.0)	9 (37.5)	15 (75.0)	5 (20.8)	7 (35.0)	13 (54.2)	44 (100.0)
Garments	10 (17.9)	46 (82.1)	10 (100.0)	31 (67.4)	4 (40.0)	8 (17.4)	2 (20.0)	24 (52.2)	56 (100.0)
Total	42 (27.6)	110 (72.4)	36 (85.7)	54 (49.1)	23 (54.8)	21 (19.1)	9 (21.4)	59 (53.6)	152 (100.0)

Note: Figures in parentheses are percentages.

Source: Tabulated from ADB (2001, 2002) and UNU–INTECH (2002) surveys using Stata 7.0 Package.

Human resource capability

Human resource (*HR*) is expected to have a positive relationship to export-incidence and wages. Unlike Kenya and Uganda, the above relationship is expected to be fairly strong owing to exports targeted strongly to developed rather than neighbouring markets. Given the low-value-added nature of assembly and processing undertaken in the three industries in Indonesia, a strong relationship is not expected between the explanatory variables and R&D activities.

Human resource capability (*HR*) was measured as:

$$HR_i = 1/3[TM_i, TE_i, CHR_i] \qquad (5.1)$$

where *TM*, *TE* and *CHR* refer to training mode, training expense as a share of payroll, and cutting-edge human resource practices used respectively. *TM* was measured as a multinomial logistic variable of 1 when staff are sent out to external organisations for training, 2 when external staff are used to train employees, 3 when staff with training responsibilities are on payroll, 4 when a separate training department is used, 5 when a separate training centre is used and 0 when no formal training is undertaken. *CHR* was measured by a score of 1 for each of the practices and totalled. The firms were asked if it was their policy to encourage team-working, small group activities to improve company performance, multi-skilling, interaction with marketing, customer service and R&D department, lifelong learning and upward mobility. HR was divided by 3, which is the number of proxies used. The proxies were normalised using the formula below:

$$\text{Normalisation score} = (X_i - X_{min})/(X_{max} - X_{min}) \qquad (5.2)$$

where X_i, X_{min} and X_{max} refer to the *i*th, minimum and maximum values of the proxy *X*.

Process technology capability

Process technology (*PT*) – being central to participation in developed export markets even in low-value-added operations – can be expected to show a positive relationship with exports. Indonesia's exports of electronics and garments go mainly to the developed markets of North America, Western Europe and Japan.

Data on three proxies facilitated the computation of *PT*, which was calculated using the formula:

$$PT_i = 1/3[EM_i, ITC_i, QC_i] \qquad (5.3)$$

where *EM*, *ITC* and *QC* refer to equipment and machinery, information technology components and quality control instruments respectively. *EM* was computed as multinomial logistic variable with average age of over five years = 0, three to five years = 1, two to less than three years = 2 and less than two years = 3. Likert scale scores ranging from 1 to 5 (least to most) were used to measure *ITC*. *QC* was measured as a dummy variable (*QC* = 1 if cutting-edge methods were used, *QC* = 0 otherwise). *PT* was divided by three, which is the number of proxies used.

R&D

Given its underdeveloped institutional and systemic facilities and the preponderance of labour-intensive assembly and processing operations in Indonesia, R&D is unlikely to produce statistically meaningful results involving the explanatory variables.

The data collected enabled the computation of two R&D proxies, i.e. R&D expenditure as a percentage of sales and R&D personnel as a share of employment. It was possible from the sample data to disentangle investment advanced between process and product R&D, but this proxy was measured to relate to both product and process R&D as:

$$RD_i = 1/2[RD_{expi}, RD_{empi}] \qquad (5.4)$$

where RD_{exp} and RD_{emp} refer to R&D expenditure as a share of sales and R&D personnel in the workforce respectively of firm *i*.

R&D was also differentiated on the basis of investment shares in sales allocated for process and product R&D, and was measured as:

RD_{proci} = R&D expenditure in process technology/sales of firm *i*,

RD_{prodi} = R&D expenditure in product technology/sales of firm *i*.

Overall technological intensity

Overall technological intensity (*TI*) was measured by adding the variables of *HR* (technology embodied in humans), *PT* (technology embodied in machinery and equipment and intangible processes) and *RD* (technology development focus embodied in products, processes and humans). Given that electronics and garment exports are generally targeted to developed markets, the high technological competence required should help produce a positive relationship between export incidence and *TI*. *TI* was measured as:

$$TI_i = HR_i + PT_i + RD_i. \qquad (5.5)$$

The residual technological variables of human resource and process technology capabilities PT (HRT), human resource and R&D capability (HRD) and process technology and R&D capability (PRD) were excluded from the equations owing to multicollinearity problems with the explanatory and control variables (see Appendix 5.1).

Wages

Owing to the relatively weak position of unions in Indonesia (see Rasiah and Chua, 1998), this chapter just used wages as the proxy of labour market conditions. Given the large reserves of labour in Indonesia, wages may not show statistically meaningful results. Nevertheless, given the premium involving skilled and knowledge workers, a positive relationship can be expected between HR and wages. Average monthly wages was used. Since it is difficult to obtain wages of workers on their own, the figure was derived by dividing the total salaries and remuneration of each company by their workforce and converting to US dollars. Average wages was used in all the regressions and was measured as:

$$W_i = \text{average wage} = \text{total payroll/(number of employees).}$$

Other critical firm-level variables

Four other important firm-level structural variables were included in the analysis, i.e. ownership, size, age and management type.

Ownership Ownership was used as a separate dummy variable and was classified using a lower foreign equity share with the exception of RD, where either a positive or a negative sign is possible for reasons advanced earlier. Given foreign electronics, and textile and garment firms' specialisation on exports to developed markets, foreign ownership can be expected to enjoy a positive relationship with HR and PT, but not with RD owing to Indonesia's underdeveloped high-tech institutions. Since it is often argued that foreign ownership in Indonesia is understated for political reasons (see Hill, 1996), the cut-off point used here was lowered to 25 per cent foreign equity. Except for two firms with 25 per cent foreign equity, the other joint-venture firms enjoyed at least 50 per cent foreign equity. Foreign ownership (FO) was measured as follows:

$$FO_i = 1 \text{ if foreign equity ownership was 25 per cent or more;}$$
$$FO = 0 \text{ otherwise.}$$

Using this criterion, local firms outnumbered foreign firms in all three industries in the sample. The breakdown by ownership was 76.9 per cent local against 23.1 per cent foreign in auto parts, 54.5 per cent local against 45.5 per cent foreign in electronics and 82.1 per cent local against 17.9 per cent foreign in garments (see Table 5.1).

Size   Employment was used as the proxy for defining size. As argued earlier, size may take both positive and negative signs or may not be statistically significant at all. Originally four categories were used, i.e.:

Micro = 50 and less
Small = >50–200
Medium = >200–500
Large = >500.

With the exception of micro firms, which did not produce statistically significant results in all the regressions, the results of the remaining regressions did not change much when the categories were reduced to two, and hence the results presented use:

SMI = 500 and less
Large = >500.

Using this criterion, large firms were generally more foreign-owned than local-owned in all three industries. The breakdown was: 33.3 per cent of foreign and 20.0 per cent of local auto parts firms; 75.0 per cent of foreign and 20.8 per cent of local electronics firms; and 40.0 per cent foreign and 17.4 per cent of local garment firms (see Table 5.1).

Age   Given that firms with longer experience are thought to enjoy greater experiential and tacit knowledge, age is considered to provide a positive relationship with exports and technological capabilities. The absolute age of the firm is used as an independent variable. The statistical relationship may not be positive if especially foreign firms using superior technology from abroad and enjoying strong access to global markets began establishing or relocating operations recently. Hence these firms already have long experience globally although their operating experience in Indonesia is short. Age is measured as follows:

$$A_i = \text{years in operation.}$$

Owner-managed firms
It is often argued that owner-managers (*OM*) impact both positively and negatively on firms' performance. On the one hand, owners are considered to

show greater drive to succeed owing to lower agency costs and the ability to make quick decisions because of the narrow chain of command. On the other hand, owner-managers are considered less professional – especially when involving big businesses – and hence may lack the instruments to succeed in export markets. Hence a neutral hypothesis with either a positive or a negative sign is expected. *OM* is measured using a dummy variable as follows:

$$OM_i = \text{if firm is managed either partly or fully by the owner;}$$
$$OM_i = 0 \text{ otherwise.}$$

Using the above criterion, local firms enjoyed a higher incidence of owner management. The breakdown was: 45.0 per cent local against no foreign auto parts firms; 54.2 per cent local against 35.0 per cent foreign electronics firms; and 52.2 per cent local against 20.0 per cent foreign garment firms (see Table 5.1).

Specific industry-level questionnaires were designed, pilot tested, translated into local Bahasa Indonesia and mailed to all firms listed in official government statistics records in Indonesia. In addition, the national consultant hired by Asian Development Bank (ADB) in Indonesia used research assistants to distribute and collect questionnaires personally in Java. Case studies of at least three firms in each industry were undertaken by the author to help extract industry-type characteristics.[5] Eighteen firms mailed questionnaires directly to the author. A total of 152 usable questionnaires were compiled (see Table 5.1). The survey and the case studies constitute the basis for the results and analysis in the study.

5.3.2   Statistical Analysis

The following basic model was specified to estimate the statistical relationships involving export incidence. Logit regressions were preferred here because of the use of a dependent dummy variable. The model was run with industry dummies:

$$\text{Logit } X = \alpha + \beta_1 TI + \beta_2 OM + \beta_3 FO + \beta_4 W + \beta_5 S + \beta_6 + \mu \qquad (5.6)$$

The determinants of three important firm-level capabilities were estimated using Tobit regressions. Tobit regressions were preferred over OLS because the dependent variables were all censored on the right and left sides of the data sets. The models were run with industry dummies:

$$\text{Tobit: } TI = \alpha + \beta_1 X + \beta_2 FO + \beta_3 OM + \beta_4 S + \beta_5 W + \beta_6 A + \mu \qquad (5.7)$$

$$\text{Tobit: } HR = \alpha + \beta_1 X + \beta_2 FO + \beta_3 OM + \beta_4 S + \beta_5 W + \beta_6 A + \mu \quad (5.8)$$

$$\text{Tobit: } PT = \alpha + \beta_1 X + \beta_2 FO + \beta_3 OM + \beta_4 S + \beta_5 W + \beta_6 A + \mu \quad (5.9)$$

$$\text{Tobit: } RD = \alpha + \beta_1 X + \beta_2 FO + \beta_3 OM + \beta_4 S + \beta_5 W + \beta_6 A + \mu \quad (5.10)$$

Models (5.6)–(5.10) did not face serious multi-collinearity problems (see Appendix 5.1), and they were also run by ownership. The logit regression involving the foreign firms' sample using model (5.6) failed owing to a high concentration of firms enjoying export experience (85.7 per cent) (see Table 5.1). Industry dummies were used in all the models but the results were not reported.

5.4   STATISTICAL RESULTS

This section compares technological capabilities of foreign and local firms, and statistical relationships involving the explanatory variables of export incidence and technological intensities while controlling for other effects.

5.4.1   Statistical Differences

Two-tail *t*-tests were used to examine the statistical significance of the technology intensity means and the results are presented in Table 5.2. Foreign firms enjoyed higher means over local firms involving all the statistically significant means. Apart from product R&D, where local firms enjoyed higher means than foreign firms, even the sample means of foreign firms exceeded that of local firms involving all the technology variables. These results could be a consequence of Indonesia's underdeveloped institutional endowments as well as the political and economic crisis that exposed local firms to severe financial problems.

Foreign firms enjoyed statistically highly significant (1 per cent level) and higher *TI* and *HR* means than local firms in electronics. Foreign firms also enjoyed a statistically highly significant (1 per cent level) and higher *HR* mean compared to local firms in auto parts. Foreign firms enjoyed a statistically significant higher *PT* mean in electronics (5 per cent level), and *TI* mean in auto parts (10 per cent level) than local firms. No obvious statistical differences existed between foreign and local firms involving *RD*, and even when broken into process and product R&D activities.

Table 5.2 Two-tail t-tests of technological intensities, Indonesia, 2001

	Foreign	Local	t		Foreign	Local	t
TI				**RD**			
Auto parts	0.943	0.698	1.73***	Auto parts	0.215	0.207	0.17
Electronics	1.035	0.735	3.21*	Electronics	0.141	0.113	0.59
Textiles & garments	1.497	1.085	1.42	Textiles & garments	0.520	0.374	1.30
HR				**RDprod**			
Auto parts	0.493	0.302	2.84*	Auto parts	0.096	0.109	-0.30
Electronics	0.628	0.425	3.80*	Electronics	0.052	0.044	0.29
Textiles & garments	0.413	0.351	0.76	Textiles & garments	0.600	0.391	1.30
PT				**RDproc**			
Auto parts	0.375	0.306	1.07	Auto parts	0.333	0.305	0.45
Electronics	0.438	0.352	1.98**	Electronics	0.231	0.181	0.61
Textiles & garments	0.367	0.361	0.07	Textiles & garments	0.440	0.357	1.30

Note: *, ** and *** refer to statistical significance at 1, 5 and 10% levels respectively.

Source: Computed from ADB (2001, 2002) and UNU–INTECH (2002) surveys using Stata 7.0 Package.

5.4.2   Statistical Relationships

Logit regressions were used to estimate the statistical relationships involving export incidence, and Tobit regressions used to estimate statistical relationships involving technological intensity variables (see Tables 5.3 and 5.4). The regressions involving the foreign firms' sample in Table 5.3 failed owing to the sample being dominated by firms with export experience, which is the dependent variable, and all foreign garment firms exported (see Table 5.1). All results presented in Tables 5.3 and 5.4 passed the White test for heteroscedacity.

Table 5.3   Relationship involving export incidence, Indonesian sample, 2001

	X	
	All	Local
TI	09.46	0.746
	(2.22)**	(1.75)***
S	1.799	1.411
	(3.06)*	(2.25)**
FO	1.373	
	(2.43)**	
OM	−0.749	−1.036
	(−1.56)	(−2.08)**
A	0.037	0.039
	(1.43)	(1.41)
W	−0.156	−0.144
	(−1.04)	(−0.92)
μ	−1.023	−0.751
	(−1.31)	(−0.92)
N	152	110
χ^2	63.21*	33.21*

Notes: *, ** and *** refer to statistical significance at 1, 5 and 10% levels respectively; export incidence too high to extract meaningful results in the foreign firms' sample; industry dummies not reported.

Source: Computed from ADB (2001, 2002) and UNU–INTECH (2002) surveys using Stata 7.0 Package.

Table 5.4   Relationship involving technological intensities, Indonesian sample, 2001

	TI			HR			PT			RD		
	All	Foreign	Local	All	Foreign	Local	All	Foreign	Local	All	Foreign	Local
X	0.212	0.263	0.239	0.099	0.243	0.084	0.125	0.268	0.125	0.067	0.016	0.088
	(2.00)**	(1.14)	(1.97)**	(2.78)*	(2.51)**	(2.21)**	(3.57)*	(2.50)**	(3.15)*	(1.14)	(0.13)	(1.31)
S	0.155	0.480	−0.034	0.082	0.043	0.068	0.078	0.110	0.073	0.023	0.261	−0.089
	(1.41)	(2.88)*	(−0.24)	(2.20)**	(0.61)	(1.50)	(2.15)**	(1.54)	(1.55)	(0.38)	(3.10)*	(−1.12)
OM	−0.306	−0.609	−0.260	−0.109	−0.247	−0.089	−0.053	−0.164	−0.046	−0.086	−0.143	−0.086
	(−3.11)*	(−3.21)*	(−2.22)**	(−3.26)*	(−3.06)*	(−2.42)**	(−1.61)	(−2.08)**	(−1.19)	(−1.57)	(−1.58)	(−1.32)
A	0.010	0.021	0.008	0.001	0.002	0.000	0.004	0.013	0.002	0.004	0.012	0.003
	(2.09)**	(2.86)*	(1.36)	(0.38)	(0.52)	(0.18)	(2.62)*	(3.94)*	(1.15)	(1.66)***	(3.22)*	(0.79)
FO	0.099			0.078			−0.042			0.026		
	(0.87)			(2.03)**			(−1.12)			(0.41)		
W	0.038	0.023	0.050	0.029	−0.005	0.045	0.004	0.021	0.000	0.005	0.013	0.006
	(1.27)	(0.49)	(1.36)	(2.85)*	(−0.28)	(3.87)*	(0.44)	(1.09)	(0.03)	(0.30)	(0.58)	(0.30)
μ	0.565	0.328	0.571	0.361	0.456	0.292	0.265	−0.052	0.293	−0.028	−0.251	0.018
	(3.52)*	(1.33)	(2.90)*	(6.67)*	(4.40)*	(4.73)*	(4.99)*	(−0.45)	(4.57)*	(−0.30)	(−1.87)***	(0.16)
N	152	42	110	152	42	110	152	42	110	152	42	110
χ^2	54.89*	31.74*	30.32*	79.97*	24.33*	46.56*	46.64*	28.70*	26.53*	53.88*	41.75*	32.35*

Notes: *, ** and *** refer to statistical significance at 1, 5 and 10% levels respectively; industry dummies not reported.

Source: Computed from ADB (2001, 2002) and UNU–INTECH (2002) surveys using Stata 7.0 Package.

Export incidence

Foreign ownership (*FO*) was statistically highly significant (1 per cent level), and its coefficient was positive and strong, confirming the higher export incidence of foreign firms compared to local firms even after controlling for other variables (see Tables 5.1 and 5.3). This result could not be compared at the ownership sample level as the foreign firms' sample involving garment firms faced perfect prediction given that all of them enjoyed export experience.

TI was statistically significant in both the overall (5 per cent level) and local firms' (10 per cent level) samples. The positive coefficient of *TI* suggests that technological intensity enjoys a positive influence on exports, i.e. firms with higher overall intensities are likely to export. Size was statistically significant in both samples, and its coefficient positive, demonstrating that larger firms enjoy higher incidence of exporting. Owner-managed firms faced an inverse statistical relationship, and its coefficient was statistically significant in the local firms' sample. Local owner-managed firms faced a lower incidence of exporting in Indonesia.

Technological capabilities

FO was statistically significant only in the *HR* regression, and its coefficient was positive (see Table 5.4). Higher export incidence and the difficult financial circumstances that have faced local firms since 1997 may have reduced their emphasis on HR practices.

Reversing the regression between *X* and *TI* produced the same results. *X* was statistically significant in the overall and local firms' samples, and the coefficients were positive. The coefficient of *X* was also positive in the foreign firms' sample, but it was statistically insignificant. Exporting firms obviously show a positive relationship with *TI*. Size was statistically highly significant only in the foreign firms' sample. Age was also statistically significant and its coefficient positive in the overall and foreign firms' samples. Owner-managed firms enjoyed an inverse relationship in all three samples, and their coefficients were statistically significant, suggesting that these firms have lower technological intensities than other firms.

Against *HR*, the explanatory variable of *X* was statistically significant in all three samples and its coefficients were positive, demonstrating that export markets attract higher emphasis on *HR* practices in firms. The higher *X* coefficient enjoyed in the foreign firms' sample compared with the local firms' sample suggests stronger emphasis in exporting foreign firms. Size was statistically significant in the overall sample, though the coefficients were positive in all three samples. *OM* was inversely correlated and its coefficients were statistically significant in all three samples, demonstrating that owner-managed firms put less emphasis on *HR* practices than other firms. Wages was statistically highly significant (1 per cent level) in the overall and local firms' samples, and its coefficients were positive, suggesting a wage premium on human resource capability in local firms. The lack of statistical significance involving the foreign firms' sample may be the consequence of a highly depreciated rupiah since foreign firms began to transact more in US dollars after the financial crisis.[6]

Against *PT*, the explanatory variable of *X* was statistically significant in all three samples, and its coefficients were positive. The higher coefficient of *X* in the foreign firms' sample compared to the other two samples suggests that export incidence has a higher influence on *PT* in foreign firms. Size was statistically significant in the overall sample, and its coefficient positive. The coefficients of size were also positive in the foreign and local firms' sample but they were statistically insignificant. Age was statistically significant in the overall and foreign firms' samples.

The low intensity of participation in R&D activities accounts for the generally weak statistical results involving *RD*. The results were weakest involving the local firms' sample. The relationship between *X* and *RD* was statistically insignificant, though the coefficient was positive in all three samples. Size was statistically significant only in the foreign firms' sample, and its coefficient was positive. Age was also statistically significant in the overall and foreign firms' sample, and its coefficients were positive.

Taken together, foreign firms generally enjoyed higher export incidence and technological intensities than local firms. Apart from product R&D in auto parts, foreign firms enjoyed higher technological intensity means than local firms in all the remaining results. However, the differences were only statistically significant involving *TI* in auto parts and electronics, *HR* in auto parts and electronics and *PT* in electronics. The econometric analysis showed a strong relationship between export incidence and overall technological, *HR* and *PT* intensities. Foreign ownership was stronger in the *HR* regression, and the coefficient of *X* stronger in the foreign firms' sample than the local firms' sample in the *HR* and *PT* regressions. The *RD* regressions generally produced statistically weak results owing to the low R&D intensity levels.

5.5 CONCLUSIONS

Overall, foreign firms enjoyed higher export incidence and technological intensities than local firms in the auto parts, electronics and garment industries in Indonesia. Foreign firms enjoyed statistically significant higher *TI* and *HR* means than local firms in auto parts and electronics. Foreign firms enjoyed a higher and statistically significant *PT* mean than local firms in electronics. With the exception of product R&D in auto parts, foreign firms also enjoyed higher but statistically insignificant means than local firms in the remaining *PT* and *RD* capabilities. The statistical results showed a strong relationship between export incidence and *TI*, *HR* and *PT*. Not only was *FO* statistically significant and its coefficient positive in the overall sample in the *HR* regression; but the coefficient of *X* was also stronger in the foreign firms' sample than in the local firms' sample. *X* was also stronger in the foreign firms' sample than in the local firms' sample involving the *PT* regression. The *RD* regressions generally produced statistically weak results owing to the low R&D intensity levels arising from Indonesia's underdeveloped high-tech infrastructure.

While taking cognisance of the impact of the financial and political crisis that may have created technological asymmetries by ownership, the results show that foreign firms generally enjoy higher technological capabilities. These results show strong potential for local firms – either through supplier relations, demonstration effect or transfer of tacit knowledge embodied in human capital – to benefit from the operations of foreign firms. Foreign firms' exposure to export markets also offers strong potential for the development of external market and domestic backward linkages for local firms. The sequencing of government focus in attracting FDI and stimulating learning and innovation must take account of the fact that export-manufacturing firms develop at the bottom of the technology ladder in host economies with weak institutions. Foreign firms act as an important vehicle in penetrating export markets and in the relocation of production knowledge (see Urata, 2001).

Given the nascent stage and the lack of institutional and systemic support and a record of government failure in the past, foreign firms seem to have internalised human resource development to support (including process technology) export manufacturing. The limited participation in R&D activities is generally directed to improving process technology. The Indonesian government will have to harness foreign–local firm synergies by creating and strengthening institutions and building links between them to stimulate learning and upgrading in the three industries, which will be extremely difficult given the weak political and macroeconomic environment that has prevailed following the financial and political crisis of 1997–98. The problem is even more severe in the fragile islands outside Java, where balkanisation is threatening a break-up of the country.

NOTES

1. A group of Berkeley economists had charted the liberal environment following the introduction of the New Order under Suharto in 1964 (Prawiro, 1998).
2. A Swiss firm replaced customs officials to control the import and export of goods, simplifying duty controls and eliminating unproductive rent seeking. Presidential Instruction No.

4   helped reduce customs-related corruption (Pangestu, 1993: 13); as a consequence, holding and inspection periods decreased by several weeks. Such reductions in customs processing time and in wasteful rents also reduced uncertainties and costs.

3.   Most of Southeast Asia and later China became beneficiaries of these developments.

4.   Batik printing enjoys a history much longer than modern garment manufacturing in Indonesia.

5.   I am grateful to Ari Kuncoro, who coordinated the survey and arranged my firm visits in late 2001.

6.   Author interview in Jakarta in February 2002.

APPENDIX 5.1

Table 5A.1 Correlation coefficient matrix involving independent variables, Indonesian sample, 2001

	TI	HR	PT	RD	FO	S	A	X	W	OM	PRD	HRD	HRT
TI	1.000												
HR	0.513*#	1.000											
PT	0.598*#	0.402*	1.000										
RD	0.851*#	0.074	0.329	1.000									
FO	0.179	0.366	0.143	−0.011	1.000								
S	0.239	0.399	0.342	0.0311	0.350	1.000							
A	0.169	0.069	0.244	0.129	0.083	0.159	1.000						
X	0.377	0.377	0.415*	0.206	0.330	0.379	0.153	1.000					
W	−0.027	0.283	0.057	−0.195	−0.033	0.099	0.005	−0.137	1.000				
OM	−0.319	−0.381	−0.219	−0.155	−0.256	−0.188	−0.096	−0.234	−0.234	1.000			
PRD	0.904*#	0.268	0.765*#	0.860*#	0.070	0.206	0.219	0.365	−0.102	−0.224	1.000		
HRD	0.940*#	0.702*#	0.496*	0.762*#	0.230	0.281	0.137	0.392	0.044	−0.357	0.788*#	1.000	
HRT	0.659*#	0.861*#	0.812*#	0.230	0.313	0.444*	0.180	0.471*	0.212	−0.365	0.595*#	0.723*#	1.000

Notes: * high correlation; # compositional overlap.

Source: Computed from ADB (2001, 2002) and UNU–INTECH (2002) surveys using Stata 7.0 Package.

6. Economic performance, local sourcing and technological intensities in Malaysia

Rajah Rasiah and Ganesh Rasagam

6.1 INTRODUCTION

Foreign direct investment (FDI) has played a major role in Malaysia's industrial development, especially in the expansion of manufactured exports since the early 1970s. Although specific instruments such as the Industrial Coordination Act of 1975 were introduced to shield foreign participation – including non-indigenous investment – in inward industries, generous incentives have targeted export-oriented manufacturing firms since the Investment Incentives Act of 1968, but especially following the opening of free trade zones in 1972 (Rasiah, 1993). From a focus on just investment and employment, the government shifted incentives to stimulate upgrading and higher-value-added activities from the 1990s. Considerable changes have since occurred in the technological dynamics of firms, as both foreign affiliates and local firms transformed operations to meet external competition and benefit from the incentive structure offered by the government. The successful development of a dynamic cluster in the state of Penang, which includes a range of local supplier firms, is now well documented (Rasiah, 1994, 1995, 1996, 2002b; Best and Rasiah, 2003; Narayanan and Lai, 2000; Mohd Nazari, 2001; Ariffin and Bell, 1999; Ariffin and Figuiredo, 2003). Related work on other industries has been scarce, although Capanelli (1999) examined supplier networks involving Japanese firms' sourcing of auto parts, and Belderbos et al. (2001) analysed linkages generated by Japanese investment in a number of countries that included Malaysia. Hobday (1996) studied innovation activities of multinationals in Malaysia. Although several studies have used dynamic methodologies to assess links between foreign and local firms, little work has been carried out to compare the technological capabilities and economic performance of foreign and local firms using firm-level data.

This chapter seeks to fill this gap and offers an example of a middle-income economy which has made recent efforts to build a high-tech infrastructure by examining technological and economic performance differences between foreign and local firms using a sample of auto parts, electronics and textile and garment firms in Malaysia. Malaysia has a developed basic infrastructure but its high-tech infrastructure is still too weak to support R&D activities in firms. Although giant transnationals (e.g. Intel, Motorola, Hewlett Packard, Seagate, Dell and Advanced Micro Devices, and the Toray Group of textile companies) are engaged in large scale production activities, the lack of institutional support has restricted their participation in R&D activities in Malaysia. Although R&D investment in gross national investment (GNI) rose from 0.1 per cent in 1988 to 0.4 per cent in 1998 (World Bank, 2002), and R&D scientists and engineers per million people rose from 85.4 in 1992 to 154.0 in 1998 – these figures were significantly lower than the commensurate figures for Korea, Taiwan and Singapore (see Rasiah, 2004). Malaysia is likely to produce results unique to economies with long production experience involving foreign firms and strong basic infrastructure. Also, rising wages, domestic content policies supporting auto parts manufacturing (which was still in place in 2003), and rationalisation involving the termination of the Multi-Fibre Agreement (MFA) in the textile and garment industries may have an impact on the Malaysian results. The lack of panel data has prevented an assessment of causation. The rest of the chapter is organised as follows. Section 6.2 discusses policy instruments and their consequent impact on FDI inflows, and manufacturing value added and exports. Section 6.3 presents the methodology and data. Section 6.4 examines statistical differences and relationships involving productivity, exports, skills, and technological and local sourcing intensities between foreign and local firms. Section 6.5 concludes.

6.2   FDI, MANUFACTURING GROWTH AND INSTITUTIONAL STRENGTH

This section discusses the significance of FDI, and the state of institutional development and manufacturing in Malaysia to locate the subsequent analysis within a structural context. Malaysia has a long history of FDI participation beginning in mining and plantation agriculture, and subsequently in manufacturing to support the primary activities and growing domestic demand for light consumer goods (Rasiah, 1995). The expansion of manufacturing in GDP became particularly important following its identification by the government as the engine of growth to engender poverty alleviation and redistribution (Malaysia, 1971). FDI was again specifically targeted to stimulate export-oriented manufacturing with significant promotional instruments contained in the Free Trade Zone Act of 1971, and the Promotion of Incentives Act of 1986. Manufacturing value added in GDP, and exports in total

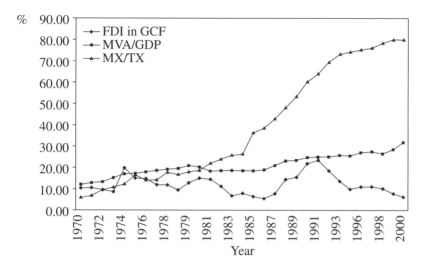

Notes: FDI – foreign direct investment; GCF – gross capital formation; MVA – manufacturing value added; GDP – gross domestic product; MX – manufactured exports; TX – total exports.

Source: Computed from World Bank (2002).

Figure 6.1 FDI, manufacturing value added and exports, Malaysia, 1970–2000

merchandise exports, rose sharply throughout the period 1972–2000 (see Figure 6.1). Although FDI levels in gross capital formation (GCF) rose strongly until 1993, they have subsequently shown a trend decline.

The introduction of import-substitution (IS) industrialisation since the enactment of the Pioneer Industry ordinance of 1958, but especially from the mid-1960s after the formation of the Malaysian Industrial Development Authority in 1964,[1] stimulated FDI participation in final goods assembly. All three industries chosen in this chapter, i.e. textiles and garments, electronics (electrical) and auto parts (automobiles) either emerged or grew from this period. Although foreign textile and garment production arrived earlier, significant participation only came from the 1950s and 1960s, and Matsushita Electric in 1965 and Volvo in 1969 pioneered the electronics and automobile industries respectively. However, FDI inflows in manufacturing slowed down substantially once the small domestic market became saturated by the late 1960s (Hoffman and Tan, 1980).

The first major wave of manufacturing FDI in Malaysia emerged in 1972–79, when export-oriented firms benefiting from the first round of export-oriented incentives pushed its share in GCF substantially (see Figure

6.1). Textiles and garments, and especially electronics experienced a massive inflow of FDI. Automobiles (in transport equipment) remained, with far less investment owing to its inward orientation. However, growing imports and the domestic IS sector continued to account for the bulk of domestic demand in the 1970s as export-oriented firms bought and sold little in the principal customs area (PCA). By the end of the 1970s, the government recognised that the export of manufactured goods was limited to a narrow range of products and there was minimum integration between the IS and export-oriented (EO) sectors. The dualistic structure led the government to launch a more aggressive plan to develop heavy industries, *inter alia*, as a means to strengthen inter-industry linkages (Rasiah, 1995: chs 4 and 5; Alavi, 1996).

Industrial emphasis from 1986 moved from increasing IS orientation to export orientation again, although both strategies were run concurrently. External developments and the Industrial Master Plan (IMP) of 1986 (implemented through the Promotion of Investment Act of 1986) helped expand manufactured exports sharply from the mid-1980s. The Plaza Accord of 1985 and the withdrawal of the generalised system of preferences (GSP) from the Asian newly industrialised economies (NIEs) in 1988 – which pushed up Northeast Asian and Singaporean currency values and reduced market access of firms in these economies in major developed markets – pressured a massive relocation of FDI into Southeast Asia. Malaysia was a major beneficiary.[2]

FDI shares in manufacturing and the three industries examined in the chapter rose in the late 1980s and early 1990s (see Figure 6.2). FDI shares in fixed asset ownership fell in the late 1990s because of rising production costs, the slowdown in electronics and subsequently the financial crisis of 1997–98. Indeed, net FDI in GCF reached its peak in 1992 (24.8 per cent) and fell gradually afterwards to 11.8 per cent in 1995 before showing some rise in the intervening years before falling further down to 8.8 per cent in 1999 (see Figure 6.1). The IMP provided a long-term plan for the development of specific subsectors, policy measures and areas of special emphasis. Twelve subsectors were given high-priority status, comprising seven resource-based industries and five non-resource-based industries. The resource-based industries were food processing, rubber, palm-oil, wood products, chemical and petrochemical, non-ferrous metal products, and non-metallic mineral products. The non-resource-based industries were electrical machinery, transport equipment, machinery and engineering products, ferrous metal and apparel. The recommendations of the IMP that were implemented included, among others, the consolidation of fiscal incentives to promote investment, with major improvements made to induce reinvestments, linkages, exports and training. Emphasis was also given to support research and development (R&D).

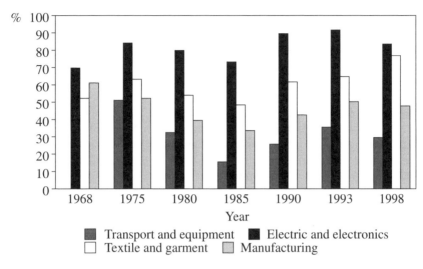

Source: Computed from Rasiah (2001b).

Figure 6.2 FDI share in fixed capital, Malaysia, 1968–98

Apart from tax and tariff holidays, other export-oriented incentives included double deductions on export credit refinancing. Among the most effective incentives was the extension of tax relief for a further five years for eligible companies that were already in operation. The eligibility criteria for double deduction for promoting exports was revised to include expenses incurred on publicity and advertisements in the media; provision of samples to prospective customers including preparation of tenders for the supply of goods to prospective customers outside Malaysia; provisions for exhibits at trade fairs or industrial exhibitions; participation in trade fairs or trade exhibitions; as well as costs incurred to maintain sales offices overseas for the promotion of exports (see Alavi, 1996). The government revamped the export credit refinancing (ECR) scheme to allow exporters greater access to subsidised interest (4 per cent) credit before or upon shipment of products. Under phase one, the limits of financing were raised from RM3 million to RM5 million. With phase two, reforms on the pre-shipment facility, the ECR ensured readily available financing to a wider range of direct and indirect exporters. The rising currencies of Japan and the Asian NIEs from 1985 and the ringgit's exchange rate management by the Central Bank added to greater export competitiveness of Malaysia's export-oriented manufacturing sector in the second half of the 1980s.[3]

The government also introduced substantial tariff reforms in the domestic market, especially involving light industries (Alavi, 1996; Malaysia, 1986:

36–8). However, state-sponsored heavy industries – of which auto parts has remained a beneficiary – continued to enjoy high IS rents. Nevertheless, these industries hardly disadvantaged export-oriented firms as they operated outside the PCA and hence did not face tariffs. The amount of incentives that flooded the EO sector can be argued to have been far too excessive as massive capital inflows, especially from 1990 (see Doraisamy and Rasiah, 2001), began to overheat the economy.

Serious labour shortages and rising wages brought extensive complaints from companies across the manufacturing sector in the early 1990s. The government began to emphasise domestic content regulations as well as institutional development to stimulate technological deepening as wages rose considerably in the early 1990s (Malaysia, 2001). A number of instruments were introduced to transform the manufacturing sector to higher-value-added and high-technology operations: e.g. the Action Plan for Industrial Technology Development (APITD) of 1990, the Human Resource Development Act of 1992, Second Industrial Master Plan (IMP2) of 1996;[4] Multimedia Super Corridor (MSC) in 1997, were some of the blueprints adopted to hasten structural change. Other institutions launched to quicken technology development in the manufacturing sector included the opening of the Malaysian Technology Development Corporation (MTDC) in 1992 and the Malaysia Industry–Government High Technology (MIGHT) in 1993 (Malaysia, 2001). The late 1990s were also gripped by rising current account deficits as rising production costs and overheating, and the emergence of attractive foreign sites (especially China and Philippines), began to reduce FDI levels in EO industries. Increasing liberalisation pressures since the formation of the World Trade Organization (WTO), the ASEAN[5] Free Trade Area (AFTA) and Asia–Pacific Economic Cooperation (APEC) also induced several domestic firms to internationalise production to cheaper sites with larger domestic markets – e.g. Eng Teknologi and Atlan.

Export-oriented policies of the early 1970s and from the mid-1980s increased the share of manufactured exports in the Malaysian economy. Manufactured exports as a percentage of total exports only accounted for about 10 per cent in 1970 but surpassed 80 per cent by 2000 (see Figure 6.1). The share of manufacturing value added in GDP rose from 12.4 per cent in 1970 to 21.6 per cent in 1980, 24.2 per cent in 1990 and 32.8 per cent in 2000. The trend values of the export–GDP ratio increased significantly since the beginning of the 1970s, from around 40 per cent in the first half of the 1970s to over 60 per cent in the second half of the 1980s and exceeding 80 per cent after 1990 (see Rasiah, 2001a, 2001b: figs 2 and 3). The gradual decline in major commodity prices (particularly tin and rubber) and the slow growth of agricultural export volume only partly explain the shift.[6] EO industrial expansion has been the most important reason for the change.

FDI acted as the prime engine of export manufacturing growth. Transnational corporations not only generated exports, but also offered the market access as they relocated the labour-intensive part of their value-added chain in Malaysia. The electrical machinery industry – where FDI accounted for over 90 per cent of ownership through much of the 1990s (see Figure 6.2) – accounted for over 71 per cent of manufactured exports in 1997. On the demand side, Malaysia's exports have been affected by FDI participation in export-processing and assembly activities to meet demand generated in developed economies (Rasiah, 1994, 1995). On the supply side, factor endowments, as well as policy instruments, have been critical in stimulating exports (Ariff and Hill, 1985). Policy instruments that attracted FDI and stimulated the expansion of EO industries included the provision of generous tax and tariff holidays, subsidised and coordinated special industrial zones and managed exchange rate float. Free trade zones (FTZ) and licensed manufacturing warehouse (LMW), in particular, were crucial in the exports of manufactured goods although their relative importance has declined since the late 1980s as tariffs facing most export-processing industries in the principal customs area declined. In addition, exporting firms were eligible for incentives irrespective of location from the late 1980s. The contribution of export-processing zones to total manufactured exports fell from 70 per cent in 1980 to 40 per cent in 1991 (Rasiah, 1993). FDI also accounted for much of other non-resource-based exports. Non-resource-based exports accounted for 74 per cent of total manufactured exports in this period, the main components being electrical machinery, textiles, clothing and footwear, metal products and transport equipment. FDI owned more than half of the fixed assets involving the textile, clothing and footwear industries.

It is against this manufacturing background with strong FDI participation and Malaysia's location in the middle-income category of the development trajectory this chapter will examine the firm-level data collected.

6.3   METHODOLOGY AND DATA

The methodology used in the chapter is explained in Chapter 1. This section presents the specific definitions used to measure and analyse the Malaysian data. The variables and their component proxies used in the chapter were measured and defined as follows.

6.3.1   Productivity and Export Performance

The proxies of labour productivity and export intensities were used to denote productivity and export performance respectively. Most firms in the sample enjoyed export experience accounting for 62 (92.5 per cent) of foreign and 39 (75.0 per cent) of local firms (see Table 6.1); the breakdown was 16 (88.9 per cent) foreign and 11 (73.3 per cent) local in auto parts; 37 (89.2 per cent) foreign and 8 (88.9 per cent) local in electronics; and 9 (75.0 per cent) foreign and 20 (71.4 per cent) local in textiles and garments. Both variables have problems but they do allow useful assessments.

$$\text{Labour productivity} = VA_i/L_i,$$

where *VA* and *L* refer to value added in 10,000 ringgit and total employees respectively of firm *i* in 2001.

$$\text{Export intensity} = X_i/Y_i,$$

where *X* and *Y* refer to exports and gross output of firm *i* in 2001.

6.3.2   Technological Capabilities

The technological capability framework advanced in Chapter 1 is employed here. Despite relatively weak institutional support for high-tech activities, especially electronics, and textile and garment firms are likely to show strong human resource and process technology intensities owing to several years of experience engaging in large scale export-oriented activities in Malaysia. However, the weak support for R&D activities is likely to produce low R&D intensities. The following broad capabilities and related composition of proxies were used.

Human resource
Two alternative proxies were used to represent human resource. However, human resource capability was used separately to measure human resource practices that denote development in firms, and hence it excluded technical, engineering and professional human resource endowments as a share of the workforce (skills intensity). The exclusion allows the differentiation of human resource capability developed by each firm and those that are acquired or poached from institutions and other firms. Both dimensions are important for driving firms' operations.

Human resource practices
Human resource (*HR*) practices is expected to have a positive relationship with labour productivity, process technology and skills intensity. Given the fairly developed nature of manufacturing undertaken in the four industries in Malaysia, a strong relationship is expected between *HR* and R&D activities.

Table 6.1 Breakdown of Malaysia sample, 2001

	Foreign	Local	Export experience Foreign	Local	Large firms Foreign	Local	Owner-managed Foreign	Local	Patents Foreign	Local	Total
Auto parts	18 (54.5)	15 (45.5)	16 (88.9)	11 (73.3)	8 (44.4)	2 (13.3)	0 (0.0)	6 (40.0)	0 (0.0)	0 (0.0)	33
Electronics	37 (80.4)	9 (19.6)	37 (89.2)	8 (88.9)	22 (59.5)	4 (44.4)	11 (29.7)	4 (44.4)	5 (13.5)	0 (0.0)	46
Textiles & garments	12 (30.0)	28 (70.0)	9 (75.0)	20 (71.4)	7 (58.3)	6 (21.4)	0 (0.0)	17 (60.7)	0 (0.0)	8 (28.6)	40
Total	67 (56.3)	52 (43.7)	62 (92.5)	39 (75.0)	37 (55.2)	12 (23.1)	11 (16.4)	27 (51.9)	5 (8.8)	8 (15.4)	119

Note: Figures in parentheses are percentages.

Source: Tabulated from UNU–INTECH (2002, 2003) Surveys using Stata 7.0 Package.

HR practices was measured as:

$$HR_i = 1/3[TM_i, TE_i, CHR_i] \tag{6.1}$$

where *TM*, *TE*, and *CHR* refer to training mode and training expense respectively as a share of payroll and cutting-edge human resource practices used respectively of firm *i*. *TM* was measured as a multinomial logistic variable of 1 when staff are sent out to external organisations for training, 2 when external staff are used to train employees, 3 when staff with training responsibilities are on payroll, 4 when a separate training department is used, 5 when a separate training centre is used and 0 when no formal training is undertaken. *CHR* was measured by a score of 1 for each of the practices. The firms were asked if it was their policy to encourage team-working, small group activities to improve company performance, multi-skilling, interaction with marketing, customer service and R&D department, lifelong learning and upward mobility. The *HR* score was divided by three, that is to say, with the total number of proxies used. The proxies were normalised using the formula below:

$$\text{Normalisation score} = (X_i - X_{min})/(X_{max} - X_{min}), \tag{6.2}$$

where x_i, X_{min} and X_{max} refer to the *i*th, minimum and maximum values respectively of the proxy, *X*.

Skills intensity
Skills intensity (*SI*) was used separately to capture the effects of different shares of managerial, professional, engineering and technical personnel in the workforce. *SI* was measured as:

$$SI = H_i/L_i,$$

where *H* and *L* refer to managers, professionals, engineers and technicians, and total employees respectively of firm *i* in 2001.

Process technology capability
Process technology (*PT*) – being central to participation in export markets even in low-value-added operations – is normally expected to show a positive relationship with exports and *HR*. However, because of the industry-specific characteristics of process technology in industries such as electronics and pharmaceuticals, and the importance of the domestic market, this relationship may not hold. The same can also be expected with R&D since foreign firms may finance R&D in product adaptation activities to meet regional markets.

Data on four proxies facilitated the computation of *PT*, which was calculated using the formula:

$$PT_i = 1/4[EM_i, PTE_i, ITC_i, QC_i] \qquad (6.3)$$

where *EM*, *PTE*, *ITC* and *QC* refer to equipment and machinery, share of process technology expense in sales, information technology components and quality control instruments of firm *i*. *EM* was computed as a multinomial logistic variable with average age of over five years = 0, five years = 1, four years = 2, three years = 3, two years = 4 and one year and less = 5. Likert scale scores ranging from 1 to 5 (least to most) were used to measure *ITC*. *QC* was measured as a dummy variable (*QC* = 1 if cutting-edge methods were used, *QC* = 0 otherwise). The *PT* score was divided by four, that is to say with the total number of the proxies used. Separate two-tail *t*-tests were run using *PTE*.

R&D capability

The Malaysian government introduced instruments to stimulate R&D in firms following the Industrial Master Plan (IMP) of 1986, and stepped it up with the launching of the Malaysian Technology Development Corporation (MTDC), Malaysia Industry–Government High Technology (MIGHT) umbrella, the IMP 2 and the Multimedia Super Corridor (MSC) in the 1990s. However, the lack of human capital and the ineffectiveness of the mechanisms used have restricted the depth of participation by firms in R&D activities (see Rasiah, 1996). Hence firm-level R&D is largely focused on process technology and product diversification and proliferation. Given Malaysia's developed basic infrastructure but underdeveloped institutional support facilities, R&D is unlikely to produce statistically significant results with the explanatory variables.

The data collected enabled the computation of two R&D proxies, i.e. R&D expenditure as a percentage of sales and R&D personnel as a share of employment. Separate two-tail *t*-tests were run using RD_{exp} in sales. It was not possible from the sample data to disentangle investment advanced between process and product R&D, and hence this proxy was measured to relate to both product and process R&D as:

$$RD_i = 1/2[RD_{expi}, RD_{empi}], \qquad (6.4)$$

where RD_{exp} and RD_{emp} refer to R&D expenditure as a share of sales and R&D personnel in workforce respectively of firm *i*.

In addition, patents filed by firms in the sample was also measured. None in auto parts had taken patents in Malaysia in 2001; 5 (13.5 per cent) foreign firms did in electronics, and 8 (28.6 per cent) local firms did in textiles and garments (see Table 6.1).

Overall Technological Intensity

For reasons advanced in Chapter 1, it can be hypothesised that the overall technological intensity (*TI*) of firms will be positively correlated with the labour productivity. *TI* was estimated as follows:

$$TI_i = HR_i + PT_i + RD_i$$

where TI_i refers to the overall technological intensity of firm *i*.

Other technology variables

Three additional technological variables were computed when examining critical relationships involving *HR*, *PT* and *RD* to avoid problems of multi-collinearity between them (see Appendix 6.1).

$$HRT_i = [HR_i + PT_i], \tag{6.5}$$

where *HRT* refers to technological influences of human and process technology resources of firm *i*.

$$HRD_i = [HR_i + RD_i], \tag{6.6}$$

where *HRD* refers to technological influences of human and R&D technology resources of firm *i*.

$$PRD_i = [PT_i + RD_i], \tag{6.7}$$

where *PRD* refers to technological influences of process and R&D technology resources of firm *i*.

Wages

Wages was used to represent labour market conditions. Given the restrictive nature of industrial relations in Malaysia, wages are unlikely to show strong correlation with productivity. Moreover, unionisation in the electronics industry is also very low. However, since there is a premium often involving professional, skilled and technical labour, average monthly wages was used. Since it is difficult to obtain wages of workers on their own, it was measured by dividing total salaries and remuneration by the workforce. Average monthly wages in thousand Malaysian ringgits was used in all the regressions and was measured as:

$$W_i = S_i/L_i,$$

where W and S refer to wages per worker and total monthly salary bill respectively of firm i.

Other firm-level variables

Five other firm-level variables were included in the analysis, i.e. local sourcing, ownership, management type, size and age. Mergers and acquisitions involving across foreign–local or reverse transfers from foreign to local in the last five years did not produce any meaningful statistical result, and hence was excluded from analysis.

Local sourcing   In contrast to the dynamic arguments of Hirschman (1958, 1987), Lall and Streeten (1977) and Rasiah (1995), which requires an assessment of linkages over time to allow supply responses, the analysis in this chapter is limited by the use of cross-sectional data. Hirschman (1972, 1984) had argued persuasively on the role export markets play in engendering backward linkages over time. Local sourcing was measured as:

$$LS_i = DI_i/OIi,$$

where LS, DI and OI refer to local sourcing, domestic inputs and overall inputs respectively of firm i.

Because foreign firms – especially transnational firms – are thought to enjoy superior connections to best-practice suppliers abroad, their relative import shares are considered higher than those involving local firms. However, because domestic content regulations were important for a long time and owing to Malaysia's experience with IS involving the automobile industry, especially following the launching of Heavy Industry Corporation of Malaysia (HICOM) in 1980, the results involving auto parts might differ from the EO industries of electronics and textiles and garments.

Ownership   Foreign ownership was defined using equity share of 50 per cent or more. Ownership was measured as:

$FO_i = 1$ if foreign equity ownership of firm i was 50 per cent or more;
$$FO = 0 \text{ otherwise,}$$

where FO refers to status of ownership of firm i. Using this definition, foreign firms constituted over half of the firms in the sample: 18 (54.5 per cent) foreign and 15 (45.5 per cent) local in auto parts; 37 (80.4 per cent) foreign and 9 (19.6 per cent) local in electronics; and 12 (30.0 per cent) foreign and 28 (70.0 per cent) local in textiles and garments (see Table 6.1).

Owner-managed firms   For the same reasons advanced in Chapters 2, 3 and 4, a neutral hypothesis with either a positive or negative sign between the performance, and technological intensities, and management type is expected. There were more local firms that were owner-managed (*OM*) compared to foreign firms: 17 local (34.7 per cent of 49 firms) and 4 foreign (10.0 per cent of 40 firms) (see Table 6.1). *OM* is measured using a dummy variable as follows:

$$OM_i = 1 \text{ if firm is managed either partly or fully by the owner;}$$
$$OM = 0 \text{ otherwise,}$$

where *OM* refers to status of management of firms *i*. Using this definition, most owner-managed firms were local: 6 (13.3 per cent) in auto parts, 11 (29.7 per cent) in electronics, and 17 (60.7 per cent) in textiles and garments (see Table 6.1). There were 11 (29.7 per cent) owner-managed foreign firms in electronics.

Size   It is interesting to examine the relationship between size, and performance and technological intensity variables in Malaysia particularly owing to the dominance of production by firms targeting exports to developed markets in electronics, and textiles and garments. For reasons advanced in Chapter 1, a neutral hypothesis was framed – simply that size has a bearing on technological capabilities.

Employment was used as the proxy for defining size and was measured as:

SMI = 500 and less
Large = >500

Using this criterion, large firms were generally more foreign-owned than local-owned in all three industries. The breakdown was: 8 (44.4 per cent) foreign and 2 (13.3 per cent) local in auto parts; 22 (59.5 per cent) foreign and 4 (44.4 per cent) local in electronics; and 7 (58.3 per cent) foreign and 6 (21.4 per cent) local in textiles and garments (see Table 6.1).

Age   Age was used as a control variable because of the potential impact of tacit and experience knowledge in the performance and technological intensity variables. The absolute age of the firm is used as an independent variable. However, the statistical relationship may not be obvious; foreign firms often access superior technology from abroad instantly when establishing or relocating operations in Malaysia. Hence, these firms already have long experience globally although their operating experience in Malaysia may be short. Age is measured as follows:

$$A_i = \text{years in operation,}$$

where A refers to age of firm i in 2001.

A total of 360 questionnaires was distributed in the key industrial location of Penang, Kelang Valley and Johor: 120 each in auto parts, electronics, and textiles and garments respectively. Overall 119 firms responded to the interview survey with sufficient information for the analysis to be carried out: 33 (27.5 per cent) auto parts, 46 (38.3 per cent) electronics and 40 textiles and garments (33.3 per cent). Case studies of three electronics, auto parts, and textiles and garments were each undertaken by the author to help extract industry-type characteristics. The survey and the case studies constitute the basis for the results and analysis in the chapter. The breakdown of the firms is shown in Table 6.1.

6.3.3 Statistical Analysis

This section presents the models specified to estimate the statistical relationships involving labour productivity, export, skills, local sourcing and technological intensities. Ordinary least squares (OLS) regressions were used when the dependent variable was value added per worker. Tobit regressions were preferred for export, skills, local sourcing and technological intensities because they are censored both on the right and the left side of the data sets. All the models were run with industry dummies:

$$\text{OLS: } VA/L = \alpha + \beta_1 X/Y + \beta_2 SI + \beta_3 TI + \beta_4 S + \beta_5 FO + \beta_6 W + \beta_7 OM + \beta_8 A + \mu \tag{6.8}$$

$$\text{Tobit: } X/Y = \alpha + \beta_1 SI + \beta_2 TI + \beta_3 S + \beta_4 FO + \beta_5 W + \beta_6 OM + \beta_7 A + \mu \tag{6.9}$$

$$\text{Tobit: } SI = \alpha + \beta_1 X/Y + \beta_2 TI + \beta_3 S + \beta_4 FO + \beta_5 W + \beta_6 OM + \beta_7 A + \mu \tag{6.10}$$

$$\text{Tobit: } LS = \alpha + \beta_1 SI + \beta_2 TI + \beta_3 S + \beta_4 FO + \beta_5 W + \beta_6 OM + \beta_7 A + \mu \tag{6.11}$$

$$\text{Tobit: } TI = \alpha + \beta_1 X/Y + \beta_2 SI + \beta_3 S + \beta_4 FO + \beta_5 W + \beta_6 OM + \beta_7 A + \mu \tag{6.12}$$

$$\text{Tobit: } HR = \alpha + \beta_1 X/Y + \beta_2 SI + \beta_3 PRD + \beta_4 S + \beta_5 FO$$
$$+ \beta_6 W + \beta_7 OM + \beta_8 A + \mu \qquad (6.13)$$

$$\text{Tobit: } PT = \alpha + \beta_1 X/Y + \beta_2 SI + \beta_3 HRD + \beta_4 S + \beta_5 FO$$
$$+ \beta_6 W + \beta_7 OM + \beta_8 A + \mu \qquad (6.14)$$

$$\text{Tobit: } RD = \alpha + \beta_1 X/Y + \beta_2 SI + \beta_3 HRT + \beta_4 S + \beta_5 FO$$
$$+ \beta_6 W + \beta_7 OM + \beta_8 A + \mu \qquad (6.15)$$

Regressions (6.8)–(6.15) were repeated using foreign and local firms' samples separately. Industry dummies were used in all the models but the results were not reported. The results of the foreign and local firms' samples in model (6.9) and foreign firms' sample in model (6.10) regressions were excluded because chi-square (χ^2) statistics was statistically insignificant.

6.4   STATISTICAL RESULTS

Two-tail t-tests and regressions controlling for the explanatory and other variables are employed here to examine the strength of the statistical relationships on firm-level productivity, and export, skills, technological and local sourcing intensities. In addition, the analysis is also carried out separately by ownership samples.

6.4.1   Statistical Differences

This section uses two-tail t-tests to examine statistical differences of the explanatory variables between foreign and local firms. These tests were run separately for all the three industries, and the results are presented in Table 6.2.

Productivity, export intensity, wages, skills and local sourcing
There were no obvious statistical differences in labour productivity, though foreign firms enjoyed a slightly higher mean in electronics and textiles and garments, and the reverse in auto parts (see Table 6.2). Although a few individual foreign firms in the sample have been much more productive than others, e.g. Intel, Motorola, Advanced Micro Devices and Penfabric, overall the differences were not obvious, suggesting that local firms have acquired considerable capabilities to compete with foreign firms.

   The lack of statistical significance involving export intensities in electronics and textiles and garments also shows that both sets of firms are exposed equally to external markets. As expected, electronics firms were significantly

Table 6.2 Two-tail t-tests of labour productivity, export, skills, local sourcing and technological intensities, Malaysia sample, 2001

	Foreign	Local	t		Foreign	Local	t
VA/L+				**HR**			
Auto parts	0.895	1.169	−1.23	Auto parts	0.385	0.361	0.58
Electronics	1.320	1.239	0.26	Electronics	0.522	0.471	0.83
Textiles and garments	1.169	0.996	0.74	Textiles and garments	0.410	0.341	1.14
X/Y				**PT**			
Auto parts	0.444	0.192	2.46**	Auto parts	0.390	0.391	−0.02
Electronics	0.542	0.449	0.67	Electronics	0.397	0.309	1.36
Textiles and garments	0.297	0.274	0.23	Textiles and garments	0.215	0.352	−2.35**
SI				**RD**			
Auto parts	0.156	0.193	−0.86	Auto parts	0.251	0.300	−0.69
Electronics	0.185	0.196	−0.20	Electronics	0.148	0.060	1.28
Textiles and garments	0.203	0.141	1.62	Textiles and garments	0.050	0.106	−1.27
LS				**RDE**			
Auto parts	0.319	0.664	−4.24*	Auto parts	2.398	3.186	−0.96
Electronics	0.385	0.540	−1.42	Electronics	0.011	0.004	1.37
Textiles and garments	0.422	0.615	−1.77***	Textiles and garments	0.125	0.647	−2.127**
TI				**RDI**			
Auto parts	1.026	1.052	−0.26	Auto parts	2.067	2.088	−0.03
Electronics	1.067	0.839	1.87***	Electronics	1.616	0.722	0.89
Textiles and garments	0.674	0.799	−0.91	Textiles and garments	0.850	1.329	−0.75

Note: *, ** and *** refer to 1, 5 and 10% levels of significance respectively. + in 10,000 ringgit.

Source: Computed from UNU–INTECH (2002, 2003) Survey using Stata 7.0 Package.

more export-intensive than auto parts and textiles and garments. However, foreign firms were significantly more export-intensive than local firms in auto parts, suggesting that local firms may not be as competitive as foreign firms in this industry. The difference could also be a consequence of local firms benefiting from supplying local assemblers which benefit in turn from the local content policies introduced to support the domestication of the auto-mobile industry.

Interestingly there was also no obvious statistical difference in skills inten-sity between foreign and local firms, though local firms enjoyed a higher mean in auto parts and electronics, and foreign firms in textiles and garments. However, not only did local firms enjoy higher local sourcing means than foreign firms; they were also statistically significant in auto parts and textiles and garments. They were statistically highly significant in auto parts, which could be a consequence of national support policies as well as foreign firms' access to global suppliers, including their parent plants.

Technological intensity
There were also no obvious statistical differences in *TI* in auto parts and textiles and garments, but the means of local firms were higher (see Table 6.2). Foreign firms enjoyed a statistically significant mean in electronics, demonstrating that local firms have yet to catch up sufficiently in this industry.

Decomposing *TI* into *HR* practices, *PT* and *RD*, and *RD* into *RDE* and *RDI* did not produce much in the way of statistically significant results. There was no statistical difference between foreign and local firms in HR practices, suggesting that these firms have acquired similar practices to compete. There were also no obvious statistical differences between foreign and local firms involving process technology in auto parts and electronics. Local firms en-joyed a statistically significant higher mean in textile and garment firms than foreign firms, which could be a consequence of less investment in machinery and equipment by foreign firms owing to the rationalisation process arising from the removal of Multi-Fibre Agreement (MFA) by the end of 2004 (WTO, 2001).

RD was statistically insignificant, though local firms enjoyed higher means in auto parts and textiles and garments, and foreign firms in electronics. R&D focus, particularly on process technology and product re-engineering in multinationals such as Intel, Motorola and AMD (see also Hobday, 1996; Rasiah, 1996; Ariffin and Bell, 1999), which is critical for firms to compete in semiconductor and telecommunication industries, largely explains the higher mean enjoyed by foreign firms. The decomposition of *RD* into R&D personnel/employment ratio (*RDE*) and R&D investment/sales ratio (*RDI*) produced largely similar results. Only involving *RDE*, local firms enjoyed a statistically significant higher mean than foreign firms in textiles and garments.

Overall, there were no obvious productivity differences between foreign and local firms. Foreign firms were more export-intensive than local firms only in auto parts, and enjoyed higher technological intensity than local firms in electronics. However, local firms enjoyed higher local sourcing intensities in auto parts and textiles and garments. Local firms also enjoyed higher PT and R&D employee intensity levels than foreign firms in textiles and garments.

6.4.2 Statistical Relationships

Apart from the regressions involving foreign and local firms' samples using X/Y, and foreign firms' sample using SI models, the remaining regressions were statistically significant. All results reported in Tables 6.3 and 6.4 also passed the White test for heteroscedascity.

Productivity, and export, skills and local sourcing intensities
Foreign ownership was statistically insignificant in the VA/L, X/Y and SI regressions, but was significant in the local sourcing regression at the 5 per cent level where the coefficient was negative (see Table 6.3). This confirms the higher propensity of local firms to source locally, which is largely a consequence of foreign firms' access to their parent firms and global suppliers.

Against VA/L, the explanatory variable of TI was statistically highly significant in all three samples, demonstrating a strong and positive relationship between technology and labour productivity. The coefficient of TI in the local firms' sample was much stronger than in the foreign firms' sample, suggesting that, to compete, local firms acquire or develop more technological capabilities within their affiliates that enjoy access to superior technology from parent plants than foreign firms. Export intensity was only positively correlated with VA/L in the foreign firms' sample and at the 10 per cent level of significance. The coefficient of X/Y in the local firms' sample was negative and strong, suggesting that local firms access higher value addition in the domestic economy and that many of their exports are in low-value-added activities. Interviews showed that local firms rely extensively on domestic consumer markets as well as supply foreign firms in Malaysia.[7] OM was also statistically significant and its coefficient positive overall, and in local firms' samples. Interestingly, owner-managed firms, which accounted for slightly over 50 per cent of the local firms' sample, enjoy higher value added than other firms. Wages had a positive coefficient in all three samples, and was statistically significant overall, and in foreign firms' samples, which is consistent with the logic that the more productive firms pay higher wages.

Table 6.3   Statistical relationships involving labour productivity, export, skills and local sourcing intensities, Malaysia sample, 2001

	VA/L			X/Y†	SI††		LS		
	All	Foreign	Local	All	All	Local	All	Foreign	Local
X/Y	-0.144	0.347	-1.295		-0.055	-0.195	-0.230	0.030	-0.611
	(-0.75)	(1.71)***	(-3.12)*		(-1.48)	(-2.89)*	(-2.62)*	(0.33)	(-3.08)*
S	-0.026	0.109	-0.195	0.145	0.014	-0.004	-0.066	0.061	-0.193
	(-0.18)	(0.71)	(-0.74)	(1.59)	(0.51)	(-0.09)	(-1.02)	(0.90)	(-1.61)
SI	0.228	0.079	-0.972	-0.386			-0.159	0.055	-0.423
	(0.47)	(0.15)	(-1.06)	(-1.26)			(0.70)	(0.24)	(-0.95)
OM	0.251	-0.064	0.621	0.103	-0.018	0.039	0.231	0.054	0.316
	(1.70)***	(-0.31)	(2.69)*	(1.08)	(-0.63)	(1.09)	(3.39)*	(0.60)	(2.91)*
A	-0.005	-0.006	-0.035	-0.000	0.003	0.002	0.005	-0.002	0.012
	(-0.56)	(-0.71)	(-1.87)***	(-0.08)	(1.80)***	(0.68)	(1.27)	(-0.62)	(1.36)
TI	0.976	1.121	1.707	-0.036	-0.017	0.055	-0.077	-0.017	-0.116
	(5.32)*	(5.10)*	(4.45)*	(-0.31)	(-0.49)	(0.90)	(-0.92)	(-0.18)	(-0.64)
FO	0.010			0.137	-0.027		-0.170		
	(0.07)			(1.38)	(-0.89)		(-2.40)**		
W	0.013	0.015	0.024	-0.002	0.003	0.006	0.003	0.009	-0.000
	(1.74)***	(1.72)***	(1.64)	(-0.32)	(2.35)**	(2.92)*	(0.98)	(2.34)**	(-0.01)
μ	0.201	-0.191	0.592	0.469	0.184	0.153	0.586	0.261	0.867
	(0.71)	(-0.67)	(1.34)	(2.72)*	(2.58)*	(2.33)**	(4.48)*	(2.06)**	(3.96)*
N	119	67	52	119	119	52	119	67	52
F, χ²	4.47*	6.00*	2.83*	20.33**	17.11**	21.12*	42.51*	8.48**	29.49*
R²	0.293	0.486	0.378						
Adj. R²	0.227	0.405	0.245						

Notes: *, ** and *** refer to 1, 5 and 10% levels of significance respectively; industry dummies were used but are not reported here; † results were statistically insignificant involving the foreign and local firms' samples; †† χ² results were statistically insignificant involving the foreign firms' sample.

Source: Computed from UNU–INTECH (2002, 2003) Survey using Stata 7.0 Package.

Table 6.4   Statistical relationships involving technological intensities, Malaysia sample, 2001

	TI			HR			PT			RD		
	All	Foreign	Local	All	Foreign	Local	All	Foreign	Local	All	Foreign	Local
X/Y	-0.085 (-0.85)	-0.234 (-1.98)**	0.415 (2.80)**	-0.015 (-0.37)	-0.092 (-1.82)***	0.049 (0.62)	-0.004 (-0.09)	-0.064 (-1.13)	0.123 (1.91)***	-0.039 (-0.53)	-0.052 (-0.53)	0.189 (1.50)
S	0.136 (1.84)***	0.120 (1.35)	0.074 (0.74)	0.012 (0.40)	-0.015 (-0.37)	0.045 (0.88)	0.105 (3.22)*	0.075 (1.75)***	0.096 (2.26)**	-0.023 (-0.41)	0.063 (0.81)	-0.080 (-1.06)
SI	-0.171 (-0.67)	0.048 (0.16)	0.195 (0.56)	0.066 (0.64)	0.147 (1.12)	0.024 (0.13)	-0.318 (-2.83)*	-0.110 (-0.75)	-0.321 (-2.12)**	0.144 (0.81)	0.021 (0.08)	0.411 (1.76)***
OM	0.054 (0.71)	0.235 (1.99)*	-0.223 (-2.68)*	0.053 (1.70)***	0.110 (2.17)**	0.064 (1.37)	0.040 (1.16)	0.089 (1.56)	-0.052 (-1.41)	-0.098 (-1.70)***	-0.010 (-0.10)	-0.209 (-3.39)*
A	0.005 (1.03)	-0.001 (-0.23)	0.023 (3.60)*	0.001 (0.29)	0.001 (0.68)	-0.002 (-0.41)	-0.004 (-1.95)**	-0.003 (-1.19)	-0.002 (-0.51)	-0.002	0.003 (0.68)	0.020 (4.29)*
PRD				0.155 (4.18)*	0.077 (1.33)	0.266 (3.97)*						
HRD							0.198 (4.73)*	0.166 (2.36)**	0.119 (2.43)**			
HRT										0.273 (2.95)*	0.125 (0.87)	0.120 (1.02)
FO	-0.064 (-0.79)			0.035 (1.05)			-0.054 (-1.51)			-0.027 (-0.44)		
W	0.007 (1.73)***	0.016 (3.42)*	-0.011 (-1.99)**	0.006 (3.80)*	0.005 (2.63)**	0.008 (2.55)*	0.003 (1.57)	0.008 (3.40)*	-0.004 (-1.89)***	-0.005	0.001 (0.26)	-0.011 (-2.84)*
μ	0.937 (7.87)*	0.897 (7.13)*	0.511 (3.38)*	0.312 (5.95)*	0.403 (6.81)*	0.256 (3.34)*	0.308 (5.38)*	0.227 (3.16)*	0.284 (4.40)*	-0.174 (-1.49)	-0.093 (0.54)	-0.345 (-2.34)**
N	119	67	52	119	67	52	119	67	52	119	67	52
χ^2	26.68*	34.06*	28.72*	57.46*	31.85*	26.94*	42.23*	40.69*	32.97*	41.87*	17.60**	46.48*

Notes: *, ** and *** refer to 1, 5 and 10% levels of significance respectively; industry dummies were used but are not reported here.

Source: Computed from UNU–INTECH (2002, 2003) Survey using Stata 7.0 Package.

135

The regressions involving export intensity were only statistically significant for interpretation in the overall firms' sample (see Table 6.3). None of the explanatory and control variables noted in the table were statistically significant, which could be a consequence of strong integration of export and domestic markets involving electronics and textiles and garments. Foreign ownership had a positive coefficient, although it was statistically insignificant. Auto parts still enjoyed considerable protection in 2001 owing to government efforts to support national automobile assemblers and local suppliers. The latter largely explains why foreign firms enjoyed a statistically significant higher X/Y mean than local firms in auto parts.

Skills intensity produced statistically significant results overall, and in local firms' samples (see Table 6.3). Foreign ownership was statistically insignificant. Export intensity had an inverse relationship with skills intensity in both the regressions, but the coefficient was statistically highly significant (at the 1 per cent level) in the local firms' sample. Local firms targeting much of their higher-value-added operations at the domestic market are obviously better equipped with human capital than those targeting low-value-added markets abroad. The explanatory variable of *TI* was statistically insignificant, which could be a consequence of the high intensity of training carried out on direct workers in electronics and textile and garment firms. Direct workers were excluded from the numerator when skills intensity was computed since it is difficult to establish a skills threshold to separate the skilled from the unskilled, especially between different industries and segments within the same value chains. It would be interesting to undertake regressions taking cognisance of this dimension of skills, but that would require far deeper participation of firms in the survey.[8] Age was statistically significant in the overall firms' sample, but its influence was marginal. Wages was statistically significant in the overall (5 per cent level) and the local firms' (1 per cent level) samples, and the positive coefficient is logical as higher wages are needed to support higher skills intensity levels.

The local sourcing regressions were all statistically significant for interpretation. Foreign ownership was significant at the 5 per cent level (see Table 6.3), and its negative coefficient showed that local firms enjoy higher propensity to source inputs locally, confirming the *t*-test results reported in Table 6.2. The explanatory variable of *TI* was statistically insignificant in all three samples. Wages was statistically significant in the foreign firms' sample, but this relationship may be spurious since there are no obvious economic reasons why wages influence firms' sourcing patterns. The removal of this variable from the equation affected the results of the foreign firms' sample and that is why it was retained in the equations.

Technological intensities

The Tobit regressions involving technological intensities were statistically significant for interpretation (see Table 6.4). Foreign ownership was not statistically significant in all the models, suggesting that there were no obvious differences in technological levels by ownership as firms installed or developed similar capability levels to compete. However, the explanatory variables showed different results when regressed by ownership samples.

Against *TI*, export intensity had a negative sign overall, and in foreign firms' samples, but a positive one in the local firms' sample. The opposite signs between the foreign and local firms' samples may explain why *X/Y* was statistically insignificant in the overall firms' sample. The negative sign of *X/Y* in the foreign firms' sample may suggest defensive withdrawal strategies used by foreign firms, especially in textile and garment firms with the revisions being undertaken for the complete removal of MFA by the end of 2004. However, the relatively lower export intensity levels in some component electronics and textiles (rather than garments) also suggest that considerable output is sold to downstream foreign and local firms (e.g. electronics components such as integrated circuits, capacitors, resistors and disk drives, and textile materials such as synthetic fibre, yarn and fabric). The statistically highly significant (1 per cent level) coefficient of *X/Y* in the local firms' sample shows that higher technology intensities are necessary for local firms to compete in export markets. *OM* was positively correlated in the foreign firms' sample, but inversely in the local firms' sample. The result in the foreign firms' sample could be spurious, especially when the incidence of *OM* was very low (see Table 6.1), but the local firms' sample result suggests that owner-managed firms have lower technological intensities. Wages was positively correlated in the overall and foreign firms' samples, which supports the hypothesis that higher wages are necessary to attract the requisite human capital to drive higher technology endowments. The inverse relationship in the local firms' sample may either be spurious or indicate that firms may have resorted to de-skilling technologies to compete in low-value-added niches and overcome problems of a high wage premium that has caused skills shortages in the country. Size was statistically significant only in the overall sample, though its coefficient was positive in all three.

The explanatory variable of *SI* was statistically insignificant in the *HR* regressions, though the coefficients were positive in all of them, suggesting that firms were exposed to similar practices irrespective of the share of human capital in the respective industries (see Table 6.4). Export intensity was negatively correlated in the foreign firms' sample, but as explained earlier with the *TI* regressions involving the foreign firms' sample, this could be either spurious or owing to a number of giant foreign firms supplying inputs to final goods assemblers who export. The coefficient of *OM* was positive in all samples, but statistically significant overall and in foreign firms' samples, suggesting that owner-managed firms have a slight preference for using HR practices than emphasising higher human capital ratios and more sophisticated process technology. The statistically highly significant and positive coefficient of *PRD* suggests that the choice of process and R&D focus had a bearing on the *HR* practices overall and in local firms' samples, but not foreign firms. Wages was statistically highly significant, and its coefficient positive in all three samples, demonstrating that firms with higher emphasis on HR practices also paid higher wages.

The explanatory variable of *X/Y* was only statistically significant in the local firms' sample involving the *PT* regressions (see Table 6.4), and its positive coefficient shows that local firms require higher process technology intensities to compete in export markets. Size was statistically significant and its coefficient was positive in all three samples, suggesting that scale was important for firms to enjoy higher process technology intensities. Skills intensity was negatively correlated with *PT* in the overall and local firms' samples, and the insignificant coefficient in the foreign firms' sample was also negative. The inverse correlations are either spurious or indicate that older firms retain slightly older equipment and process techniques compared to newer firms. The negative coefficient of age may suggest this inference. The residual *TI* left, i.e. *HRD* technologies, enjoyed a statistically significant and positive relationship with *PT*, suggesting that process technologies are driven strongly by *HR* and *RD* practices in firms. Wages was positively correlated with *PT* in the foreign firms' sample, and its coefficient was positive but statistically insignificant in the overall sample. Foreign firms with higher process technologies also paid higher wages. The statistically significant coefficient involving local firms may be spurious.

Apart from skills intensity and wages, none of the remaining explanatory variables was significant in the *RD* regressions, which could be a result of low R&D intensities (see Table 6.4). *SI* was statistically significant at the 10 per cent level in the local firms' sample, though its coefficient was positive in all three samples. Higher skill intensities seem important in the local firms' participation in R&D activities. *OM* was statistically significant and its coefficient was negative in the overall and local firms' samples, suggesting that owners enjoy higher freedom to make R&D decisions in local firms. Age was statistically highly significant in the local firms' sample, suggesting that the older firms have enjoyed enough learning to participate in R&D activities. Although *HRT* had a positive coefficient in all three samples, it was statistically highly significant (1 per cent level) only in the overall sample. Wages was statistically significant in the overall and local firms' samples, but its coefficient was negative. This result is either spurious or indicates that local firms engaged in R&D activities are in low-value-added activities.

Taken together, *TI* showed a strong and statistically highly significant relationship with labour productivity in all three samples, but the coefficient was strongest in the local firms' sample. Export intensity had an inverse relationship with *TI* and *HR* in the foreign firms' sample, which could be a result of high-tech firms supplying to export-oriented downstream firms. However, further information on the firms involving the production segment of firms in the value chains in each of the industries is necessary to confirm this. Although the foreign firms that replied to this question in the questionnaire used supplied components, yarn and fabric to exporting firms, the response rate was too small for a related dummy to be introduced in the regressions. Export intensity also had an inverse relationship with labour productivity, skills intensity and local sourcing in the local firms' sample, suggesting a greater focus by local firms on the domestic market. Although foreign firms on average were more export-intensive than local firms, the gap was big in auto parts. Foreign ownership enjoyed little statistical relationship with the key variables when controlled for the only explanatory and control variables except for local sourcing, where the statistically significant negative sign confirms the *t*-test results reported earlier. Wages was statistically correlated with *HR* in all three samples, labour productivity in the overall and foreign firms' samples, skills intensity in the overall and local firms' samples, and *PT* and local sourcing in the foreign firms' samples. The coefficients of the explanatory variables in the *RD* regressions were generally statistically insignificant, except for *SI* in the local firms' sample. The positive coefficient in the local firms suggests that human capital has been important in driving R&D in local firms.

6.5   CONCLUSIONS

Overall, the statistical tests showed no obvious productivity differences between foreign and local firms. Although foreign firms on average were more export-intensive than local firms, they were statistically significant only in auto parts. Foreign firms enjoyed higher technological intensity than local firms in electronics. However, local firms enjoyed higher *RD*, *PT* and *LS* intensities than foreign firms in textiles and garments. Local firms also enjoyed higher *LS* intensities than foreign firms in auto parts.

TI showed a strong and statistically highly significant relationship with labour productivity in all three samples, but the coefficient was strongest in the local firms' sample. Export intensity had an inverse relationship with *TI* and *HR* in the foreign firms' sample, which could be a result of high-tech electronic components and textile firms supplying export-oriented downstream firms in consumer and industrial electronics, and garment firms. However, further information on the segment of production in the value chains in each of the industries is necessary to confirm this. Export intensity also had an inverse relationship with labour productivity, skills intensity and local sourcing in the local firms' sample, suggesting a greater focus by local firms on domestic markets. Wages was statistically correlated with *HR* in all three samples, labour productivity in the overall and foreign firms' samples, skills intensity in the overall and local firms' samples, and *PT* and local sourcing in the foreign firms' samples. The coefficients of the explanatory variables in the *RD* regressions were generally statistically insignificant, except for *SI* in the local firms' sample. The positive coefficient in the local firms suggests that human capital is an important driver of R&D activities in local firms. The negative coefficient of wages in the *PT* and *RD* regressions in the local firms' sample is likely to be spurious.

While stimulating the diffusion of process technology capabilities to local firms is still useful, local firms' R&D capabilities should be strengthened further with government support. Foreign firms can still play a complementary role as interviews showed that a considerable amount of tacit knowledge developed in foreign firms have moved out to start local firms (see also Rasiah, 2002). Local firms appear to access much of the value added in the domestic market, particularly auto parts firms, which is expected to attract problems from increased liberalisation pressures. The auto parts industry is currently facing increased competition following the government's efforts to implement the deregulation initiatives required under the ASEAN Free Trade Agreement (AFTA). High tariffs imposed to shelter national assemblers will have to be reduced to 20 per cent in 2005 and eventually to 5 per cent in 2008. Whereas foreign firms can continue to access technology from parent plants, local firms must strengthen their R&D facilities to support higher-value-added activities. This has become increasingly necessary owing to rising wages and the integration of low wage sites in the international division of labour (e.g. China, the Philippines and Indonesia).

NOTES

1. MIDA was originally known as the Federal Industrial Development Authority (FIDA) (Rasiah, 1995: ch. 4).
2. These forces also drove massive FDI inflows into Indonesia and Thailand (see Rasiah, 2003a).
3. The ringgit was depreciated in 1986 (Malaysia, 1988).
4. The IMP2 emphasised the development of clusters.
5. ASEAN stands for Association of Southeast Asian Nations.
6. Tin crashed in the early 1980s (Jomo, 1990).
7. Author interviews conducted in 2002 in Penang and Kuala Lumpur.
8. An attempt to measure skills intensity along these lines was made during pilot tests, but some managers reported that these responses would be unreliable owing to differences in classifications used by the different industries.

APPENDIX 6.1

Table 6A.1   *Correlation coefficient matrix of independent variables, Malaysia sample, 2001*

	TI	X/Y	SI	HR	PT	RD	PRD	HRD	HRT	FO	S	W	OM	A
TI	1.000													
X/Y	0.029	1.000												
SI	0.058	-0.095	1.000											
HR	0.673*#	0.092	0.150	1.000										
PT	0.749*#	0.066	-0.150	0.365	1.000									
RD	0.636*#	-0.089	0.112	0.052	0.203	1.000								
PRD	0.826*#	-0.085	-0.024	0.233	0.643*#	0.800*#	1.000							
HRD	0.836*#	-0.077	0.123	0.562*#	0.365	0.771*#	0.853*#	1.000						
HRT	0.861*#	0.096	0.000	0.827*#	0.826*#	0.154	0.530*#	0.561*#	1.000					
FO	0.146	0.277	0.055	0.278	0.020	0.010	-0.103	0.020	0.180	1.000				
S	0.243	0.224	0.127	0.234	0.235	0.041	0.069	0.073	0.284	0.324	1.000			
W	0.048	-0.176	0.190	0.110	0.008	-0.016	0.041	0.094	0.071	0.123	0.067	1.000		
OM	-0.074	0.009	-0.133	-0.032	0.024	-0.136	-0.054	-0.085	-0.005	-0.378	-0.207	-0.304	1.000	
A	0.011	-0.125	0.154	-0.014	-0.089	0.115	0.140	0.185	-0.062	-0.094	0.247	0.308	-0.060	1.000

Notes: * high correlation; # compositional overlap.

Source: Computed from UNU–INTECH (2002; 2003) Survey using Stata 7.0 Package.

141

7. Productivity, export, local sourcing and technology in Brazil

Rajah Rasiah

7.1 INTRODUCTION

Brazil is the largest economy in Latin America and has enjoyed a long history of government support in the development of producer goods industries under import substitution (IS). The large domestic economy, fairly developed science and technology (S&T) infrastructure, ownership regulation and domestic content requirements – the latter two applied varyingly since the 1950s – helped create an industrial structure with strong participation by both foreign and local capital in manufacturing.

Empirical and analytical accounts examining the role of FDI in technological capabilities in Brazil are dominated by focus on process equipment R&D capabilities. Government policy instruments are argued to have influenced foreign firms' participation in R&D activities to access opportunities to sell in the domestic market and incentives. A number of studies have compared technological capabilities of foreign and local firms. Katz (1999), Katz and Bercovich (1993), Lastres and Cassiolato (2000) and Costa (2001) presented empirical evidence to show that foreign firms' R&D activities are limited to process technology and modification of machinery and equipment. Ariffin and Figueiredo (2003), using a dynamic methodology that locates firms on the basis of differentiation of technological activities in respect of their degree and depth of intensity, showed no difference between foreign and local consumer firms in Manaus, Brazil.

This chapter attempts to add to this literature and offer an example of a middle-income economy with some strong high-tech institutions in the development trajectory by examining technological and economic performance differences and relationships using a sample of firms from the auto parts, electronics, pharmaceutical and textile and garment firms in Brazil. Given Brazil's relatively developed S&T infrastructure in the more developed states such as São Paulo, the gap between foreign and local firms may be small. The rest of the chapter is organised as follows. Section 7.2 discusses the evolving role of institutional support, FDI and export manufacturing in Brazil. Section

7.3 presents the methodology and data. Section 7.4 examines technological characteristics of the firms in the sample and the statistical differences and relationships involving productivity, exports, skills, and technological and local sourcing intensities between foreign and local firms. Section 7.5 offers conclusions and policy implications.

7.2 INSTITUTIONS, STRENGTH, FDI AND MANUFACTURING

Brazil has enjoyed institutional development of R&D in agriculture, health and mining from the eighteenth century (Dahlman and Fristak, 1993: 416). Although industrialisation began to evolve from the early twentieth century, rapid growth only took place from the mid-twentieth century. Government-promoted IS automobile manufacturing began in 1957, though assembly and sales can be traced to the 1920s. Following the disastrous economic outcome of economic liberalism in the 1960s and increased concerns over national security, the military strengthened state control of heavy industries since the 1970s (Adler, 1987; Baptista and Cassiolato, 1994). The military regimes gradually gravitated towards greater nationalism and local technology development. Despite a number of weaknesses, the government focused extensively on institutional development for military and strategic reasons. Especially informatics, telecommunications (Telebras), defence, aviation and nuclear energy became major targets of promotion and investment (Dahlman and Fristak, 1993: 419; Mytelka, 1999: 121; Goldstein, 2002). Although massive investment in state-controlled enterprises and the restrictionary FDI policies of the 1970s exacerbated current account deficits and foreign debt, these institutions helped strengthen tacit knowledge in local employees as well as other forms of learning. Heavy investment in technical and vocational education helped compensate shortfalls in the formal education system and offered firms considerable human capital to expand manufacturing (Dahlman and Fristak, 1993: 439). Especially automobile, automotive parts and machine tool firms benefited considerably from the technical and vocational training programmes.[1] Brazil ranked as a middle-income country and with a moderately developed S&T infrastructure. It had a GDP per capita in PPP measures of US$7625 in 2000, and 168 scientists and engineers per million people in 1995 (World Bank, 2002). Although R&D expenditure in GNP in Brazil (0.8 per cent) in 1996 was much lower than the shares in the developed economies of Japan (2.7 per cent), the United States (2.6 per cent) and the UK (1.9 per cent), and the newly industrialised economy of Korea (2.6 per cent), it was still higher than the middle-income economies of Mexico (0.3 per cent) and Malaysia (0.2 per cent) (World Bank, 2002).

Although FDI levels in Brazil are moderate, almost 75 per cent was concentrated in manufacturing as early as 1987 (Dahlman and Fristak, 1993: 433). Liberalisation, especially from the late 1990s, has revived strong FDI inflows, which have benefited from the large domestic market and domestic capabilities engendered in the country to participate in export manufacturing. Foreign firms reported that a critical slice of their R&D personnel had developed their tacit knowledge from working in government-supported R&D institutions such as the Centre for Telecommunications Research and Development (CPqD) of Telebras (telecommunication firms), and universities (pharmaceutical firms) in the state of São Paulo.[2]

Brazil is an interesting case of IS where its large domestic economy encouraged government focus on industrial development. However, cumbersome government policy and balance of payment problems – assisting in some ways and hindering in others, as described by Evans (1995) – helped create the high-tech infrastructure to support innovative activities but lacked the dynamism to sustain rapid new firm creation. Government policy instruments – e.g. incentives tying tax exemptions with R&D linkages with local universities – and the outflow of R&D personnel from government institutions to private firms have been significant. Hence, whereas foreign and large local firms engaged in manufacturing have benefited from a strong high-tech infrastructure particularly in the developed states such as São Paulo, high interest rates and a lack of strong inter-firm links has reduced knowledge flows and new firm creation. Nevertheless, despite strong IS policies and the relative stagnation of value added in GDP, manufactured exports has continued to show a trend rise in overall exports.

FDI took advantage of the large domestic market to appropriate rents from high tariff protection against imports and special sectoral benefits (Mortimore, 1998). The automobile, machinery and electronics industries were some of those that benefited from such market-seeking FDI inflows (Newfarmer and Mueller, 1975; Evans, 1995), but generally expanding rentier and internationally inefficient operations (Cardoso and Faletto, 1979; Gereffi and Evans, 1981; Newfarmer, 1985; Jenkins, 1984, 1987; Mortimore, 1998). Balance of payment deficits and debt service problems led the Brazilian government to introduce performance requirements such as local content, export targets and foreign exchange limits (Mortimore, 1985, 1991), which drove TNCs to increase domestic sourcing, but key inputs were accessed from imports or TNC subsidiaries (see Jenkins, 1987). While liberalisation and stabilisation have intensified FDI inflows – a significant amount has emerged through mergers and acquisitions since the mid-1990s – Cimoli and Katz (2003) argue that it has also aggravated domestic capability building owing to increased imports (see also Figure 7.1). FDI inflows in gross fixed capital formation in Brazil have expanded sharply since the late 1990s (see Figure

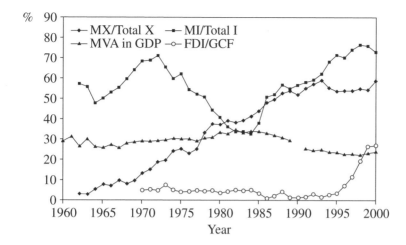

Notes: FDI – foreign direct investment; GCF – gross capital formation; MX – manufactured exports; MI – manufactured imports; MVA – manufacturing value added.

Source: Computed from World Bank (2002).

Figure 7.1 Key FDI and manufacturing statistics, Brazil, 1960–2000

7.1). TNC investment in the Brazilian automobile industry boomed in the period 1995–99 following the introduction of *Regime Automotivo* by the federal government (Quadros, 2003). However, its impact on the auto parts industry might change owing to compliance with the World Trade Organization's (WTO) agreement on Trade Related Investment Measures (TRIMs), which calls for an end to local content regulations. The consequences may be destructive given that increased liberalisation and international integration of production have already inhibited local R&D activities (see Cimoli and Katz, 2003).

It is against this analytic framework and industrial background that the data involving foreign and local manufacturing firms will be examined. Given the long experience with manufacturing growth – particularly since the 1950s – many of the implications may be useful for large developing economies with fairly developed institutional support. The industries of auto parts, pharmaceuticals, electronics and textiles and garments were chosen for analysis. Machine tools was dropped owing to too few responses. All the industries chosen have fairly strong participation of foreign and local firms, and with the exception of pharmaceuticals enjoyed a manufacturing value added share exceeding 5 per cent in 2001.[3] Pharmaceuticals was added to the list owing to its increasing importance globally and the modernisation of the industry in Brazil since the enactment of the Intellectual Property Law in 1996.

7.3   METHODOLOGY AND DATA

The chapter uses the technological capability framework advanced in Chapter 1. The component proxies used to analyse the variables in section 7.4 were measured and defined as follows.

7.3.1   Productivity and Export Performance

The proxies of labour productivity and export intensities were used to denote productivity and export performance respectively. Firms enjoying export experience accounted for 83.1 per cent of the 89 firms (see Table 7.1). Both variables have problems but they do allow useful assessments. Labour productivity was measured as:

$$\text{Labour productivity} = VA_i/L_i,$$

where VA and L refer to value added in 10,000 Real and total employees respectively of firm i in 2001. Export intensity was measured as:

$$\text{Export intensity} = X_i/Y_i,$$

where X and Y refer to exports and gross output of firm i in 2001.

7.3.2   Technological Capabilities

As advanced in Chapter 1, the technological capability framework is used to estimate technological intensities here. Firms are likely to show relatively higher levels of technological capability in Brazil owing to the long industrialisation experience, fairly strong high tech institutions in the state of São Paulo where the responding firms are located and the large domestic market in the country.

Human resource
Two alternative proxies were used to represent human resource. However, human resource capability was used separately to measure human resource practices that denote development in firms, and hence it excluded technical, engineering and professional human resource endowments as a share of the workforce (skills intensity). The exclusion allows the differentiation of

Table 7.1   *Breakdown of firms, Brazil sample, 2001*

	Ownership		Unions		Export experience		Owner-managed		Mergers & acquisitions		Total firms
	Foreign	Local	Foreign	Local	Foreign	Local	Foreign	Local	Foreign	Local	
Auto parts	13	18	11 (84.6)	12 (66.7)	12 (92.3)	16 (88.9)	0 (0.0)	4 (12.9)	7 (53.8)	2 (11.1)	31
Electronics	12	4	8 (66.7)	4 (100.0)	8 (66.7)	4 (100.0)	0 (0.0)	0 (0.0)	8 (66.7)	0 (0.0)	16
Pharmaceuticals	9	7	4 (44.4)	5 (71.4)	9 (100.0)	5 (71.4)	0 (0.0)	5 (71.4)	4 (44.4)	4 (57.1)	16
Textiles & garments	6	20	6 (100.0)	20 (100.0)	6 (100.0)	14 (70.0)	4 (66.7)	8 (40.0)	4 (66.7)	4 (20.0)	26
Total	40	49	29 (72.5)	41 (83.7)	36 (90.0)	39 (80.0)	4 (10.0)	17 (34.7)	23 (57.5)	10 (20.4)	89

Note: Figures in parentheses refer to percentage intensities.

Source: Tabulated from UNU–INTECH Interview and Survey (2002, 2003) using Stata 7.0 Package.

human resource capability developed by each firm and those that are acquired or poached from institutions and other firms. Both dimensions are important for driving firms' operations.

Human resource practices

Given the fairly developed nature of manufacturing undertaken in the four industries in Brazil, human resource (*HR*) practices is expected to have a positive relationship with labour productivity, process technology and skills intensity.

HR was measured as:

$$HR_i = 1/3[TM_i, TE_i, CHR_i], \qquad (7.1)$$

where *TM*, *TE* and *CHR* refer to training mode, training expense as a share of payroll and cutting-edge human resource practices used respectively of firm *i*. *TM* was measured as a multinomial logistic variable of 1 when staff are sent out to external organisations for training, 2 when external staff are used to train employees, 3 when staff with training responsibilities are on payroll, 4 when a separate training department is used, 5 when a separate training centre is used and 0 when no formal training is undertaken. *CHR* was measured by a score of 1 for each of the practices and divided by the total number of practices. The firms were asked if it was their policy to encourage team-working, small group activities to improve company performance, multi-skilling, interaction with marketing, customer service and R&D department, lifelong learning and upward mobility. Separate two-tail *t*-tests were run using *TE*. The proxies were normalised using the formula below:

$$\text{Normalisation score} = (X_i - X_{\min})/(X_{\max} - X_{\min}), \qquad (7.2)$$

where X_i, $X_{\min}$ and $X_{\max}$ refer to the *i*th, minimum and maximum values respectively of the proxy *X*.

Skills intensity

Skills intensity (*SI*) was used separately to capture the effects of different shares of managerial, professional, engineering and technical personnel in the workforce. *SI* was measured as:

$$SI = H_i/L_i,$$

where *H* and *L* refer to managers, professionals, engineers and technicians and total employees respectively of firm *i* in 2001.

Process technology capability

Process technology (*PT*) – being central to participation in export markets even in low-value-added operations – is normally expected to show a positive relationship with exports and *HR*. However, because of the industry-specific characteristics of process technology in industries such as electronics and pharmaceuticals, and given Brazil's fairly developed domestic market, this relationship may not hold. The same can also be expected with R&D since foreign firms may finance R&D in product adaptation activities to meet domestic final markets and process technology to take advantage of Brazil's structure of factor markets.

Data on four proxies facilitated the computation of *PT*, which was calculated using the formula:

$$PT_i = 1/4[EM_i, PTE_i, ITC_i, QC_i], \qquad (7.3)$$

where *EM*, *PTE*, *ITC* and *QC* refer to equipment and machinery, process technology expense in sales, information technology components and quality control instruments respectively of firm *i*. *EM* was computed as a multinomial logistic variable with average age of over five years = 0, five years = 1, four years = 2, three years = 3, two years = 4 and one year and less = 5. Likert scale scores ranging from 1 to 5 (least to most) were used to measure *ITC*. *QC* was measured as a dummy variable (*QC* = 1 if cutting-edge methods were used, *QC* = 0 otherwise). The *PT* score was divided by four, which is the number of proxies used. Separate two-tail *t*-tests were run using *PTE*.

R&D capability

Given Brazil's fairly developed high-tech institutions especially in the state of São Paulo from where the firms were drawn and its huge domestic market, R&D is likely to produce statistically significant results, though there may not be obvious differences between foreign and local firms.

The data collected enabled the computation of two R&D proxies, i.e. R&D expenditure as a percentage of sales and R&D personnel as a share of employment. It was not possible from the sample data to disentangle investment advanced between process and product R&D, and hence this proxy was measured to relate to both product and process R&D as:

$$RD_i = 1/2[RD_{expi}, RD_{empi}], \qquad (7.4)$$

where RD_{exp} and RD_{emp} refer to R&D expenditure as a share of sales and R&D personnel in the workforce respectively of firm *i*. Separate two-tail *t*-tests were run using RD_{exp} in sales.

Other technology variables

Three additional technological variables were computed when examining critical relationships involving *HR*, *PT* and *RD* to avert problems of collinearity between them (see Appendix 7.1).

$$HRT_i = [HR_i + PT_i], \tag{7.5}$$

where *HRT* refers to technological influences of human and process technology resources of firm *i*.

$$HRD_i = [HR_i + RD_i], \tag{7.6}$$

where *HRD* refers to technological influences of human and R&D technology resources of firm *i*.

$$PRD_i = [PT_i + RD_i], \tag{7.7}$$

where *PRD* refers to technological influences of process and R&D technology resources of firm *i*.

Wages

Wages was used to represent labour market conditions. Unions was dropped for reasons advanced in Chapter 1. Although the incidence of firms having unionised workers was very high, the density of unionisation among workers between the firms was not very high; overall 72.5 per cent foreign and 83.7 per cent of local firms in the sample had unionised workers (see Table 7.1). Including the union variable did not produce any statistically significant results, which could be a consequence of the high incidence of unionisation.

Given the premium involving skilled and knowledge workers, a positive relationship can be expected between productivity and wages. Average monthly wages was used. Since it is difficult to obtain wages of workers on their own, it was measured by dividing total salaries and remuneration by the workforce. Average monthly wages in thousand Brazilian real was used in all the regressions and was measured as:

$$W_i = S_i/L_i,$$

where *W* and *S* refer to wages per worker and total monthly salary bill respectively of firm *i*.

Overall technological intensity

For reasons advanced in Chapter 1, and given Brazil's fairly developed industrial structure, it can be hypothesised that the overall technological intensity (*TI*) of firms will be positively correlated with the labour productivity. *TI* was estimated as follows:

$$TI_i = HR_i + PT_i + RD_i,$$

where TI_i refers to the overall technological intensity of firm *i*.

Local sourcing

Given the experience of Brazil where *IS* engendered considerable industrial expansion for several decades owing primarily to its large domestic markets, local sourcing intensities in the country may produce statistically meaningful relationships. However, the cross-sectional data used here does not provide a time trend and hence its impact on the diffusion of knowledge involving the domestic economy as argued by Hirschman (1987) and examined by Rasiah (1995) cannot be examined here. Because foreign firms – especially transnationals – are thought to enjoy superior connections to best practice suppliers abroad, their relative import shares are considered higher than those involving local firms. However, because domestic content regulations were important until 2000, strong backward linkages may have emerged in Brazil. Thus, local sourcing is estimated in the usual conventional way, and was measured as:

$$LS_i = DI_i/OI_i,$$

where *LS*, *DI* and *IO* refer to local sourcing, domestic inputs and overall inputs respectively of firm *i*.

Other critical firm-level variables

Three other important firm-level variables were included in the analysis, i.e. size, ownership and management type. Age was dropped owing to a lack of statistical significance in all the regressions run for this chapter. Mergers and acquisitions involving cross foreign–local or reverse transfers from foreign to local in the last five years also did not produce any meaningful statistical result, but the data were presented to show the relatively high incidence of M&A among foreign firms compared to local firms.

Size   As argued in Chapter 1, it was not possible to identify *ex ante* the nature of relationship between size and the performance and technology variables. Size was measured in the chapter as:

$S_i = 1$ if employment exceeded 500; $S_i = 0$ otherwise.

where S refers to size of firm i in 2001.

Unlike the least developed economies of Kenya and Uganda, where it is extremely difficult to find large manufacturing firms, Brazil's long history of industrialization allows an easy definition of size categories using an employment size cut-off point of 500.

In auto parts manufacturing, 67.7 per cent of the 31 firms had an employment size exceeding 500 employees. Although this breakdown was atypical of the global auto parts industry, it is unavoidable owing to the difficulty of accessing primary data from firms. The breakdown for textile and garments – typically dominated by large employment size in developing economies – was 76.9 per cent with employment size exceeding 500 employees. The commensurate figures for electronics and pharmaceuticals were 50 per cent each of 16 firms respectively exceeding 500 employees.

Ownership   Foreign ownership was defined using equity share of 50 per cent or more. Using this criterion, foreign ownership in the sample was highest in the electronics industry (75.0 per cent of 16 firms), followed by pharmaceuticals (56.3 per cent of 16 firms), auto parts (41.9 per cent of 31 firms) and textiles and garments (23.1 per cent of 26 firms) (see Table 7. 1). Ownership was measured as:

$FO_i = 1$ if foreign equity ownership of firm i was 50 per cent or more;
$FO = 0$ otherwise,

where FO refers to status of ownership of firm i.

Mergers and acquisitions   The increase in mergers and acquisitions over the last two decades has raised the emphasis on its role in capability building, productivity and exports (see UNCTAD, 2002). Mergers or majority share acquisition by foreign firms of local or foreign firms in the last five years was particularly strong, accounting for 57.5 per cent of the 40 foreign firms in the sample. Mergers and acquisitions by local firms of local or foreign firms accounted for only 20.4 per cent of the 49 firms (see Table 7.1).

Owner-managed firms   As discussed in earlier chapters owner-managers (*OM*) impact have produced both positive and negative relationships on firms' performance. On the one hand, the lower agency cost is considered to offer them the freedom to make quick decisions. On the other hand, owner-managers are considered less professional, especially lacking corporate knowledge of big businesses, and hence may lack the instruments to succeed in competitive markets. Hence a neutral hypothesis with either a positive or negative sign is expected. There were more local firms with OM management compared to foreign firms: 17 local (34.7 per cent of 49 firms) and 4 foreign (10.0 per cent of 40 firms) (see Table 7.1). *OM* is measured using a dummy variable as follows:

$$OM_i = 1 \text{ if firm is managed either partly or fully by the owner;}$$
$$OM = 0 \text{ otherwise,}$$

where *OM* refers to status of management of firm *i*.

7.3.3   Statistical Analysis

This section presents the models specified to estimate the statistical relationships involving labour productivity, export, skills, local sourcing and technological intensities. OLS regressions were used when the dependent variable was value added per worker. Tobit regressions were preferred for export, skills, local sourcing and technological intensities because they are censored both on the right and the left side of the data sets. All the models were run with industry dummies:

$$\text{OLS: } VA/L = \alpha + \beta_1 X/Y + \beta_2 TI + \beta_3 S + \beta_4 FO + \beta_5 W + \beta_6 OM + \mu \tag{7.8}$$

$$\text{Tobit: } X/Y = \alpha + \beta_1 TI + \beta_2 S + \beta_3 FO + \beta_4 W + \beta_5 OM + \mu \tag{7.9}$$

$$\text{Tobit: } SI = \alpha + \beta_1 X/Y + \beta_2 TI + \beta_3 S + \beta_4 FO + \beta_5 W + \beta_6 OM + \mu \tag{7.10}$$

$$\text{Tobit: } LS = \alpha + \beta_1 X/Y + \beta_2 TI + \beta_3 S + \beta_4 FO + \beta_5 W + \beta_6 OM + \mu \tag{7.11}$$

$$\text{Tobit: } TI = \alpha + \beta_1 X/Y + \beta_2 SI + \beta_3 S + \beta_4 FO + \beta_5 OM + \mu \tag{7.12}$$

$$\text{Tobit: } HR = \alpha + \beta_1 X/Y + \beta_2 SI + \beta_3 S + \beta_4 PRD + \beta_5 FO + \beta_6 W + \beta_7 OM + \mu \tag{7.13}$$

$$\text{Tobit: } PT = \alpha + \beta_1 X/Y + \beta_2 HRD + \beta_3 S + \beta_4 FO + \beta_5 W + \beta_6 OM + \mu \tag{7.14}$$

$$\text{Tobit: } RD = \alpha + \beta_1 X/Y + \beta_2 HRT + \beta_3 S + \beta_4 FO + \beta_5 W$$
$$+ \beta_6 OM + \mu \qquad\qquad (7.15)$$

Regressions (7.8)–(7.15) were repeated using foreign and local firm samples separately. The variable of *OM* was dropped in these regressions because of its low incidence in the foreign firms' decomposed sample.

Overall 103 firms responded to the interview survey, but 14 responses were dropped owing to incomplete information for analysis. Although the São Paulo state sampling frame was not used, data collection was carried out randomly. A total of 89 filled questionnaires was obtained. Case studies of three electronics, auto parts, and textiles and garments were each undertaken by the author to help extract industry-type characteristics. No case studies were conducted on the pharmaceutical firms. The survey and the case studies constitute the basis for the results and analysis in the chapter. The breakdown of the firms is shown in Table 7.1.

7.4   STATISTICAL RESULTS

This section analyses the statistical results comparing foreign and local firms, and the statistical relationships involving them. Also discussed are important indicators of firms' participation in higher-value-added activities: e.g. incidence of involvement in original equipment manufacturing (OEM), original design manufacturing (ODM) and original brand manufacturing (OBM); and firms' take-up of patents.

The breakdown of the sample by the depth of manufacturing showed few firms engaged in OBM and ODM activities. Only local firms in the sample participated in OBM and ODM activities, albeit the incidence was very small (see Table 7.2). Two pharmaceutical and four textile and garment firms enjoyed OBM operations. All the four local firms engaged in ODM activities were in textile and garment manufacturing. Two of the foreign electronics firms that did not have OBM or ODM activities had R&D operations registered under separate subsidiaries in Brazil. The number of firms engaged in OEM was much higher. Foreign firms showed higher incidence of participation: 17 foreign firms (42.5 per cent) compared to 12 local firms (24.5 per cent). Local firms enjoyed a slightly higher take up of patents than foreign firms: 13 foreign (32.5 per cent) and 16 local (32.7 per cent). However, in the absence of ODM activities, it is likely that foreign firms' patents resulted from R&D undertaken abroad.

Table 7.2 Manufacturing technology characteristics, Brazil sample, 2001

	OBM			ODM			OEM			Patents		
	Foreign	Local	Total	Foreign	Local	Total	Foreign	Local	Total	Foreign	Local	Total
Auto parts	0	0	0	0	0	0	3	4	7	3	5	8
Electronics	0	0	0	0	0	0	8	4	12	4	4	8
Pharmaceuticals	0	2	2	0	0	0	4	2	6	4	3	7
Textiles & garments	0	4	4	0	4	4	2	2	4	2	4	6
Total	0	6	6	0	4	4	17	12	29	13	16	29

Note: Figures refer to number of firms involved.

Source: Tabulated from UNU–INTECH Interview and Survey (2002, 2003) using Stata 7.0 Package.

7.4.1   Statistical Differences

This section uses two-tail *t*-tests to examine statistical differences of the explanatory variables between foreign and local firms. These tests were run separately for all the four industries, and the results are presented in Table 7.3.

Productivity, export intensity, wages, skills and local sourcing
The *t*-tests produced mixed results involving labour productivity, export intensity, skills intensity, local sourcing and wages. Labour productivity was only statistically significant in the electronics industry at the 1 per cent level: foreign firms enjoyed a higher productivity level than local firms. Export intensity differences were statistically significant involving electronics (5 per cent level) and pharmaceutical firms (10 per cent level): foreign firms enjoyed higher export intensities in these industries than local firms. Wage differentials were statistically significant in electronics (at 1 per cent level) and pharmaceutical (at 5 per cent level) firms: local firms enjoyed higher wages than foreign firms in electronics firms but the reverse held for pharmaceutical firms. The statistical results in the auto parts and textiles and garments subsamples were not significant. The electronics (5 per cent level) and textiles and garments (5 per cent level) subsamples enjoyed statistically significant differences in skills intensities: foreign firms generally enjoyed higher skills intensities than local firms.

Local sourcing intensities involving electronics (1 per cent level) and textiles and garments (1 per cent level) were statistically significant. Local firms enjoyed higher local sourcing levels than foreign firms in these industries. Hence, as noted earlier, foreign firms' generally greater access to global suppliers continue to hold in these two industries. However, the results involving auto parts and pharmaceutical industries were statistically insignificant. Strong focus by the Brazilian government under *IS* over several decades, and performance and local content requirements especially from the late 1980s seem to have caused an evening-out effect between foreign and local firms.

Technological intensity
The statistically significant technological intensity variables generally favoured foreign firms. Foreign firms enjoyed higher and statistically highly significant (1 per cent level) *TI* levels than local firms in the electronics, and textile and garment industries. The decomposed *TI* variables of *HR* and *PT* also produced generally similar results: foreign firms enjoyed higher *HR* levels in the electronics (10 per cent level) and textiles and garments (1 per cent level) and higher *PT* levels in the electronics (1 per cent level) and

Table 7.3 Two-tail t-tests of productivity, and wages and export, skills, local sourcing and technology intensities, Brazil sample, 2001

	Foreign	Local	t
VA/L#			
Auto parts	3.57	3.39	0.49
Electronics	5.59	3.43	3.26*
Pharmaceuticals	2.62	2.95	-1.01
Textiles & garments	3.42	2.95	0.82
X/Y			
Auto parts	0.58	0.42	1.34
Electronics	0.13	0.02	2.13**
Pharmaceuticals	0.31	0.10	1.77***
Textiles & garments	0.34	0.19	1.13
W+			
Auto parts	13.18	7.35	1.40
Electronics	2.23	6.10	-5.71*
Pharmaceuticals	5.35	2.79	2.11**
Textiles & garments	4.72	3.05	0.79
SI			
Auto parts	0.20	0.18	0.35
Electronics	0.51	0.20	2.21**
Pharmaceuticals	0.29	0.35	-1.67
Textiles & garments	0.14	0.07	2.09**

	Foreign	Local	t
TI			
Auto parts	1.07	1.00	0.74
Electronics	1.27	0.64	2.84*
Pharmaceuticals	0.71	0.84	1.41
Textiles & garments	1.05	0.74	3.86*
HR			
Auto parts	0.58	0.52	1.21
Electronics	0.56	0.42	1.99***
Pharmaceuticals	0.41	0.53	-1.94***
Textiles & garments	0.59	0.39	3.45*
PT			
Auto parts	0.39	0.38	0.26
Electronics	0.52	0.20	10.25*
Pharmaceuticals	0.30	0.30	0.11
Textiles & garments	0.45	0.33	2.51**
RD			
Auto parts	0.10	0.10	0.13
Electronics	0.19	0.02	1.40
Pharmaceuticals	0.00	0.02	-1.57
Textiles & garments	0.01	0.03	-0.81

	Foreign	Local	t
TE			
Auto parts	4.50	4.56	-0.03
Electronics	3.00	3.00	0.00
Pharmaceuticals	3.86	5.34	1.21
Textiles & garments	3.63	1.66	2.54**
PTE			
Auto parts	2.93	3.48	0.51
Electronics	3.33	3.00	0.37
Pharmaceuticals	7.67	8.57	0.36
Textiles & garments	2.00	3.49	-1.24
RDE			
Auto parts	1.09	0.13	1.54
Electronics	0.04	0.02	2.46**
Pharmaceuticals	0.01	0.02	-0.91
Textiles & garments	0.01	0.02	-1.03
LS			
Auto parts	0.69	0.78	-1.16
Electronics	0.38	0.91	-3.63*
Pharmaceuticals	0.42	0.49	-1.42
Textiles & garments	0.56	0.80	-2.90*

Notes: *, ** and *** refer to 1, 5 and 10% levels of significance; # in 10 000 real; + in 1000 real per month.

Source: Computed from UNU–INTECH Interview and Survey (2002, 2003) using Stata 7.0 Package.

textiles and garments (5 per cent level) subsamples. Local firms enjoyed a statistically significant (10 per cent level) advantage in *HR* levels. The results involving auto parts remained statistically insignificant. The *t*-tests involving *RD* produced no statistically significant results, suggesting that there is no apparent difference in R&D intensities between foreign and local firms. Whereas typically foreign firms rely on their parent plants abroad for R&D support, conditional government incentives seem to have raised their R&D participation in Brazil to levels similar to local firms. Interviews with three electronics firms support this view.[4]

Separate two-tail *t*-tests using the typically used proxies of *TE*, *PTE* and RD_{exp} produced far less statistically significant differences between foreign and local firms. Foreign firms enjoyed statistically significant and higher *TE* levels in textiles and garments, and *RDE* levels in the electronics subsamples. Apart from these, the results suggest that there are few differences in technological expenditures in sales between foreign and local firms.

Overall, the statistical analysis produced mixed results. Foreign firms were generally more productive in electronics. The difference between foreign and local firms was insignificant in the remaining three subsamples. Foreign firms enjoyed higher export intensities than local firms in electronics and pharmaceuticals. Foreign firms also paid higher wages than local firms in pharmaceuticals, but the reverse occurred in electronics. Local firms enjoyed higher local sourcing intensities than foreign firms in electronics and textiles and garments. The statistical differences were not obvious in auto parts and pharmaceuticals. Foreign firms enjoyed higher overall technological and process technology intensities than local firms in electronics and textiles and garments subsamples. Local firms enjoyed slightly higher *HR* intensity than foreign firms in pharmaceuticals. R&D produced no statistically meaningful result except for *RDE* of electronics firms, where foreign firms made higher expenditures than local firms. Foreign firms spent more on HR training than local firms in textiles and garments.

7.4.2   Statistical Relationships

Having identified differences involving the sample data by ownership in the previous section, this section evaluates the statistical relationships involving labour productivity, and export, skills and local-sourcing intensities, and the technological variables controlling for wages, age, management type and ownership.

Productivity, and export, skills and local sourcing intensities
Table 7.4 presents the econometric results establishing the statistical relationships involving labour productivity, and export, skills and local sourcing

Table 7.4   Relationships involving productivity and export, skills and local sourcing intensities, Brazil sample, 2001

	V/L			X/Y			SI			LS		
	All	Foreign	Local	All	Foreign	Local	All	Foreign	Local	All	Foreign	Local
X/Y	-0.290	-1.136	0.122				-0.118	-0.200	0.001	4.639	7.562	5.239
	(-0.74)	(-2.74)*	(0.20)				(-1.77)***	(-1.58)	(0.02)	(1.08)	(0.99)	(1.15)
TI	2.672	2.349	2.429	-0.035	0.104	-0.130	0.252	0.249	0.080	0.602	24.556	5.913
	(7.59)*	(5.03)*	(3.43)*	(-0.28)	(0.50)	(-0.53)	(4.42)*	(1.73)***	(1.20)	(0.16)	(2.84)*	(1.09)
S	-0.073	0.055	0.219	0.331	0.248	0.396	-0.080	-0.027	-0.079	-3.465	-22.947	-3.012
	(-0.32)	(0.17)	(0.54)	(4.16)*	(1.81)***	(2.96)*	(-2.14)**	(-0.27)	(-2.08)**	(-1.35)	(-3.86)*	(-0.97)
OM	-0.281			0.021			0.061			-0.924		
	(-1.17)			(0.25)			(1.57)			(-0.35)		
FO	-0.039			0.207			0.048			0.880		
	(-0.18)			(2.78)*			(1.35)			(0.36)		
W	0.000	0.000	0.000	-0.000	0.000	0.000	0.000	-0.000	0.011	0.000	0.000	-0.000
	(0.94)	(0.94)	(1.54)	(-0.50)	(0.45)	(-0.64)	(0.71)	(-0.95)	(5.51)*	(0.78)	(0.72)	(-0.24)
μ	0.863	1.561	0.506	0.236	0.320	0.282	0.000	0.100	0.083	-0.940	-19.437	-4.720
	(2.24)**	(3.35)*	(0.69)	(1.83)***	(1.63)	(1.18)	(0.000)	(0.70)	(1.21)	(-0.22)	(-2.27)**	(-0.84)
N	89	40	49	89	40	49	89	40	49	89	40	49
F, χ²	15.55*	34.68*	3.62*	46.58*	30.13*	19.10*	74.60*	31.17*	51.96*	29.97*	31.39*	6.12**
R²	0.639	0.884	0.382									
Adj. R²	0.598	0.858	0.276									

Note: *, ** and *** refer to 1, 5 and 10% levels of significance.

Source: Computed from UNU–INTECH Interview and Survey (2002, 2003) using Stata 7.0 Package.

intensities using models (7.8)–(7.11) formulated in section 7.3. These regressions were also run separately by ownership samples. With the exception of the local firms' sample involving the local sourcing model (7.11) above, not only was the overall model fit (F, χ^2-stats) of the remaining models statistically significant; all the regressions also easily passed the Cook–Weisberg tests for heteroscedascity.

Against labour productivity as the dependent variable, foreign ownership was statistically insignificant when controlled for size, export orientation, technological intensity, wages, *OM* and industry. *TI* was statistically highly significant (1 per cent level) and its coefficient was positive and strong, demonstrating an extremely strong link between *TI* and productivity. The strength of this relationship was similar between foreign and local firms. *X/Y* was statistically highly significant in the foreign firms' sample, but its negative coefficient suggests that foreign firms enjoyed higher rents selling in the domestic market than abroad. Although the coefficient involving wages was positive, it was statistically insignificant in all three samples. The high incidence of unions may have ensured a right wage structure across firms rather than productivity standards (see Table 7.1).

FO's relationship with *X/Y* was statistically highly significant and its coefficient positive. Despite the importance of the domestic market and fairly similar export incidence by ownership (see Table 7.1), foreign firms were more export-intensive than local firms when controlled for size, *TI*, wages, *OM* and industry. *TI* was statistically insignificant in all three *X/Y* regressions, suggesting that export markets had little influence on the choice of technology. Size was statistically significant, and the coefficients were positive, suggesting that scale mattered in the exporting activities. Wages was statistically insignificant.

The relationship between *SI* and *TI* was statistically significant, and their coefficients positive in the overall and foreign firms' samples. This relationship was statistically insignificant involving the local firms' sample, though the *TI* coefficient was positive. Size was statistically significant in the overall and local firms' samples: the negative coefficient shows that small and medium firms enjoy higher skill intensities than the labour-intensive large firms. The results were not significant in the foreign firms' sample. Wages was statistically highly significant in the local firms' sample and its coefficient positive. Wages was insignificant in the overall and foreign firms' samples.

Although the two-tail *t*-tests showed local firms to have higher local sourcing intensities than foreign firms in electronics and textile firms, the results are not obvious when controlled for export intensity, *TI*, *S*, *OM*, wages and industry. *TI* enjoyed a statistically highly significant and positive influence on local sourcing in foreign firms. Foreign firms with higher *TI* levels are likely to source more locally than those with low levels, suggesting the presence of selected high-tech suppliers domestically. Perhaps the low-value-added inputs are imported from lower-wage economies such as Argentina and Peru. Size was inversely correlated, suggesting that foreign small and medium firms source more inputs locally than large foreign firms. The local sample failed the chi-square statistics for model fit.

Technological intensities

Table 7.5 presents the econometric results establishing the statistical relationships involving the technological intensity variables – *TI*, *HR*, *PT* and *RD* – using models (8.12)–(8.15) formulated in section 7.3. These regressions were also run using ownership samples. Not only was the overall model fit (chi-square statistics) of these remaining models statistically significant; all the regressions also easily passed the Cook–Weisberg tests for heteroscedascity.

The relationship between *FO* and *TI* was statistically highly significant and its coefficient positive, which shows that foreign firms enjoy higher *TI* levels even after controlling for size, export intensity, management type, wages and industry. Size was statistically significant and its coefficient positive in all three samples but its coefficient in the foreign firms' sample was significantly higher than the local firms' sample. Export intensity was statistically insignificant in all three samples, demonstrating that reversing the relationship still did not produce a statistically significant relationship. Wages was only significant in the local firms' sample, and its positive coefficient suggests a positive influence on technology.

The relationship between *FO* and *HR* was statistically marginally significant and its coefficient positive. Foreign firms enjoyed slightly higher *HR* levels than local firms after controlling for *X/Y*, *PRD*, *OM*, wages and industry. *X/Y* was highly significant statistically and its coefficient positive in the foreign firms' sample. The relationship was inverse involving local firms. Whereas export markets seem to have encouraged foreign firms to strengthen their *HR* practices, the opposite relationship is found with local firms, which could be the result of foreign firms' targeting developed markets whilst local firms may be exporting more into regional markets. More empirical evidence is essential to confirm this. The statistically strong and positive relationship with *PRD* in all three samples shows that HR practices are influenced simultaneously by process and product technology endowments in firms. Size was only statistically significant and positive in the local firms' sample. Management type (*OM*) was also statistically significant in the overall sample, but its positive coefficient was only marginally significant.

The relationship between *FO* and *PT* was statistically highly significant and its coefficient positive. Foreign firms enjoyed slightly higher *PT* levels than local firms after controlling for export intensity, *HRD*, *OM*, wages and industry. *X/Y* was statistically insignificant involving all three samples. Size

Table 7.5   Relationships involving technological intensities, Brazil sample, 2001

	TI			HR			PT			RD		
	All	Foreign	Local	All	Foreign	Local	All	Foreign	Local	All	Foreign	Local
X/Y	0.031 (0.27)	0.083 (0.58)	-0.107 (-0.85)	-0.011 (0.63)	0.305 (4.67)*	-0.161 (-2.42)**	0.017 (0.38)	-0.037 (-0.73)	0.059 (0.94)	0.069 (1.13)	-0.141 (-1.16)	0.060 (1.76)***
SI	0.821 (4.49)*	0.407 (2.15)**	0.297 (0.86)	0.060 (0.63)	0.189 (2.30)**	0.008 (0.04)						
PRD				0.280 (3.65)*	0.285 (2.91)*	0.310 (2.54)**						
HRD							0.239 (4.51)*	0.048 (0.73)	0.304 (2.83)*			
HRT	0.240 (3.71)*	0.572 (6.56)*	0.180 (2.09)**							0.370 (4.86)*	0.593 (2.18)**	0.157 (3.37)*
S	0.010 (0.14)			0.040 (1.24)	-0.042 (-0.81)	0.097 (2.08)**	-0.003 (-0.10)	0.134 (3.75)*	-0.031 (-0.72)	0.037 (1.00)	0.165 (1.57)	0.030 (1.33)
OM				0.048 (1.45)			-0.036 (-1.29)			0.029 (0.82)		
FO	0.138 (2.21)**			0.047 (1.58)			0.062 (2.51)*			-0.062 (-1.71)***		
W	-0.000 (-1.04)	-0.000 (-0.10)	0.000 (1.05)	0.000 (0.11)	0.000 (0.65)	-0.000 (-0.05)	-0.000 (-2.75)**	-0.000 (-3.25)*	0.000 (0.14)	0.000 (2.73)*	0.011 (2.60)*	0.000 (4.24)*
μ	0.667 (8.28)*	0.632 (5.92)*	0.811 (8.11)*	0.345 (8.04)*	0.229 (3.87)*	0.360 (5.39)*	0.242 (6.36)*	0.359 (8.33)*	0.200 (2.93)*	-0.348 (-4.54)*	-0.635 (-2.33)**	-0.138 (-2.95)*
N	89	40	49	89	40	49	89	40	49	89	40	49
χ^2	54.00*	63.53*	22.59*	40.56*	49.91*	25.19*	46.52*	53.25*	18.26*	56.10*	48.24*	43.35*

Note: *, ** and *** refer to 1, 5 and 10% levels of significance.

Source: Computed from UNU–INTECH Interview and Survey (2002, 2003) using Stata 7.0 Package.

was only statistically significant in the foreign firms' sample: large foreign firms enjoyed higher *PT* levels than small and medium foreign firms. Although the relationship between *PT* and *HRD* was statistically highly significant and positive, the link was only reproduced in the local firms' sample. *HRD* was statistically insignificant in the foreign firms' sample.

The relationship between *FO* and *RD* was statistically significant but only marginally, and its coefficient was negative, which shows that local firms have only a slight advantage over foreign firms in R&D levels when controlled for size, export intensity, *HRT*, *OM*, wages and industry. *HRT* and wages were statistically highly significant in all three samples and their coefficients positive, demonstrating that *RD* levels are simultaneously and positively correlated strongly with *HR* and process technologies and wages. Export intensity was marginally statistically significant and its coefficient positive in the local firms' sample, suggesting that external markets have a positive influence on local firms' *RD* capabilities. The lack of such a relationship in the foreign firms' sample suggests that their R&D activities may be geared more towards meeting government regulations to access incentives and domestic market requirements.

A few important conclusions emerge from the regressions. First, ownership did not matter on labour productivity, skills and local sourcing intensities when controlled for size, and export and technology intensities, wages, *OM* and industry. Export intensity was inversely correlated with *X/Y* in the foreign firms' sample, suggesting that foreign firms appropriate more rents from the domestic economy than in export markets. Foreign firms were more export-intensive than local firms after controlling for *TI*, size, wage, *OM* and industry. *FO* enjoyed a stronger relationship with *TI* and *PT* levels than local firms after controlling for export intensity, size, wages, *OM* and industry. Against *TI*, *LS* was highly significant in the foreign firms' sample, which is likely to be a reflection of domestic content regulations imposed by the government, export intensity was statistically insignificant against *TI* and *PT*, suggesting that export markets had no significant influence on overall technological and process technology capabilities. Ownership was not statistically correlated with *HR*. Interestingly, export intensity was strongly and positively correlated with *HR* in the foreign firms' sample, whereas this relationship was reversed in the local firms' sample. *FO* showed a marginally significant but inverse relationship with *RD*. The positive and significant relationship between *X/Y* and *RD* in the local firms' sample supports further this marginal relationship.

7.5   CONCLUSIONS

The evidence in the chapter shows that foreign firms show high levels of production and process-related capabilities, but no participation in OBM and ODM activities. Although the evidence generally supports the findings of Katz (1999), Katz and Bercovich (1993), Lastres and Cassiolato (2000) and Costa (2001), local firms only showed slightly higher R&D intensities than foreign firms when controlled for other variables, and the *t*-tests showed no obvious differences in R&D intensities. The share of the sampled firms participating in OBM and ODM activities and the number of firms with experience of patent take-up was extremely low. Foreign firms' intensity of participation in OEM was higher than in local firms, but only local firms participated in OBM and ODM activities. Local firms enjoyed a slightly higher incidence of patent take up than foreign firms.

The statistical analysis produced mixed results. Foreign firms were generally more productive only in electronics. The difference between foreign and local firms was insignificant in the remaining three subsamples. In addition, the pooled regression results on labour productivity, controlling for other variables, was statistically insignificant. Foreign firms enjoyed higher export intensities than local firms in electronics and pharmaceuticals, which were statistically significant even when controlled for other variables. Foreign firms paid higher wages in pharmaceuticals, but local firms enjoyed higher wages in electronics. Local firms enjoyed higher local sourcing intensities than foreign firms in electronics and textiles and garments, but the results were statistically insignificant when controlled for other variables. Foreign firms enjoyed higher overall technological and process technology intensities than local firms in electronics and textiles and garments subsamples, even when controlled for other variables. Local firms enjoyed slightly higher HR intensity than foreign firms in pharmaceuticals, but the results were insignificant in the pooled sample when controlled for other variables. However, foreign firms spent more on HR training than local firms in textiles and garments. R&D produced no statistically meaningful result except for R&D expenditure of electronics firms, where foreign firms spent higher expenditures than local firms. However, local firms enjoyed a slight advantage over foreign firms when controlled for other variables. Also, only local firms in the sample were engaged in OBM and ODM activities. No statistically significant difference existed between foreign and local firms in auto parts.

The results suggest that while stimulating the diffusion of process technology capabilities to local firms is still useful, local firms' R&D capabilities in Brazil should be strengthened further with government support. Although the current spate of liberalisation has made the world less tolerant and, as Cimoli and Katz (2003) have argued, have already undermined industrial policy instruments in the country, efforts must be made to strengthen initiatives to stimulate local firms' participation in such innovative entrepreneurial activities.

NOTES

1. Interviews by the author in June 2002 in São Paulo.
2. Interview by the author in June 2002 in São Paulo.
3. UNIDO (2002).
4. Conducted by the author in São Paulo in June 2002.

APPENDIX 7.1

Table 7A.1 Correlation matrix of independent variables, Brazil sample, 2001

	X/Y	TI	HR	PT	RD	OM	S	SI	W	PRD	HRD	HRT
X/Y	1.000											
TI	0.1882	1.000										
HR	0.175	0.8156*#	1.000									
PT	0.1213	0.7555*#	0.4399*	1.000								
RD	0.1448	0.7866*#	0.4560*	0.3857	1.000							
OM	-0.0283	-0.1399	-0.0408	-0.2106	-0.0904	1.000						
S	0.3649	0.2588	0.2094	0.0624	0.3265	0.0997	1.000					
SI	-0.2010	0.4288*#	0.3075	0.3088	0.3947	-0.0522	-0.2437	1.000				
W	0.1378	0.1087	0.1131	-0.1314	0.2547	-0.0741	0.2589	0.0703	1.000			
PRD	0.1604	0.9267*#	0.4383*	0.8146*#	0.8493*#	-0.1773	0.2410	0.4248*	0.0849	1.000		
HRD	0.1877	0.9391*#	0.8583*#	0.4842	0.8480*#	-0.0764	0.3129	0.4106*	0.2141	0.8102*#	1.000	
HRT	0.1765	0.9273*#	0.8687*#	0.8270*#	0.2982	-0.1417	0.1655	0.3628	-0.0017	0.7863*#	0.8045*#	1.000

Note: * highly correlated, # overlapping composition.

Source: Computed from UNU–INTECH (2002) Survey using Stata 7.0 Package.

8. Intel-driven enterprise linkages in Costa Rica

Jorge Monge

8.1 INTRODUCTION

The promotion of small and medium enterprises (SMEs) in economies requires a conducive environment: policies, functioning markets and services tailored to their real needs as well as to identifying niches to match their capacities, such as forging dynamic linkages between local and multinational firms. Past works on multinational-rooted linkages include Rasiah (1994, 2002a, 2002b), Ernst and Guerrieri (2001) and Lin and Rasiah (2003). This chapter discusses the role of one of the world's most famous firms – whom some consider as among developmental and entrepreneurial firms (see Best, 2001; Best and Rasiah, 2003) – in rooting supply synergies in a developing site. This chapter draws on a research conceived jointly with Eric Hershberg.

Since paving the way for the PC revolution by marketing the world's first microprocessor in 1971, Intel has spearheaded a computer revolution that has changed the world. Ninety per cent of personal computers in use today are based on Intel-architecture microprocessors. In addition to the popular Pentium® processor, Intel manufactures networking and communications products as well as semiconductor products used in automobile engines, home appliances and laser printers. Intel has become the world's largest supplier of microprocessors with 60–75 per cent of the global market and nearly 85 per cent of PCs have an Intel processor, 'Intel Inside' (see Mendez, 1999; Ortiz, 1998). Intel's total income rose from US$16.2 billion in 1995 to US$26.3 billion in 1998. These figures reveal the corporation to be one of the most profitable companies in the world: Intel paid over $3.7 billion in income taxes in 1997 (see NASBIC, 1998). In late 2001 the company employed approximately 80 000 people in 45 countries around the world. Intel's distinctive position in the semiconductor industry has led the company to pioneer an equally distinctive strategy for operations and investment. The strategy is driven by cutting-edge technology and blistering speed of implementation. Every nine months or so, Intel builds a new plant. Nearly all of these plants are built to meet future, rather than existing, demand (see Spar, 1998). For instance, following the explosion of E-commerce (projected at $1 billion in 2002) and multimedia applications, Intel oriented its products – since Pentium III – to Internet-based applications (see *La Nacion Digital*, 2000).

The intensity of multinational corporations' linkages with SMEs and the ability of countries and individual firms to exploit such linkages for technological upgrading depend on the interaction of several factors: e.g. SMEs' ability to meet high-quality standards or at least have the potential to achieve them. Other factors include multinational corporate strategies, which may be conducive to the development of local SMEs, and dynamic public policies in attracting foreign direct investment (FDI) and stimulating technology capability building in local firms. Prahalad and Doz (1987), Bartlett and Goshal (1989) and Birkinshaw et al. (1998) discussed the important initiatives taken by multinational affiliates seeking to participate actively in the local environment. Such initiatives take on tremendous technological implications when the affiliates involved require strong embedding institutions, network cohesion and supplier firms (Rasiah, 2002b; Best and Rasiah, 2003). Intel's relocation has shaken the Costa Rican economy to respond to such opportunities. Mortimore and Vergara (2003) and Mytelka and Barclay (2003) have discussed extensively the strategic implications of Intel's relocation in Costa Rica. However, these works have focused more on the government's strategic policy approach to attract Intel rather than the supplier network that has emerged in the country.

This chapter attempts to fill the gap by examining the above processes and the development of supplier synergies in Costa Rica. Intel's decision to locate an assembly and test facility in Costa Rica marked a watershed in the country's economic development. Since it began operation, the composition of Costa Rican exports has been transformed; nearly a billion dollars' worth of chips were exported in the firm's first year of operation. The synergies created by its operation, including the relocation of numerous global service providers (GSPs) to supply the flagship firm, have expanded exports further. From non-production-related activities, local suppliers have increasingly become inserted in Intel's value chain in high-technology segments such as software development. The rest of the chapter is organised as follows. Section 8.2 presents the methodology used to examine the development of suppliers in Costa Rica. Section 8.3 discusses the dynamism associated with Intel's operations and the electronics industry as a whole. Section 8.4 examines the supplier linkages that have developed from Intel's operations in Costa Rica. Section 8.5 concludes with a focus on policy implications.

8.2 METHODOLOGY AND DATA

As explained in Chapter 1, an attempt to examine the conduct and performance of a firm requires knowledge of its embedding structure. An adapted version of the methodology advanced in Chapter 1 is presented in Figure 8.1. Given Costa Rica's small size of 3.8 million people in 2000 (World Bank, 2002), its integration into Intel's global value chain has also had a major impact on its economy. Thus the government in Costa Rica has organised its policy framework at one level to attract strategic firms such as Intel, and at another level to engender the environment for small and medium suppliers to integrate into their complementary segments. There has been a strong emphasis on the creation of a diversified base of knowledge for technology diversification to facilitate upgrading in the strategic firms as well as among the small and medium firms supplying them.

SME promotional policies that integrate the different facets of development – e.g. industrial promotion, trade, technology and FDI – have to be viewed together (Figure 8.2). Business development services (BDS) has become an extremely important instrument to support the development of local suppliers. BDS has assisted *ex ante* integration, monitoring and *ex post* appraisal of suppliers' participation in such dynamic value chains to support integration, expansion, diversification and competitiveness.

Governments often play an important role by framing attractive policies to stimulate the relocation of strategic multinationals that enjoy the dynamism

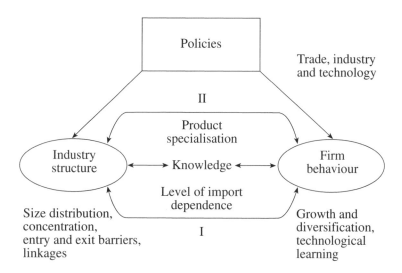

Figure 8.1   Co-evolution of industry structure and firm behaviour

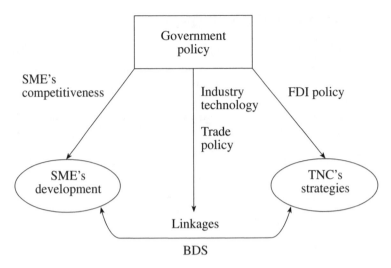

Figure 8.2   SMEs' development and TNCs' strategies

to stimulate strong linkages. SMEs' regulatory and legal framework should promote industrial upgrading and develop through a business–government coordination process the needed institutional framework. Indeed, the role of BDS in strengthening government–firm coordination has proved effective in the appropriation of multinational synergies. A related but more detailed methodology was used by Rasiah (1994) to trace supplier networks in Malaysia.

The data used in the chapter were collected by the author through case study interviews. Given the focus on Intel's supplier networks, the suppliers were traced from links with the firm.

8.3   INTEL'S RELOCATION AND ELECTRONICS INDUSTRY DYNAMICS

Costa Rica is a Central American republic that had depended traditionally on coffee, bananas, tourism and a handful of non-traditional exports for its revenue. By Intel's decision to open assembly and test operations in Costa Rica, the pioneering US microprocessor firm helped make manufacturing a major revenue earner. Intel's exports alone accounted for around one-fifth of national exports when it began operations in 1998. When the indirect exports of Intel are included – from global service providers (GSPs) who relocated to service the firm – the shares will be much higher. GSPs supply flagship enterprises with components and specialised activities and services. In addition to the upgrading opportunities that GSPs bring, it has encouraged the emergence and growth of a local software industry offering the promise of developing into a high-technology cluster.

The viability of a high-technology path to prosperity has far-reaching implications for Costa Rica. Long the most prosperous and peaceful of the Central American republics, the agrarian underpinnings of Costa Rica's unique formula for stability are no longer sufficient to generate the resources needed to meet the needs of the populace or to fund the benevolent democratic welfare state that has evolved since the late 1940s. Tourism offers one noteworthy growth opportunity, particularly as the country continues to upgrade into eco-tourism and other specialised niches, but that quintessentially non-traditional export can only be part of the solution to the long-term development challenges facing Costa Rica. Cognisant of the need to pursue new avenues for growth, both major political parties have sought to promote manufactured exports through the creation of *zonas francas* (export-processing zones – EPZs), in which foreign firms are exempted from tariffs and controls on investment and repatriation of capital. Concentrated primarily in the outskirts of the capital city San José, in proximity to the international airport, EPZs have attracted manufacturing investment in several industries.

Notwithstanding successes in attracting FDI from US, European and Asian firms during the 1980s and 1990s, Costa Rica's EPZs exhibit problems commonly associated with *maquila* production. Companies operating in the EPZs typically import an overwhelming percentage of inputs and, after conducting assembly operations in Costa Rica, ship finished goods abroad, with local value added being limited almost exclusively to that which takes place within the assembly plant. Significantly, the drawbacks to the EPZ model appear to have been true for potentially 'high-end' industries such as electronics, in which investment first began to trickle into Costa Rica two decades ago, as well as for 'low-end' sectors more typically associated with *maquila* production, such as garments and consumer goods.

Substantial public investments in primary and secondary education have endowed Costa Rica with a workforce that is far better educated than that of neighbouring countries and that indeed is among the most developed in Latin America. While *zonas francas* boosted exports and created some employment for relatively low-skilled workers and a handful of managers, their overall contribution to the local economy before Intel's arrival on the scene has been disappointing. Yet the most optimistic accounts hold that the investments undertaken by Intel and by the GSPs that accompanied it to Costa Rica will have qualitatively superior effects on the country's prospects. In the popular press and in the discourse of politicians, arrival of chip manufacturing has been understood to imply the dawn of an era in which Costa Ricans will prosper because of their expertise as engineers and technicians, and as highly skilled workers reaping the fruits of comparative advantage in human capital. A country whose path to peaceful development could be attributed to the century-long predominance of small farm-based coffee production would thus renew its ticket to prosperity in a new era: by producing engineering and technical expertise for the global market in semiconductors, software and related high-value-added products.

The Challenge of Upgrading

Costa Rica's wager on the electronics industry as a springboard of economic success can be analysed in terms of the challenges faced by any locality, whether national, regional or local in scale, seeking to engage in the processes of globalisation. However, to suggest that countries share an interest in becoming linked to the global economy alone is not enough to achieve this objective, or to ensure that they will benefit equally from it. It is through complex interactions between global and local dynamics that we come to understand the ways in which globalisation offers opportunities for improving economic conditions in some settings, stagnation in some and decline in others.

Indeed, as impressive as the scale of Intel's activities in Costa Rica may be, this is not sufficient to ensure development of an 'agglomeration economy' in which firms clustered closely to one another create an environment conducive to learning and innovation. Whether this and the associated dynamics of 'industrial upgrading' take hold will depend on a number of intertwined factors. These encompass exogenous questions, such as the evolving structure and performance of the electronics industry, the role of Costa Rican operations in Intel's global strategies, and the degree to which locally based firms will be considered as potential partners by Intel and its global suppliers. Endogenous factors – matters that may be amenable to the influence of public and private institutions in Costa Rica – are also likely to weigh heavily on eventual outcomes. These factors include the ability of local firms to meet the exacting standards of multinational firms and to branch out into related areas of production and services, as well as workplace dynamics that emerge in the firms and their local suppliers.

Industrial upgrading can follow various paths, but invariably it entails increasing the complexity and specificity of activities undertaken in the particular setting. Moving from one level of activity to another within a single global chain constitutes one approach to upgrading. The unprecedented decentralisation of highly integrated economic activities implies that particular actors may specialise in a limited number of functions along a given global value chain or cross-national production network (see Borrus et al., 2000; Gereffi and Tam, forthcoming). For example, a hierarchy of activities was identified (see Gereffi and Fonda, 1992) in the apparel and light manufacturing sectors – from simple assembly at one end of the spectrum to design and engineering at the other – through which the successful Asian export economies moved over the decades beginning in the 1960s. Similarly, in the computer industry, the most advanced of East Asia's National Innovation Centres (NICs) have developed design capabilities previously enjoyed only by US and Japanese firms and have shifted manufacturing of relatively simple components to other countries in the region. Mathews and Cho (2000) describe a parallel process in the East Asian semiconductor industry from the late 1970s through the 1990s, a period during which countries such as Singapore entered the sector as relatively low-wage assemblers for multinationals but progressed to a point where domestic enterprises could occupy some of the most desirable niches in the value chain, turning over to less developed neighbours activities that rely primarily on low-cost production capabilities. Typically, such intrasectoral upgrading entails the adoption of new technologies or enhanced production processes, or shifting niches based on improved knowledge, either of changing patterns of demand in highly segmented markets or of the key points at which actors can exercise control over the chain. While we suggest below that there is evidence of some intrasectoral upgrading in Costa Rican electronics, the growing reliance of large firms such as Intel on GSPs, which establish operations wherever new plants are established, signals a narrowing of space for such forms of upgrading.

An alternative approach to upgrading is to take advantage of the experience gained through participation in a given chain to shift into other, perhaps related, sectors. In the Costa Rican case, the emerging software industry would seem to offer an especially promising opportunity for such intersectoral upgrading, which takes on particular importance given that semiconductors are the subject of unparalleled volatility in demand and sharp downward pressure on prices. More generally, Costa Rican firms and workers may acquire new capabilities through exposure to the global electronics environment, and these capabilities may be deployed in a variety of economic activities. There is also the possibility that efforts by public and private institutions to facilitate upgrading of local industry in order to engage in electronics-related activity may have important spillover effects that will enable domestic actors to thrive in a variety of industries.

Whether intra- or intersectoral in nature, upgrading involves processes of organisational learning and technological and managerial advances that result from exposure to the risky universe of global value chains. As evident in the experience with EPZs, actors incur real risks when they enter a given chain at a relatively low level. And in sectors as volatile as electronics, it is easy to become trapped in low-value-added niches. In this regard, a key concern of this section is whether the activities undertaken by Intel in Costa Rica will differ substantially in nature from those that characterise production elsewhere in *zonas francas*. That is, we must determine whether the value added will be limited to assembly and testing operations, the location of which is determined largely by cost considerations, or whether such activities may be supplemented by engagement with other segments of the chain or by shifts into new industries. As outlined further below, the distinction between assembly and other functions is relevant for semiconductors in much the same way as for relatively low-technology manufacturing: the portion of value added associated with the assembly and testing stage of the semiconductor chain is relatively low, and is likely to narrow further over time, thus magnifying the importance of Costa Rica's upgrading into higher stages of the chain or establishing niches in related industries.

The next section outlines the principal characteristics of the electronics industry, situates Intel in the rapidly changing landscape of the sector, discussing the specific role played by Costa Rican activities in the globally dispersed activities of the industry and in the strategies of Intel. Also examined are the roles of foreign and local firms engaged in the chain, highlighting obstacles and opportunities for upgrading.

Internationalisation of Electronics Firms

The electronics industry has been one of the fastest growing and most rapidly expanding industries in the world, and until recently the sector was expected to continue growing at annual rates of nearly 9 per cent, with worldwide production of electronics equipment topping US$1 trillion by the end of 2000 (see FIAS, 1996a, 1998b; Gonzalez et al., 1997). Semiconductors, which are important to almost all electronic products (including computers, consumer electronic goods, transportation equipment, telecommunications apparatus, and industrial machinery hardware), accounted for 12.5 per cent of the total value of electronic equipment sales (see ITS, 1993), and employed an estimated four million people worldwide in 1997.

Many countries have sought to develop an electronics industry in hopes of benefiting from soaring demand for high-technology products and establishing a new source of domestic value added (see USEPA, 1995; Vieto, 1998). Growth in electronics equipment production has been concentrated in North America, Europe and East Asia, where the so-called 'Four Tigers' – Hong Kong, Taiwan, South Korea and Singapore – have gained access to highly profitable niches of the industry. To date, Latin America's role in the electronics industry has been very modest, with production concentrated in Brazil and Mexico. The region accounts for only about 3 per cent of worldwide

*Table 8.1   Worldwide electronic systems: annual production (US$ millions)
and annual growth rates*

	1994	1995	1994–1995 (%)	1995–2000 (%)
Semiconductors	110 000	125 000	13.6	20.0
Consumer electronics	157 096	170 746	8.7	6.2
Telecommunications	127 200	148 668	16.9	11.6
Computers	208 590	236 747	13.5	10.4
Software	77 000	86 000	11.7	12.0

Source: S&P (1996).

semiconductor production. Table 8.1 shows annual production levels and growth rates of worldwide electronic systems.

Semiconductors

Almost all contemporary industrial products, ranging from consumer electronic goods, consumer durables and industrial robots to smart missiles, require semiconductors, or integrated circuits, and their production requires varying levels of technical sophistication. Semiconductor devices are essential to information and communication equipment industries and to the development of virtually all other high-tech industries (see Sung, 1999). Integrated circuits production has grown dramatically over the past 40 years, from US$100 million in the late 1950s to US$150 billion in 1995.

The industry is remarkably volatile: while global semiconductor sales decreased 8.4 per cent in 1998, they rebounded in 1999, rising 19 per cent, and soared during the first three months of 2000, when sales rose by 28.4 per cent compared to the previous year. Intense competition between leading companies in the industry and the pace of technological innovation have combined to reduce most product life cycles to two to three years, compared with seven to eight years in the mid-1970s. To remain competitive, semiconductor companies were forced to spend about 25 per cent of sales revenues on R&D. These high R&D costs, as well as economies of scale in production, mean that companies must maintain large market shares in order to survive.

During the 1990s, semiconductor technology propelled the direction of change as well as growth patterns of the worldwide electronics industry. Until the unexpectedly sharp slowdown that began during the second half of 2000 and that has accelerated since then, it appeared that this trend would continue during the coming years, as wireless communications join networked personal computers, home PCs and consumer electronics emerged as globally pervasive applications for these components.

Semiconductor manufacturing encompasses multiple processes, of varying levels of technical sophistication. Outside the US, Japan and Europe, only Taiwan, South Korea and Singapore have been able to develop wafer fabrication facilities, the segment of the chain for which barriers to entry are highest. This was possible only because of the technical skill and business networks provided by expatriate populations working for leading US semiconductor companies (see Ernst, 2000a), and it is doubtful that this achievement can be replicated under present circumstances, for both the scale of production and the capital requirements for establishing wafer fabrication plants are growing at an astonishing pace (see Leachman and Leachman, 2001).

Apart from the demand for highly skilled personnel, it would cost around US$2 billion to build an 8-inch wafer fabrication plant using 0.5 micron technologies and today firms are switching to 12 inches wafer and 0.25 to 0.18 microns etching lines – that consume 40 per cent less energy and water per chip than the 8-inch process (Figure 8.3). No Latin American country is

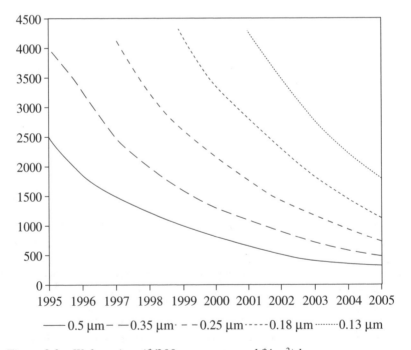

Figure 8.3   Wafer prices ($/200 mm wager and $/cm²) by process technology

likely to combine access to the necessary pool of capital with a sufficiently large stock of trained technicians capable of implementing such an advanced manufacturing process. Malaysia, with a long history of semiconductor assembly and testing, and two wafer fabrication plants in operation by 2003, still lacks human capital endowments to support new product development (see Rasiah, 2002b).

Several Asian countries have developed assembly and test facilities similar to those established by Intel in Costa Rica. These operations require the least qualified personnel and lowest paid workers in the value chain of the semiconductor industry. A typical worker in a semiconductor assembly and test facility is paid close to US$1 per hour in Malaysia. That worker would earn slightly less in the Philippines, and about half as much in China. As companies diversify away from Malaysia, which until recently has been the primary location for semiconductor assembly and testing, a large number of assembly and test facilities are now being developed in China, Indonesia and the Philippines.

Costa Rica's Electronics Industry

Before Intel's arrival in 1998, Costa Rica experienced three clearly defined waves of FDI in the electronic components industry. During the 1970s five foreign companies established facilities in the country, including Motorola, Trimpot (an affiliate of Bourns Inc.) and Square D; during the late 1980s and very early 1990s six more companies established facilities, including Espion (an affiliate of C&K Components) and Reliability. The third wave of electronic FDI dates from 1994 to 1996, with the establishment of nine firms, among them Protek and DSC Communications (which closed local operations in 1999 due to merger and acquisitions strategy). Most firms in the sector were established through foreign investment, especially from the United States, with one-third of the companies exporting directly to the US, in most instances exclusively to their parent companies (see Hsing, 1996a, 1996b).

In November of 1996, Intel announced plans to construct a semiconductor assembly and test plant – called A6/T6 – in Costa Rica with an investment of $300–$500 million, to produce and test nearly 20–30 per cent of its Pentium II chips. The announcement was the country's main economic news that year which was echoed throughout the region considering this was the first Intel plant in Latin America and competition to attract the investment had been intense. The structure of Costa Rican exports has changed drastically since the arrival of Intel, putting electronics products in first place ahead of all earlier traditional and non-traditional exports. In 1998, the first year of Intel production, Intel Costa Rica exported $985.31 million, representing 18 per cent of national exports, with modular circuits and microstructures as the main exports (see *El Financiero*, 1999).

What attracted Intel to Costa Rica

Several factors explain Intel's relocation in Costa Rica. The country's positive international image – it had enjoyed half a century of liberal democracy and a stable record of economic growth, and had achieved some of the best indicators of social well-being in the developing world. The country had also launched various initiatives to attract foreign investments: FDI was encouraged by legislation that places no limitations on foreign property ownership or for conducting business; by a constitution that gives equal rights and obligations to foreigners and nationals and by-laws that place no restrictions on repatriation or transfer of capital. Intellectual property laws in accordance with World Trade Organization (WTO) guidelines are in place, as are agreements with several countries for investment promotion and protection. Costa Rica has also instituted a free trade regime (FTR) with attractive incentives for foreign investment. For instance, there is a 100 per cent exemption on import duties for raw materials, components and equipment, on export taxes, excise taxes and profit repatriation taxes as well as on income taxes for eight years with a 50 per cent exemption for the following four years. In addition, there are no restrictions on capital or profit repatriation and companies can sell to exporters within Costa Rica and 25 per cent to the local market (see CINDE, 2000). Realising that some textile manufacturers have moved to neighbouring countries in part because of the country's higher wages and benefits compared to theirs, the Costa Rican government sought companies by focusing on the nation's more mature, sophisticated and technologically advanced labour pool. The high-technology human capital endowment was an important differentiating variable in the selection of Costa Rica.

Intel's initial list of possible locations for the planned new facility included around ten countries worldwide; among the Latin American options were Brazil, Chile and Mexico. A combination of different factors contributed to Costa Rica's eventual selection. To be considered at all, a stable political, economic and pro-business environment was essential. The winning candidate needed to ensure that the critical institutions necessary to support Intel's operations were developed. Costa Rica offered the initial base with good basic infrastructure and educational institutions that could supply technical and professional human resource. Intel also sought a non-union labour environment, incentives, free trade regime, exoneration, privileges and fast-track permits. Like other cutting-edge technology firms, because Intel relies on a dependable and well-educated labour pool, it only builds plants where it is assured access to a highly trainable supply of labour. The previous establishment in Costa Rica of an important number of foreign electronics firms was another positive factor for Intel's decision (see Gonzalez et al., 1997).

Two additional factors were also important in swinging Intel's decision to relocate in Costa Rica: negotiation tactics and specific concessions (see Spar, 1998). During the selection process, several major concerns emerged. The first was simply Costa Rica's small size and limited resources. Initial projections indicated that the planned plant might require up to 30 per cent of Costa Rica's power capability, although it turns out that actual usage has represented only about 5 per cent[1] of Costa Rican capacity (see I&A, 1998; *La Republica*, 1996). Cargo facilities were a major concern since the firm's output has to be exported frequently by air. While the physical infrastructure of Costa Rica's airport at San José was more than adequate, the frequency of flights and airport efficiency were not. The Costa Rican government provided assurance on both issues. Regulations also required that environmental standards were observed at the Costa Rica plant, and hence the authorities ensured that wastewater discharge and hazardous industrial waste management standards were met (see Spar, 1998; Vieto, 1998).

The efforts of local institutions to accommodate the magnitude of the project and the requirements of the corporation required exceptional and explicit measures, which had never before taken place in Costa Rica. The active participation of the nation's president and a team of senior government officials provided a clear signal of their interest in Intel's investment. In fact, among the negotiating tactics and actions of Costa Rican authorities during the decision-making process, bargains were struck and problems were resolved through unified response and extensive personal involvement of key government officials. Government authorities also successfully addressed the three immediate demands sought by Intel, i.e. guarantees on physical infrastructure, educational infrastructure, and favourable financial terms for the proposed investment.

As noted earlier, Intel was also attracted by Costa Rica's relatively well-educated, skilled and easily trainable labour force, which benefited from long-term investment in public education by the government. The country enjoyed a literacy rate of 94 per cent in 2001 and many workers continue to seek additional specialised training. The National Vocational Training Institute (INA) and private sector groups provide technical and vocational training. Costa Rica's ample pool of professionals, educated at both Costa Rican and foreign universities, is among the largest and most diversified in Latin America (see USITC, 1993).

Costa Rica also provided a fairly compliant industrial relations environment. The Costa Rican Labour Code of 1943 governs labour–management relations, including wages, working hours and conditions as well as employment termination and provides for the resolution of labour disputes in labour courts. The National Wage Council, composed of government, labour,. and private sector representatives, establishes minimum wage rates for the private sector semi-annually. According to the Labour Ministry, about 15 per cent of Costa Rica's workforce were unionised in 2001, a figure that has remained relatively constant. While the vast majority of union members are in the public sector, many private sector workers are affiliated with so-called solidarity associations. Under such associations, employers provide access to credit unions and savings plans in return for agreements to avoid strikes and other types of confrontations. Overall, more Costa Rican workers belong to solidarity associations than to unions. The strong technical intensity of the labour force and the pro-business environment corresponded to Intel's preferences.

8.4   INTEL-ROOTED SUPPLIER NETWORKS

Intel relocated assembly and test operations in Costa Rica, which is less expensive and more labour-intensive than wafer fabrication. The first Costa Rican Intel plant (CR1) was built in 1997 by assembling and testing Pentium II processors as well as Pentium Pro, Pentium MMX, Celeron and SEC cartridges, which integrated microprocessor and memory. Intel opened a new plant (CR3), which began operations in January 1999 to assemble and test Pentium III processors and OLGA, one of its main components, and has since started plans to assemble and test Pentium IV processors (see Corcoran, 1999; *La Nacion*, 1997, 1998).

Relocation of Suppliers

According to government official records from *Coalición de Iniciativas para el Desarrollo* (CINDE), which is a government institution established to attract FDI, there are more than 30 firms in electronics and related industries with manufacturing operations in Costa Rica. These companies are primarily foreign firms established under FTR undertaking a broad range of electronics activities. The presence of several leading firms created a positive environment for stimulating capability building in local firms, including complementary backward and forward linkages in different sectors (see Doner and Hershberg, 1999).

The large companies established before Intel's arrival included C&K Components (formerly known as Espion), which manufactures miniature switches. Bourns Inc. (formerly Trimpot) provides PC board assembly and testing. Panduit supplies wire and cable accessories, Protek Electronics provides digital metering equipment. Tico Pride Electronics (TPE), an electronic contract manufacturing services firm, started operations in 1994 with its sales and marketing office in Orange, California. Its activities include printed circuit board assembly using surface mount technology (SMT) and through hole technology, and assembly of wiring and harnesses for electro-motors used in aviation. Several of these companies underwent rapid expansion in the late 1990s (see FR, 2000).

Intel's operation in Costa Rica consists of the A6/T6 plant, which undertakes assembly and test with the main processor components imported from other Intel plants (*fab*) located abroad and from other high-technology providers. On-site specialised services delivered by its foreign equipment providers are required for the operation of Intel's Costa Rican plant, as are basic services and supplies provided by local firms.

Foreign high-technology companies arrived along with Intel to provide accessories as well as specialised services. Initially, Intel's plant was expected to bring to Costa Rica an additional US$500 million worth of associated investment by approximately forty firms to engage in support and supply activities (see FIAS, 1996a, 1996b); however, the scale of investment has not reached the expected level. Among the electronic companies attracted by Intel are Photocircuits (circuit boards), Pycon (test boards), AeTec (circuit boards) (see Ward, 1999), Anixter (data communications, cable and wires), Tiros (curing systems), Entex (systems management), HP-Agilent (instrumentation), Alphasem (die attach and sort systems), RVSI (automation), Schlumberger (testing), which established operations in 1998 and early 1999 (see Table 8.2).

As stated by Wong (2000), who was the vice-president and managing director of Intel Penang in 2001:

> Intel suppliers need to meet several critical capabilities, which first and foremost means technical competencies, manufacturing capabilities and the ability to respond to multiple and sudden changes almost instantly. The latter issue reflects the nature of Intel's business where market dynamics change quickly, which also require suppliers to be responsive to that change in the same rhythm in which Intel operates, i.e. 24 hours a day and 7 days a week. In addition suppliers need to be able to meet Intel's stringent environment, health and safety (EHS) requirements. Since Intel has become a global player with manufacturing sites in various locations world wide, SME suppliers have to be able to support this global network. Last but not least, Intel suppliers need to be competitive from a total cost perspective.

It is easier to understand Intel-driven suppliers by locating them in Intel's value chain, which is examined in the next section.

Table 8.2   Intel-CR high-technology products and service providers

Company	Activity
AeTec Intl.	Circuit board production, media cleaning process (trays)
HP–Agilent	Instrumentation, measurement and semiconductor equipment
AK Precision	Material injection, trays for pick and place equipment (moulds)
Alphasem	Fully automatic die attach and die sort systems
Anixter	Data communications products and electrical wire and cable
DEK Printing Machines Ltd	Precision screen printing systems and pre-placement solutions
EMC Technology, Inc.	Electronic components for satellite telecommunications (microwave)
Entex	E-business consulting and management of LAN/WAN/desktop
Fema	Fixtures for pick and place equipment and magazine walls
LKT	Automatic loading systems – boats transfer – from/to magazines carts
Mecsoft	Software and design involved in trays for pick and place equipment
OPM Micro Precision	Micro precision products for pick and place equipment (moulds)
Panduit Corporation	Cable tying and accessories, electronic components, labelling
Photocircuits	Circuit boards
Pycon	Electronic boards calibration, test during burn-in systems
Reliability	DC to DC converters and burn-in and test equipment
Robotic Vision Systems Inc.	Automated inspection, packages, machine-vision-based scrutiny
Sawtek	Radio and intermediate frequency, filters for digital wireless phones
Schlumberger	Systems and services for testing semiconductors devices
Sykes	Call center/support services
Tiros Thermal Solutions	Design and manufacture of automated curing system, vertical cure ovens

Source: Monge (2001).

Input–Output Dynamics

Although physics and electronics engineering are the underlying technologies of semiconductors, the manufacture of semiconductors also requires skills in chemistry, chemical engineering and metallurgy. In the manufacture of semiconductors there are four stages: design, wafer production and wafer fabrication, assembly and test, and sales (see FIAS, 1996a, 1996b; Spar, 1998; USITC, 1993; Vieto, 1998). The Costa Rican operations only carry out assembly and test.

Intel Costa Rica specialises in assembly and test operations, i.e. back end preparation, probe test, die cut, wire bonding, encapsulation and burn-in. Compared to fabrication, assembly and testing of semiconductors is more labour-intensive, and is often conducted in developing countries endowed with large reserves of low-wage labour. The assembly process in Intel-CR1 consists of attaching the processor and other components, such as cache memory and RAM memory, on to wafers (purified polycrystalline silicon) using a welding process. The Intel-CR1 production line consists of 25 machines arranged along a line 180 metres long (see *La Nacion*, 1998). In the test operation, a robot places 30 semiconductor chips (boards) into a test machine controlled by a technical worker who uses a computer and his analytic knowledge to re-programme the test if needed (see I&A, 1998). The inputs needed for Intel CR operations in phase I are classified by sector in: electronics and non-electronics components, chemicals (solid, liquid and gases), packaging material, energy and water, and others. Machinery, equipment, technological knowledge, know-how, services, maintenance and different labour skill levels are among the inputs required.

The production process typically constitutes 2 per cent of value added in the semiconductor chain, with wafer fabrication representing 26 per cent, assembly and test 10 per cent, and customisation, sales and profit 62 per cent. Assembly and test facilities are obviously the least technology-intensive and hence do not allow the appropriation of Costa Rica's educated workers effectively. According to FIAS (1996a, 1996b), the assembly and test operations of Costa Rican plant represent about 10 per cent of total sales value of chips and the value added is provided by the least qualified personnel and lowest paid workers in the semiconductors' value chain. Once other expenses are added, the local value added incurred by Intel over the first two years of operation in Costa Rica amounted to about 18–20 per cent, including labour, services and electricity, among others. For an assembly and test facility such as A6/T6, wage costs are the most important variable cost, typically accounting for 25–30 per cent of total operating costs (see *La Nacion*, 1999; *La Republica*, 1999; Mendez, 1999; Spar, 1998).

High-Technology Suppliers

The data collected allowed a discussion of the nature of suppliers linked to Intel. Suppliers can be distinguished as high-technology-based and others. Table 8.2 presents a list of firms interviewed and the services they provide Intel in Costa Rica. These firms are essentially GSPs. It can be seen that although Costa Rican activities constitute the lowest segment in Intel's global value chain, it is still fairly sophisticated, and the GSPs it has attracted are also engaged in high-value-added activities.

Other Suppliers

In addition to the high-technology firms, local companies offer other services to Intel's A6/T6 Costa Rica plant. According to data (see *La Republica*, 1999), 76 per cent of Intel's local purchases represent services in 1999. Table 8.3 presents a list of such suppliers interviewed and the services they offer Intel. Logistics among other factors offer Costa Rican firms significant advantages over foreign firms in supplying Intel with these non-high-technology services.

Table 8.3   Intel-CR products and services providers not related to high technology

Company	Activity
Electroplast	Plastic products
Corbel	Boxes, corrugated boxes
Econopak	Wood boxes
PRAXAIR de Costa Rica	Nitrogen
Capris	Hardware store, industrial equipment and machinery
Universal	Office supplies
Wackenhut	Security services for facilities
InHealth	Food
CORMAR–AEI–Danzas	Transportation/custom service
Metro Servicios	Occupational safety and health products
Metrologia Consultores	Equipment calibration
ICE	Electric power
Vargas Mejia y Asociados	Security services
A y A	Water

Source: Monge (2001).

Intel-driven Chain

Intel is the driver in the value chain, using its flagship microprocessors network to control critical resources and capabilities along the productive chain, determining the participation and opportunities of other participants, and coordinating activities through its international linkages. Intel facilities around the world act as a 'virtual factory'. As is typical of flagships (Ernst, 2000b), Intel locates different activities of the production chain wherever they can be carried out most effectively, wherever they improve access to resources and capabilities and wherever such activities are needed to facilitate the penetration of important growth markets. Figure 8.4 shows the A6/T6 segment of the chain in Costa Rica.

The establishment of Intel at its Costa Rican location motivated the arrival of GSPs to support Intel's production through different services and products. These GSPs were already part of Intel's global value chain and had previous contracts with Intel at other plants with longstanding relationships developed over many years. Some of these firms were established through Intel's strategy of fostering outsourcing to accomplish manufacturing needs, mainly cost reduction and speed to market. Although most of these firms continue to serve Intel Costa Rica, some have expanded to export.

For the purpose of the Intel-CR chain's study, firms' activities were classified – according to the products or services required by Intel's production

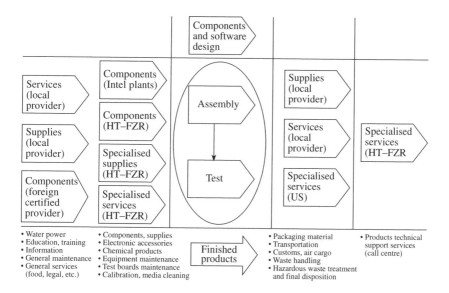

Figure 8.4   A6/T6 chain at Costa Rican location

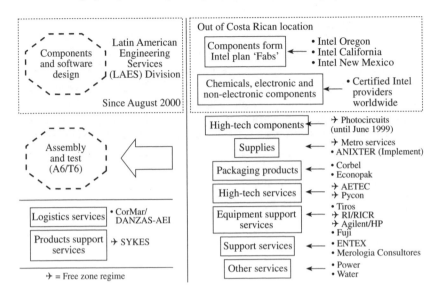

Figure 8.5   Clusters in Intel plant A6/T6

chain – as follows: high-technology components, equipment support services, high-technology services, support services, supplies, packaging products, logistics services, other production and product support services (Figure 8.5).

Intel's productive chain activities and the variable status of providers along the chain is presented in Table 8.4, which helps to integrate the analysis in four variables (see Ernst, 2000c) to explain how specialisation affects market structure and upgrading potential.

High-tech components, equipment components and services, high-tech services and product support activities, which have high product and process specialisation, present highly complex production structures. Thus, while the potential for upgrading is higher, so too are the entry barriers, and linkages are low along the chain. Instead, support services, supplies, packaging products and logistics services activities with low product specialisation and a relatively high process flexibility specialisation (reflected in the speed of response) present low complex production structures and hence low potential for upgrading (see also Appendix 8.1).

For instance, in high-tech components, a US firm which arrived as Intel's provider and whose contract ended, decided to continue operations in Costa Rica. It upgraded to a higher end of the chain by moving to tooling, where printed circuit boards are designed using CAD software. The firm had carried out *maquila* activities for Intel with 300 employees when its contract ended in 1999. Resuming initially with ten employees with an upgraded plant to

Table 8.4   Specialisation–upgrading matrix, Intel production chain, Costa Rica

Firm activity	Explanatory variables		Dependent variables	
	Product specialization	Process specialization	Market structure	Upgrading potential
High-tech components				
From other Intel plants	High	High	High	High
Printed circuit boards	High	Low	Low	Low
Equipment component and services				
Cure semiconductors	High	High	High	Medium
Chamber to test processors	High	High	High	Medium
IBT and AXI	High	High	High	Medium
Pick and place	High	High	High	Medium
High-tech services				
Handling media cleaning	High	High	High	Medium
Repair of boards/testing processors	High	High	High	High
Product support				
Product support	High	High	High	High
Support services				
Hardware and software tech support	Low	High	Low	Low
Equipment calibration services	Low	High	Low	Low
Supplies				
Clean room/electrostatics control	Low	High	Low	Low
Data communication products (distribution)	Low	High	Low	Low
Packaging products				
Corrugated boxes	Low	Low	Low	Low
Wood boxes, wooden pallets	Low	Low	Low	Low
Logistics services				
Freight transportation/ logistics	Low	High	Low	Low

supply a higher-end segment of Intel's value chain, the firm grew rapidly to employ 250 employees in 2001.

In equipment component and services, local companies are becoming providers by successfully surmounting high technological entry barriers. For example, a local firm upgraded to become Intel's supplier of high-technology products through a business development service (BDS) provider using SUDIAC© tools[2] for selling products to Motorola. This linkage benefited from a national programme for the development of local providers linked to multinationals. The firm's product is currently being tested in three different facilities in the US and Asia, offering local firms the opportunity to graduate into GSPs. Other examples involving horizontal linkages among local SMEs to supply products to meet Intel's requirements, involving material injection, precision machining and software design capabilities. These firms had already started an arrangement to supply Abbot, which is another multinational. One of them had been part of the SUDIAC–BDS application programme (see Monge, 1994, 1999).

Multinational suppliers engaged in high-tech services are broadening their local knowledge base through subcontract relations and training personnel. GSPs' activities in Costa Rica have grown fivefold since their arrival, supplying not just Intel and the other multinationals in Costa Rica, but also those located in the neighbouring economies. The agglomeration of international firms in Costa Rica has helped spin off local firms in metal precision, clean room, static and occupational health and safety as well as in metrology services and equipment maintenance and repair.

Logistic services presented a high entry barrier for potential competitors due to Intel's preference for GSPs, which are able to deliver services with global coverage. To be considered by Intel as a provider of these services, a local customs broker and airfreight forwarder with a regional position in the market successfully became Intel's provider to manage high-speed inventory, and deliver sales orders to Intel customers and supporting distribution-related services.

Local Product Support Services is a differentiated firm, based on information communication technology (ICT) development where close interaction with customers is needed and the barriers to entry are high since it is a post-sell service with significant value generation. The potential for upgrading is high on the basis of substantial possibilities to deepen the local knowledge base and strengthen forward linkages. Intel's local provider was already established in Costa Rica and has diversified its operations to offer services to other multinationals in Costa Rica.

Deepening Efforts

Intel's plans to deepen and integrate newer versions of its microprocessor has generated considerable implications for further upgrading in Costa Rica. Technological deepening at the Intel plant in Costa Rica will continue to be incremental towards the latest technology, even if it is limited to assembly and test operations. These developments generate implications for upgrading supplier activities as well. A number of these developments have already produced results in Costa Rica.

The Latin American Engineering Service Group, comprising 22 engineers from Costa Rica, six from Colombia, one from Venezuela and one from Brazil, is working at a California design centre using very large system integration technology (VLSI) to improve the speed of Pentium IV, using the profile of electronic engineers with programming skills for microprocessor design. This could represent a niche area such as the one in software. In fact, recently, Intel formed a software group directed to take advantage of the country's capacities in this sector (see Monge, 2002).

Intel invested recently in Artinsoft, a Costa Rican company, whose flagship product is a computer language translator that allows business to update software and systems rather than replace them. The core technology, software with artificial intelligence characteristics, can be adapted to Intel products, or to work in designing a program to enable companies to migrate to Intel's Internet and operating systems, i.e. transition from 32-bit to 64-bit architecture. Intel has invested in over 200 firms recently, and the list of these firms and their products helps to put in perspective the investment made in the Costa Rican software company (see Albrink et al., 2000; Corcoran, 1999; Malik, 2001; Reindhart, 2000; Takahashi, 2001). Among the examples is a German software company with a leading-edge product in supply chain management that complements Intel's capacity to work as a virtual factory. Another Costa Rican software company developed an inventory management software based on Internet applications, which will be tested in four assembly and testing facilities as a building block for supply chain management in Intel's virtual factory system. Wong (2000) succinctly captured Intel's rationale for these investments:

> Intel turns to new suppliers when they use or possess a promising technology or new capabilities which are not available at Intel – when performance issues, such as quality, delivery or price competitiveness attract Intel's attention – or when Intel faces capacity constraints that could be bridged by outside suppliers.

As with successful examples (see Fransman, 1985; Lin and Rasiah, 2003), nationally coordinated programmes are needed to assist local firms to appropriate the synergies associated with Intel's deepening activities in Costa

Rica. The role of Penang Development Corporation as a key intermediary organisation supporting strong state–business coordination was central in the growth of suppliers to harness synergies from Intel's operations in Penang (see Rasiah, 1994, 1996). In Costa Rica, the National Centre for High Technology (CENAT) and the *Provee* programme to facilitate local SME links with high-technology multinationals constitute important steps to support such developments. In addition, national coordination efforts were also established through the *Impulso* programme promoted directly by the President's Office. This development is a dynamic process that requires the combination of critical and innovative thinking by stakeholders and strong developmental organisations that promote inter-firm linkages.

Overall, it can be seen that Intel's relocation in Costa Rica has not only on its own generated demand for the relocation of foreign GSPs and local firms to provide services directly, but also indirectly through the expansion of the suppliers and their own suppliers, meeting demand domestically as well in export markets. Given Costa Rica's high-technology endowments and government initiatives, the view of the country as a potentially strong emerging cluster appears very realistic.

8.5   CONCLUSIONS

This chapter presented a glowing account of how the relocation of a developmental multinational helped attract supplier synergies – both foreign and local – and laid the foundations for continuing upgrading and differentiation and division of labour in Costa Rica. Government policies were important in providing both basic and high-tech infrastructure, as well as coordination and support for local suppliers. Hence, even though the segment located in Costa Rica constitutes the shallowest part of Intel's global chain in microprocessors, it has engendered considerable synergies to attract high-tech suppliers and similar supply responses from local firms. In addition, the assembly and test operations in microprocessors are fairly sophisticated if compared with typical manufacturing in Latin America.

While recognising the contribution Intel has made to the local economy, it is important to note a number of issues that the government and the other local actors will have to overcome to sustain and integrate further Intel's operations in the country. Obviously Costa Rica is a special case given the country's small size and Intel's huge influence. The metaphor that comes to mind is that of B. Perlman, one of Intel's vice-presidents: 'a whale in a swimming pool' (see Spar, 1998). It will be interesting to see for how long Intel will retain operations in Costa Rica.

NOTES

1. Data sources vary in a range from 2 per cent to 8 per cent.
2. The author developed SUDIAC© (Unified Industrial Diagnosis System for Competitiveness Improvement) and applied it in over 100 SMEs in Latin America and Africa, as well as the Business Development Services (BDS) Management System applied in several BDS organisations in Latin America and Africa.

APPENDIX 8.1

Table 8A.1   *Specialisation–upgrading matrix:[a] trial application to Intel production chain at Costa Rican location*

	Product specialisation									
	Low complexity/uncertainty					High complexity/uncertainty				
	Homogeneous (commodities)					Differentiated				
Activities/function part of Intel / Chain at Costa Rica location	Mature technology	Established design	East to duplicate	Predictable changes in demand & tech	Limited interaction with customers	New technology	Fluid design	Difficult to replicate	Unpredictable changes	Close interaction with customers
High-Tech Components										
From other Intel plants						S	S	S	S	S
Printed circuit boards	S			S			S	S		S
Equipment Support Services										
Cure semiconductors						S	S	S	S	S
Chamber to test processors						S	S	S	S	S
IBT and AXI						S	S	S	S	S
Pick and place						S	S	S	S	S
High Tech Services										
Handling media cleaning						S	S	S	S	S
Repair of boards/testing processors						S	S	S	S	S
Support Services										
Hardware and software tech support	S	S	S	S	S					
Equipment calibration services	S	S	S	S	S					
Supplies										
Clean room/electrostatics control	S	S	S	S	S					
Data communication products (distribution)	S	S	S	S	S					
Packaging Products										
Corrugated boxes	S	S	S	S	S					
Wood boxes, stands	S	S	S	S	S					
Logistics Services										
Freight transportation/ logistics	S	S	S	S	S					
Product Support										
Product support		S				S		S	S	S

Note: [a] Applied from Ernst (2000b) to the research case.

Process specialisation — Low (MP) — Economies of scale and scope	Process specialisation — High (FS) — Speed of response	Market structure — Low complexity/uncertainty — Low entry barriers	Price competition	Limited value generation	Market structure — High complexity/uncertainty — High entry barriers	Premium prices	Significant value generation	Upgrading potential — Low complexity/uncertainty — Limited technological learning requirements	Limited pressure to develop forward and backward linkages	Upgrading potential — High complexity/uncertainty — Substantial pressure to broaden and deepen local knowledge base	Substantial pressure to broaden and deepen linkages
	S				S	S	S			S	S
S			S	S	S			S	S		
	S			S	S	S			S	S	
	S			S	S	S			S	S	
	S			S	S	S			S	S	
	S			S	S	S			S	S	
	S			S	S	S			S	S	
	S			S	S	S				S	S
	S	S	S	S				S	S		
	S	S	S	S				S	S		
	S	S	S	S				S	S		
	S	S	S	S				S	S		
	S				S	S	S	S	S		
S		S	S	S				S	S		
S		S	S	S				S	S		
	S	S	S	S				S	S		
	S			S	S	S				S	S

Table 8A.2　Specialisation–upgrading matrix[a] relation between explanatory and dependent variables

					Explanatory		
						Product	
					Low complexity/uncertainty		
					Homogeneous (commodities)		
Dependent variables			Mature technology	Established design	Easy to replicate	Predictable changes in demand & tech.	Limited interaction with customers
Market structure	Low complexity/ uncertainty	Low entry barriers	X	X	X	X	X
		Price competition	X	X	X	X	X
		Limited value generation	X	X	X	X	X
	High complexity/ uncertainty	High entry barriers					
		Premium pricing					
		Significant value generation					
Upgrading potential	Low complexity/ uncertainty	Limited technological learning requirements	X	X	X	X	X
		Limited pressure to develop forward and backward linkages	X	X	X	X	X
	High complexity/ uncertainty	Substantial pressure to broaden and deepen local knowledge base					
		Substantial pressure to broaden and deepen linkages					

Note:　[a] Applied from Ernst (2000b) to the research case.

variables						
specialisation					Process specialisation	
High complexity/uncertainty					Low	High
Differentiated					MP	FS
New technology	Fluid design	Difficult to replicate	Unpredictable changes	Close interaction with customers	Economies of scale & scope	Speed of response
					X	
					X	
					X	
X	X	X	X	X		X
X	X	X	X	X		X
X	X	X	X	X		X
					X	
					X	
X	X	X	X	X		X
X	X	X	X	X		X

Bibliography

Abramovitz, M. (1956), 'Resource and output trends in the United States since 1870', *American Economic Review*, **46**, 5–23.

ADB (2001), *Asian Development Outlook*, Manila: Asian Development Bank.

Adler, E. (1987), *The Power of Ideology: The Quest for Technological Autonomy in Argentina and Brazil*, Berkeley, CA: University of California Press.

Agarwal, J.P. (1976), 'Factor proportions in foreign and domestic firms in Indian manufacturing', *Economic Journal*, **86**: 589–94.

Aitken, B., and A.E. Harrison (1992), 'Does proximity to foreign firms induce technology spillovers?', World Bank and International Monetary Fund mimeo.

Aitken, B.J., and A. Harrison (1999), 'Do foreign firms benefit from direct foreign investment? Evidence from Venezuela', *American Economic Review*, **89**(3): 605–18.

Aitken, B.J., G. Hansen and A.E. Harrison (1997), 'Spillovers, foreign investment and export behavior', *Journal of International Economics*, **43**, 103–32.

Aitken, B.J., G. Hansen and A.E. Harrison (1999), 'Do domestic firms benefit from direct foreign investment? Evidence from Venezuela', *American Economic Review*, **89**(3), 103–32.

Akamatsu, K. (1962), 'Historical pattern of economic growth in developing countries', *Developing Economics*, **1**: 3–25.

Alavi, R. (1996), *Import Substitution Industrialisation: Infant Industries in Malaysia*, London: Routledge.

Albrink, J., G. Irwin, G. Neilson and D. Sasina (2000), 'From bricks to clicks. The four stages of E-volution', *Strategy + Business:* 3.

Allen, G.C., and A.G. Donnithorne (1957), *Western Enterprise in Indonesia and Malaya*, London: Allen & Unwin.

Amin, S. (1976), *Unequal Development*, New York: Monthly Review Press.

Amsden, A., T. Tschang and A. Goto (2001), 'Do foreign companies conduct R&D in developing countries?', ADB Institute working paper, no. 14, March.

Amsden, A.O. (1989), *Asia's Next Giant, South Korea and Late Industrialization*, New York: Oxford University Press.

Andersson, U., M. Forgren and U. Holm (2002), 'The strategic impact of external networks: subsidiary performance and competence development in the multinational corporation', *Strategic Management Journal*, **23**: 979–96.

Aoki, M. (2001), *Toward a Comparative Institutional Analysis*, Cambridge, MA: MIT Press.

Ariff, M., and Hal Hill (1985), *Export-Oriented Industrialisation – The ASEAN Experience*, Sydney: Allen and Unwin.

Ariffin, N., and M. Bell (1999), 'Firms, politics and political economy: patterns of subsidiary–parent linkages and technological capability-building in electronics TNC subsidiaries in Malaysia', in K.S. Jomo, G. Felker and R. Rasiah (eds), *Industrial Technology Development in Malaysia*, London: Routledge.

Ariffin, N., and Figueiredo, P. (2003), 'Internationalisation of innovative capabilities: counter-evidence from the electronics industry in Malaysia and Brazil', conference paper for DRUID's Knowledge Conference, June.

Arrow, K. (1962), 'The economic significance of learning by doing', *Review of Economic Studies*, **29**: 155–73.

Audretsch, D. (2002), 'The dynamic role of small firms: evidence from U.S.', *Small Business Economics*, **18**(1–3): 13–40.

Audretsch, D., and Z. Acs (1991), *Innovation and Technological Change: An International Comparison*, Ann Arbor, MI: University of Michigan Press.

Babbage, C. (1832), *On the Economy of Machinery and Manufactures*, London: Charles Knight.

Bain, J. (1968), *Industrial Organization*, New York: John Wiley and Sons.

Balassa, B. (1991), *Economic Policies in the Pacific Area Developing Countries*, London: Macmillan.

Bank of Uganda (2003), 'Unpublished statistics', Bank of Uganda, Kampala.

Baptista, M., and J. Cassiolato (1994), 'Liberalization and the recent development of the Brazilian information industry', paper presented at the conference Liberalization and Competitiveness, University of California, San Diego, 5–7 May.

Baran, P. (1957), *Political Economy of Growth*, New York: Monthly Review Press.

Baran, P. (1973), 'Political economy of backwardness', in C.K. Wilber (ed.), *Political Economy of Development and Underdevelopment*, New York: Random House.

Barnes, J., and J. Lorentzen (2003), 'Learning upgrading, and innovation in the South African automotive industry', paper presented at the International Workshop FDI-Assisted Development, Oslo, 22–24 May.

Bartlett, C.A., and S. Ghoshal (1989), *Managing Across Borders: The Transnational Solution*, Boston, MA: Harvard Business School Press.

Behrman, J.N., and W.A. Fischer (1980), *Overseas R&D Activity of Transnational Companies*, Cambridge, MA: Oelgeschlager, Gun and Hain.

Belderbos, R., G. Capannelli and K. Fukao (2001), 'Backward vertical linkages of foreign manufacturing affiliates: evidence from Japanese multinationals', *World Development*, **29**(1): 189–208.

Bell, M., and K. Pavitt (1995), 'The development of technological capabilities', in I.U. Haque (ed.), *Trade, Technology and International Competitiveness*, Washington, DC: World Bank.

Best, M. (1990), *The New Competition*, Cambridge, MA: Harvard University Press.

Best, M. (2001), *The New Competitive Advantage*, Oxford: Oxford University Press.

Best, M., and R. Rasiah (2001), 'Malaysian electronics in transition', report prepared for the Malaysian Government, Kuala Lumpur.

Best, M., and R. Rasiah (2003), 'Malaysian electronics: at the crossroads', UNIDO working paper no. 12, Geneva.

Bhagwati, J. (1979), 'International factor movements and national advantage', *Indian Economic Review*, **14**(2): 73–100.

Bigsten, A., and P. Kimuyu (eds) (2002), *Structure and Performance of Manufacturing in Kenya*, London: Palgrave.

Birkinshaw, J.M., N. Hood and S. Johnsson (1998), 'Building firm-specific advantages in multinational corporations: the role of subsidiary initiatives', *Strategic Management Journal*, **19**: 221–41.

Black, A. (2001), 'Globalization and restructuring in the South African automotive industry', *Journal of International Development*, **13**(6): 779–96.

Blalock, G. (2002), 'Technology from foreign direct investment: strategic transfer through supply chains', mimeo, Haas School of Business, Berkeley.

Blomström, M. (1986), 'Foreign investment and productive efficiency: the case of Mexico', *Journal of Industrial Economics*, **35**(1): 97–110.

Blomström, M., and A. Kokko (1998), 'Multinational corporations and spillovers', *Journal of Economic Surveys*, **12**(3): 247–77.

Blomström, M., and H. Persson (1983), 'Foreign investment and spillover efficiency in an underdeveloped economy: evidence from the Mexican manufacturing industry', *World Development*, **11**(6): 493–501.

Blomström, M., and F. Sjoholm (1999), 'Technology transfer and spillovers: does local participation with multinationals matter?', *European Economic Review*, **43**: 915–23.

Blomström, M., and E. Wolff (1994), 'Multinational corporations and productivity convergence in Mexico', in W. Baumol, R. Nelson and E. Wolff (eds), *Convergence of Productivity: Cross-National Studies and Historical Evidence*, Oxford: Oxford University Press.

Booth, A. (1998), *The Indonesian Economy in the Nineteenth and Twentieth Centuries: A History of Missed Opportunities*, Basingstoke: Macmillan.

Booth, A. (1999), 'Initial conditions and miraculous growth: why is South East Asia different from Taiwan and South Korea?', *World Development*, **27**(2): 301–22.

Borenzstein, E.J., J. De Gregorio and J.W. Lee (1998), 'How does foreign direct investment affect economic growth?', *Journal of International Economics*, **45**: 115–35.

Borrus, M., D. Ernst and S. Haggard (eds) (2000), *International Production Networks in Asia: Rivalry or Riches?*, London: Routledge.

Cantwell, J. (1995), 'The globalization of technology: what remains of the product cycle model?', *Cambridge Journal of Economics*, **19**: 155–74.

Cantwell, J., and R. Mudambi (2001), 'MNE competence-creating subsidiary mandates: an empirical investigation', Reading University, International Investment and Management discussion paper, no. 285.

Capannelli, G. (1999), 'Technology transfer from Japanese consumer electronic firms via buyer–supplier relations', in K.S. Jomo, G. Felker and R. Rasiah (eds), *Industrial Technology Development in Malaysia: Industry and Firm Studies*, London: Routledge.

Cardoso, F.H. (1977), 'The consumption of dependency theory in the United States', *Latin American Research Review*, **12**(3): 7–24.

Cardoso, F., and E. Faletto (1979), *Dependency and Development in Latin America*, Berkeley, CA: University of California Press.

Caves, R. (1974a), 'Causes of direct investment: foreign firms' share in Canadian and United Kingdom manufacturing industries', *Review of Economics and Statistics*, **56**: 272–93.

Caves, R. (1974b), 'Multinational firms, competition and productivity in host-country industries', *Economica*, **41**: 176–93.

Caves, R. (1982), *Multinational Enterprise and Economic Analysis*, Cambridge: Cambridge University Press.

Chandler, A. (1961), *Strategy and Structure: Chapters in the History of the American Industrial Enterprise*, Cambridge, MA: MIT Press.

Chandler, A. (1977), *The Visible Hand: The Managerial Revolution in American Business*, Cambridge, MA: Harvard University Press.

Cimoli, M., and J. Katz (2003), 'Structural reforms, technological gaps and economic development: a Latin American perspective', *Industrial and Corporate Change*, **12**(2): 387–411.

CINDE (2000), *Costa Rican Investment Board: Costa Rica Unexplored Business Opportunities. Key advantages of operating in Costa Rica*, San José: Costa Rican Investment Board.

Corcoran, E. (1999), 'Reinventing Intel', *Forbes*: 155–59.

Correa, C. (1999), *Technology Transfer in the WTO Agreement, A Positive Agenda for Developing Economies*, Geneva: UNCTAD.

Costa, I. (2001), 'Ownership and technological capabilities in Brazil', paper presented at the DRUID Academy winter conference, Aalborg, 18–20 January.

Coughlin, P., and G.K. Ikiara (eds) (1988), *Industrialisation in Kenya: In Search of a Strategy*, London: Heinemann.

Crankovic, M., and R. Levine (2000), 'Does foreign direct investment accelerate economic growth?', University of Minnesota working paper.

Creamer, D.B. (1976), *Overseas Research and Development by United States Multinationals 1966–1975*, New York: Conference Board.

Dahlman, C., and C. Fristak (1993), 'National systems supporting technical advance in industry: the Brazilian experience', in R. Nelson (ed.), *National Innovation Systems: A Comparative Analysis*, New York: Oxford University Press.

Davies, H. (1977), 'Technological transfer through commercial transactions', *Journal of Industrial Economics*, **26**: 165–71.

De Mello, L.R. (1999), 'Foreign direct investment-led growth: evidence from time series and panel data', *Oxford Economic Papers*, **51**: 133–51.

Deyo, F.C. (ed.) (1987), *The Political Economy of the New Asian Industrialism*, Ithaca, NY: Cornell University Press.

Dhanani, S. (2000), 'Indonesia: strategy for manufacturing competitivensss', vol. II: main report, UNIDO/UNDP project, Jakarta.

Dolan, C., and J. Humphrey (2000), 'Governance and trade in fresh vegetables: the impact of UK supermarkets on the African horticulture industry', *Journal of Development Studies*, **37**(2): 147–76.

Doner, R. (2001), 'Institutions and the tasks of economic upgrading', paper prepared for delivery at the 2001 annual meeting of the American Political Science Association, San Francisco, 30 August–2 September.

Doner, R., and E. Hershberg (1999), 'Flexible production and political decentralization in the developing world: elective affinities in the pursuit of competitiveness?', *Studies in Comparative International Development*, **33**(4): 45–82.

Doraisamy, A., and R. Rasiah (2001), 'Fiscal incentives for promotion of manufactured exports in Malaysia', in K.S. Jomo (ed), *Southeast Asia's Industrialization: Industrial Policy, Capabilities and Sustainability*, London: Palgrave.

Dosi, G. (1982), 'Technological paradigms and technological trajectories', *Research Policy*, **11**(3): 147–62.

Dunning, J.H. (1958), *American Investment in British Manufacturing Industry*, London: Allen & Unwin.

Dunning, J.H. (1971), *The Multinational Enterprise*, London: Allen & Unwin.

Dunning, J.H. (1974), *Economic Analysis and the Multinational Enterprise*, London: Allen & Unwin.

Dunning, J. (1981), 'Explaining the international direct investment position of countries: towards a dynamic or developmental approach', *Weltwirtschaftliches Archiv*, **117**, 30–64.

Dunning, J.H. (1994a), 'Re-evaluating the benefits of foreign direct investment', *Transnational Corporations*, **3**(1): 23–52.

Dunning, J.H. (1994b), 'Multinational enterprises and globalisation of innovation capacity', *Research Policy*, **23**(1): 67–88.

Dunning, J.H. (1997), *Alliance Capitalism and Global Business*, London: Routledge.

Dunning, J.H. (2003), 'Relational assets, networks and international business activity', in J.H. Dunning and G. Boyd (eds), *Alliance Capitalism and Corporate Management: Entrepreneurial Cooperation in Knowledge Based Economies*, Cheltenham, UK and Northampton, USA: Edward Elgar.

El Financiero (1999), 'Inversion de Intel en Costa Rica', San José: La Nacion Publicaciones.

Emmanuel, A. (1989), *Appropriate or Underdeveloped Technology*, Paris: John Wiley.

Enwright, M.J. (2000), 'Globalization, regionalization and knowledge based economy in Hong Kong', in J.H. Dunning (ed.), *Regions, Globalization and the Knowledge Based Economy*, Oxford: Oxford University Press.

Ernst, D. (1998), 'Externalization and inter-organizational networks: how globalization transforms the Japanese model', in D. Dirk (ed.), *Japanese Management in the Low Growth Era: Between External Shocks and Internal Evolution*, Berlin and New York: Springer Verlag.

Ernst, D. (2000a), 'Inter-organisational knowledge outsourcing: what permits small Taiwanese firms to compete in the computer industry?', *Asia Pacific Journal of Management*: John Wiley, **17**(2), 223–55.

Ernst, D. (2000b), 'Internet, global production networks and industrial upgrading a knowledge-centered conceptual framework', paper presented at Industrial Upgrading and Equity Workshop, San José.

Ernst, D. (2000c), 'The economics of electronics industry: competitive dynamics and industrial organisation', Economic series working paper no. 7 East-West Center, Honolulu.

Ernst, D. (2003), 'Global production networks and local development', research proposal mimeo.

Ernst, D., and P. Guerrieri (1998), 'International production networks and changing trade patterns in East Asia: the case of the electronics industry', *Oxford Development Studies*, **26**(2), 191–212.

Ernst, D., T. Ganiatsos and L. Mytelka (eds) (1998), 'Technological Capabilities and Export Success: Lessons from East Asia', London: Routledge.

Evans, P. (1979), *Dependent Development: The Alliance of Multinational, State and Local Capital in Brazil*, Princeton, NJ: Princeton University Press.

Evans, P. (1995), *Embedded Autonomy: States and Industrial Transformation*, Princeton, NJ: Princeton University Press.

FIAS (1996a), *Costa Rica. A Strategy for Foreign Investment in Costa Rica's Electronics Industry*, Washington, DC: Foreign Investment Advisory Services.

FIAS (1996b), *FDI News Industry Focus: The Electronics Industry*, Washington, DC: Foreign Investment Advisory Services.

Figueiredo, P.N. (2002), 'Learning processes features and technological capability accumulation: explaining inter-firm differences', *Technovation*, **22**: 685–98.

FR (2000), *Field Research Interviews*, San José: Codeti.

Frank, A.G. (1973), 'Development of underdevelopment', in C.K. Wilber (ed.), *Political Economy of Development and Underdevelopment*, New York: Random House.

Fransman, M. (1985), 'International competitiveness, technical change and the state: the machine tool industries in Taiwan and Japan', *World Development*, **14**(12): 1375–96.

Freeman, C. (1989), 'New technology and catching-up', *European Journal of Development Research*, **1**(1): 85–99.

Frobel, F., J. Heinrich and O. Kreye (1980), *The New International Division of Labour*, Cambridge: Cambridge University Press.

Fukasaku, K. (2001), 'Foreign direct investment and development: where do we stand', first draft, Paris: OECD Development Centre.

Furtado, C. (1973), 'The structure of external dependence', in C.K. Wilber (ed.), *Political Economy of Development and Underdevelopment*, New York: Random House.

Gachino, G. (2003), 'Foreign direct investment, export performance and capability building: evidence from Kenyan manufacturing industry', paper presented at the International Workshop on Transnational Corporations, Technological Capabilities and Competitiveness: Evidence from Africa, Asia and Latin America, Institute for New Technologies, United Nations University, Maastricht, 19–20 May.

Gachino, G., and R. Rasiah (2003), 'Labor productivity, exports and skills formation: comparing foreign and local firms in Kenyan manufacturing', paper presented at the International Workshop FDI-Assisted Development, Oslo, 22–24 May.

Gelb, S. (2002), 'Foreign companies in South Africa: entry, performance and impact: an overview', The Edge Institute, accessed at www.the.edge.org.za.

Gerrefi, G. (1994), 'Organization of buyer-driven global commodity chains:

how U.S. retailers shape overseas production networks', in G. Gereffi and M. Korzeniewicz (eds), *Commodity Chains and Global Capitalism*, Westport, CT: Praeger.

Gerrefi, G. (2002), 'International competitiveness in the global apparel commodity chain', *International Journal of Business Society*, **3**(1): 1–23.

Gerrefi, G. (2003), 'International competitiveness of Asian firms in the global apparel commodity chain', *International Journal of Business Society*, **4**(2): 71–110.

Gerrefi, G., and P. Evans (1981), 'Transnational corporations, dependent development and state policy in the semiperiphery: a comparison of Brazil and Mexico', *Latin American Research Review*, **16**(3): 31–64.

Gereffi, G., and S. Fonda (1992), 'Regional paths of development', *American Review of Sociology*, **18**: 419–43.

Gereffi, G., and T. Tam (forthcoming) *Who Gets Ahead in the Global Economy?: Industrial Upgrading, Value Chains and Development.*

Gerschenkron, A. (1962), *Economic Backwardness in Historical Perspective*, Cambridge, MA: Harvard University Press.

Ghose, A.K. (2003), *Jobs and Incomes in a Globalizing World*, Geneva: International Labour Organization.

Glenday, G., and David Ndii (2000), 'Export platforms in Kenya', African Economic Policy discussion paper no. 44.

Goldstein, A. (2002), 'The political economy of high-tech industries in developing countries: aerospace in Brazil, Indonesia and South Africa', *Cambridge Journal of Economics*, **26**: 521–38.

Gonzalez, A., L. Marshall and J. Marshall (1997), *Atracción de Inversión Productiva en Centroamérica, Análisis y Discusión de Temas Relevantes*, San José: Incae-Clacds.

Greer, D. (1992), *Industrial Organization and Public Policy*, New York: Macmillan.

Guerrieri, P., and C. Pietrobelli (2003), 'Industrial districts' evolution and technological regimes: Italy and Taiwan', *Technovation*, forthcoming.

Gujarati, D. (1988), *Basic Econometrics*, New York: McGraw-Hill.

Haddad, M., and A. Harrison (1993), 'Are there positive spillovers from direct foreign investment? Evidence from panel data for Mexico', *Journal of Development Economics*, **42**: 51–74.

Hamilton, A. (1791), 'Report on manufactures', reprinted in H.C. Syrett (ed.), *The Papers of Alexander Hamilton*, vol. 1, New York: Columbia University Press.

Harris, J. (1971), 'Nigerian entrepreneurship in industry', in P. Kilby (ed.), *Entrepreneurship and Economic Development*, New York: Fine Press.

Helleiner, G.K. (1973), 'Manufactured exports from less developed countries and multinational firms', *Economic Journal*, **83**: 21–47.

Helleiner, G.K. (1975), 'The role of multinational corporations in the less developed countries' trade technology', *World Development*, **3**(4): 161–89.

Hershberg, E., and J. Monge (2001), 'Industrial upgrading and equity in Costa Rica', paper presented at the SSRC-FLACSO-CODETI workshop, San José.

Hill, H. (1988), *Foreign Investment and Industrialisation in Indonesia*, Singapore: Oxford University Press.

Hill, H. (1995), *The Indonesian Economy since 1966: Southeast Asia's Emerging Giant*, Cambridge: Cambridge University Press.

Hill, H. (1996), 'Indonesia's industrial policy and performance: "orthodoxy" vindicated', *Economic Development and Cultural Change*, **45**(1): 147–74.

Hirschman, A. (1958), *The Strategy of Economic Development*, New Haven, CT: Yale University Press.

Hirschman, A. (1968), 'The political economy of import-substituting industrialization in Latin America', *Quarterly Journal of Economics*, **82**(2): 1–32.

Hirschman, A. (1972), *Exit, Voice and Loyalty: Responses to Decline in Firms, Organizations, and States*, Cambridge, MA: Harvard University Press.

Hirschman, A. (1977), 'A generalized linkage approach to development with special reference to staples', in M. Nash (ed.), 'Essays on economic development and cultural change in honour of Bert H. Hoselitz', *Economic Development and Cultural Change*, **25**: 67–98.

Hirschman, A. (1984), 'The on and off connections between political and economic progress', *American Economic Review*, **84**: 343–8.

Hobday, M. (1995), *Innovations in East Asia*, Cheltenham, UK and Brookfield, US: Edward Elgar.

Hobday, M. (1996), 'Innovation in South-East Asia: lessons for Europe', *Management Decision*, **34**(9): 71–81.

Hoffman, L., and T.N. Tan (1980), *Industrial Growth, Employment and Foreign Investment in Malaysia*, Kuala Lumpur: Oxford University Press.

Hsing, Y.T. (1996a), 'Thicker than water: interpersonal relations and Taiwanese investment in southern China', *Environment and Planning*, **28**: 2241–61.

Hsing, Y.T. (1996b), *Making Capitalism in China: The Taiwan Connection*, New York: Oxford University Press.

Hughes, H., and P.S. You (eds) (1969), *Foreign Investment and Industrialisation in Singapore*, Canberra: Australian National University Press.

Hymer, S. (1960), 'The international operations of national firms: a study of direct foreign investment', Ph.D. dissertation, MIT (published by MIT Press in 1976).

Hymer, S. (1972), 'The multinational corporation and the law of uneven development', New Haven Economic Growth Center, Yale University, occasional paper no. 181, pp. 113–40.

I&A (1998), *Ingeniería & Arquitectura*, (5), 4–23.

ITS (1993), *Industry Trade Summary*, Washington, DC: US International Trade Commission.

Ikiara, G.K. (1988), 'The role of government institutions in Kenya's industrialisation', in P. Coughlin and G.K. Ikiara (eds), *Industrialisation in Kenya: In Search of a strategy*, Nairobi: Heinemann.

Ikiara, G.K., and W. Odhiambo (2001), 'A review of the first decade of Kenya's export processing zones, 1990–2000', report presented to the Export Processing Zone Authority (EPZA), Nairobi.

Jenkins, R. (1984), *Transnational Corporations and Industrial Transformation in Latin America*, New York: St Martin's Press.

Jenkins, R. (1987), *Transnational Corporations and the Latin American Automobile Industry*, London: Macmillan.

Johnson, C. (1982), *MITI and the Japanese Miracle*, Stanford, CA: Stanford University Press.

Jomo, K.S. (1990), *Growth and Structural Change in the Malaysian Economy*, London: Macmillan.

Kaldor, N. (1957), 'A model of economic growth', *Economic Journal*, **67**: 591–624.

Kaldor, N. (1967), *Strategic Factors in Economic Development*, Ithaca, NY: Cornell University Press.

Kalecki, M. (1976), *Essays on Developing Economies*, Hassocks, UK: Harvester.

Kaplinsky, R. (1978), 'Technical change and the multinational corporation: some British multinationals in Kenya', in R. Kaplinsky (ed.), *Readings on the Multinational Corporation in Kenya*, Nairobi: Heineman.

Kasekende, L.A. (2000a), 'Capital account liberalisation and poverty', mimeo, Kampala.

Kasekende, L.A. (2000b), 'Liberalisation of the Ugandan economy and its effects', 5th Seminar of the Institute of Certified Public Accountants of Uganda.

Katz, J.M. (ed.) (1987), *Technology Generation in Latin American Manufacturing Industries*, Basingstoke: Macmillan.

Katz, J.M. (1999), 'Structural reforms and technological behaviour: the sources and nature of technological change in Latin America in the 1990s', paper presented at the International Conference, The Political Economy of Technology in Developing Countries, Brighton.

Katz, J.M., and N.A. Bercovich (1993), 'National systems of innovation supporting technical advance in industry: the case of Argentina', in R.R.

Nelson (ed.), *National Innovation Systems: A Comparative Analysis*, New York: Oxford University Press.

Kenya (1998), *Economic Survey*, Nairobi: Government of Kenya.

Kessing, D.B. (1983), 'Linking up to distant markets: south to north exports of manufactured consumer goods', *American Economic Review*, **73**: 338–42.

Kilby, P. (1965), *African Enterprise: The Nigerian Bread Industry*, Stanford, CA: Stanford University Press.

Kilby, P. (1969), *Industrialisation in an Open Economy: Nigeria, 1945–1966*, Cambridge: Cambridge University Press.

Kim, L. (1997), *From Imitation to Innovation*, Cambridge, MA: Harvard Business School Press.

Kim, L. (2003), 'The dynamics of technology development: lessons from the Korean experience', in S. Lall and S. Urata (eds), *Competitiveness, FDI and Technological Activity in East Asia*, Cheltenham, UK and Northampton, USA: Edward Elgar.

Kimuyu, P. (1999), 'Structure and performance of the manufacturing sector in Kenya', in P. Kimuyu, M. Wagacha and O. Abagi (eds), *Kenya's Strategic Policies for the 21st Century: Macroeconomic and Sectoral Choices*, Nairobi: Institute of Public Policy Analysis and Research (IPAR).

Kitching, G. (1982), *Backwardness in Historical Perspective*, London: Methuen.

Kmenta, J. (1971), *Elements of Econometrics*, New York: Macmillan.

Kojima, K. (1975), 'International trade and foreign investment: substitutes or complements', *Hitotsubashi Journal of Economics*, **16**: 1–12.

Kraemer, K.L., and J. Dedrick (2003), 'The information technology sector and international competitiveness', *International Journal of Business and Society*, **4**(2): 111–34.

Krugman, P. (1979), 'A model of innovation, technology transfer, and the world distribution of income', *Journal of Political Economy*, **87**: 253–66.

Krugman, P. (1996), 'The myth of Asia's miracle', *Foreign Affairs*, **73**(6): 63–78.

Lall, S. (1978), 'Transnationals, domestic enterprises, and industrial structure in host LDCs: a survey', *Oxford Economic Papers*, **30**: 217–48.

Lall, S. (1979a), 'Multinationals and market structure in an open developing economy: the case of Malaysia', *Weltwirtschaftliches Archiv*, **115**(2): 325–50.

Lall, S. (1979b), 'The international allocation of research activity by U.S. multinationals', *Oxford Bulletin of Economics and Statistics*, **41**: 313–31.

Lall, S. (1980a), 'Monopolistic advantages and foreign involvement by U.S. manufacturing industry', *Oxford Economic Papers*, **32**: 102–22.

Lall, S. (1980b), *The Multinational Corporation*, London: Macmillan.

Lall, S. (1992), 'Technological capabilities and industrialisation', *World Development*, **20**(2): 165–86.

Lall, S. (1996), *Learning from the Asian Tigers*, Basingstoke: Macmillan.

Lall, S. (2001), *Competitiveness, Technology and Skills*, Cheltenham, UK and Northampton, USA: Edward Elgar.

Lall, S. (2003), 'Foreign direct investment, technology development and competitiveness: issues and evidence', in S. Lall and S. Urata (eds), *Competitiveness, FDI and Technological Activity in East Asia*, Cheltenham, UK and Northampton, USA: Edward Elgar.

Lall, S., and P. Streeten (1977), *Foreign Investment, Transnationals and Developing Countries*, Basingstoke: Macmillan.

Lall, S., and G. Wignaraja (1998), 'Mauritius: dynamising export competitiveness', Commonwealth Secretariat economic paper no. 33, London.

Langdon, S. (1978), 'The multinational corporation in the Kenya political economy', in R. Kaplinsky (ed.), *Readings on the Multinational Corporation in Kenya*, Nairobi: Heineman.

Lastres, H.M.M., and J.E. Cassiolato (2000), 'From clusters to innovation systems: cases from Brazil', paper prepared for the Second Annual Global Development Network Conference, Beyond Economics: Multidisciplinary Approaches to Development, Tokyo, December.

Leachman, R., and C. Leachman (2001), 'Globalization of Semiconductor Manufacturing', Competitive Semiconductor Manufacturing Program, University of Berkeley.

Lenin, V.I. (1965), *Imperialism the Highest Stage of Capitalism*, Beijing: Foreign Language Press.

Lewis, A. (1955), *The Theory of Economic Growth*, London: Allen & Unwin.

Leys, C. (1975), *Underdevelopment in Kenya: The Political Economy of Neo-Colonialism*, Nairobi: Heinemann.

Lim, L.Y.C., and E.F. Pang (1979), 'The electronics industry in Singapore: structure, employment, technology and linkages', National University of Singapore, working paper no. 16, Singapore.

Lin, Y., and R. Rasiah (2003), 'Structure, technical change and government intervention: the development of the information hardware electronics industry in Taiwan', *International Journal of Business and Society*, **4**(2): 135–71.

Linsu Kim (1997), *From Imitation to Innovation*, Cambridge, MA: Harvard Business School Press.

Linsu Kim and R. Nelson (eds) (2001), *Technology, Learning and Innovation: Experiences of Newly Industrializing Countries*, Cambridge: Cambridge University Press.

List, F. (1885), *The National System of Political Economy*, London: Longmans, Green and Co.

Lucas, R.E. (1988), 'On the mechanics of economic development', *Journal of Monetary Economics*, **22**: 3–22.

Lundvall, B.A. (1992), *National Systems of Innovation: Towards a Theory of Innovation and Interactive Learning*, London: Frances Pinter.

Luxemburg, R. (1963), *The Accumulation of Capital*, London: Routledge and Kegan Paul.

Malaysia (1971), *Second Malaysia Plan 1971–1975*, Kuala Lumpur: Government Printers.

Malaysia (1986), *Industrial Master Plan*, Kuala Lumpur: Malaysian Industrial Development Authority.

Malaysia (1988), *Mid-Term Review of Fifth Malaysia Plan 1986–1990*, Kuala Lumpur: Government Printers.

Malaysia (2001), *Eighth Malaysia Plan 2001–2005*, Kuala Lumpur: Government Printers.

Malik, O. (2001), 'Absorb & conquer', *Red Herring* (3).

Manning, C. (1998), *Indonesian Labour in Transition: An East Asian Success Story?* Cambridge: Cambridge University Press.

Mansfield, E. (1985), 'How fast does new industrial technology leak out?', *Journal of Industrial Economics*, **34**(2): 217–24.

Mansfield, E., D.J. Teece and A. Romeo (1979), 'Overseas research and development by US-based firms', *Economica*, **46**: 187–96.

Markusen, A. (1996), 'Sticky places in slippery space: a typology of industrial districts', *Economic Geography*, **72**: 293–313.

Markusen, J.R. (1991), 'The theory of the multinational enterprise: a common analytical framework', in E. Ramstetter (ed.), *Direct Foreign Investment in Asia's Developing Economies and Structural Change in the Asia-Pacific Region*, Boulder, CO: Westview.

Marshall, A. (1890), *Principles of Economics*, London: Macmillan.

Marshall, A. (1927), *Industry and Trade*, London: Macmillan.

Marx, K. (1964), *Pre-capitalist Economic Formations*, London: Lawrence and Wishart.

Marx, K. (1965), *Capital: A Critical Analysis of Capitalist Production*, vol. 1, Moscow: Progress Publishers.

Marx, K. (1967), *Capital*, vol. 2, London: Lawrence and Wishart.

Mathews, J.A. (1996), 'High technology industrialisation in East Asia', *Journal of Industry Studies*, **3**(2): 1–77.

Mathews, J.A. (1997), 'A Silicon Valley of the East: creating Taiwan's semiconductor industry', *California Management Review*, **39**(4): 26–54.

Mathews, J.A., and D.S. Cho (2000), *Tiger Technology: The Creation of a Semiconductor Industry in East Asia*, Cambridge: Cambridge University Press.

Mendez, P. (1999), 'Intel a la cabeza del desarrollo tecnológico', *Actualidad Económica*, **205**(13): 30–38.

Mill, J.S. (1848), *Principles of Political Economy with some of their Applications to Social Policy*, London: John Parker and West Strand.

Mohd Nazari, I. (2001), 'Foreign direct investments and development: the Malaysian electronics sector', Chr. Michelsen Institute, working paper no. 4, Bergen, Norway.

Monge, J. (1994), *SUDIAC Unified Industrial Diagnosis System for Improvement of Competitiveness*, San José: Codeti.

Monge, J. (1999), *BDS Business Development Services Management System*, San José: Codeti.

Monge, J. (2001), 'Industrial upgrading in Costa Rica. Implications of Intel investment', paper presented at SSRC-FLACSO-CODETI workshop, San José.

Monge, J. (2002), 'Software sector and industrial upgrading in Costa Rica', in J.P. Perez-Sainz (ed.), *Global Chains and Enterprises in Central America*, San José: FLACSO.

Morawetz, D. (1981), *Why the Emperor's New Clothes are Made in Colombia*, London: Oxford University Press.

Mortimore, M. (1985), 'The subsidiary role of FDI in industrialization: the Colombian manufacturing sector', *NU-CEPAL Review*, no. 25, Santiago, April.

Mortimore, M. (1991), *Transnational Banks and the International Debt Crisis*, New York: United Nations Center on Transnational Corporations.

Mortimore, M. (1998), 'Getting a lift: modernizing industry by way of Latin American integration schemes. The example of automobiles', *Transnational Corporations*, **7**(2): 97–136.

Mortimore, M., and S. Vergara (2004), 'Targeting winners: can FDI policy help developing countries industrialize?', *European Journal of Development Research*, in press.

Moxon, R.W. (1975), 'The Motivation for Investment in Offshore Plants: The Case of the U.S. Electronics Industry', *Journal of International Business Studies*, **6**(1): 51–66.

Murray, R. (1973), 'The internationalisation of capital and the nation state', *New Left Review*, **67**: 84–109.

Muto, I. (1977), 'The trade zone and mystique of export-oriented industrialization', *AMPO: Asia Quarterly*, 9–32.

Myrdal, G. (1957), *Economic Theory and Underdeveloped Regions*, New York: Methuen.

Mytelka, L.K. (ed.) (1999), *Competition, Innovation and Competitiveness in Developing Countries*, Paris: OECD.

Mytelka, L.K. (2003), 'New wave technologies: their emergence, diffusion and impact, the case of hydrogen fuel cell technology and the developing world', UNU–INTECH discussion paper no. 3, Maastricht.

Mytelka, L.K., and F. Farinelli (2000), 'Local clusters, innovation systems and sustained competitiveness', UNU–INTECH discussion paper no. 5, Maastricht.

Mytelka, L.K., and L.A. Barclay (2003), 'Using foreign investment strategically for innovation', paper presented for the Conference on Understanding FDI-Assisted Economic Development, TIK Centre, University of Oslo, Norway, 22–25 May.

La Nacion (1997), *La Nacion & La Nacion Digital Publicaciones Periodicas*, San José.

Nagesh, K. (1990), *Multinational Enterprises in India: Industrial Distribution*, London: Routledge.

Narayanan, S., and Y.W. Lai (2000), 'Technological maturity and development without research: the challenge for Malaysian manufacturing', *Development and Change*, **31**(2): 435–57.

Narula, R. (1996), *Multinational Investment and Economic Structure: Globalisation and Competitiveness*, London: Routledge.

Narula, R. (2002), 'Innovation systems and "inertia" in R&D location: Norwegian firms and the role of systemic lock-in', *Research Policy*, **31**(5): 795–816.

Narula, R., and R. Dunning (2000), 'Industrial development, globalisation and multinational enterprises: new realities for developing countries', *Oxford Development Studies*, **28**(2): 141–67.

NASBIC (1998), *America's Small Business Partners Success Stories: Intel Corporation*, Washington, DC: National Association of Small Business Investment Companies.

Nelson, R. (ed.) (1993), *National Innovation Systems*, New York: Oxford University Press.

Nelson, R.R., and S.G. Winter (1982a), 'The Schumpeterian trade-off revisited', *American Economic Review*, **72**(1): 114–32.

Nelson, R.R., and S.G. Winter (1982b), *An Evolutionary Theory of Economic Change*, Cambridge, MA: Harvard University Press.

Newfarmer, R. (1985), *Profits, Progress and Poverty: Case Studies of International Industries in Latin America*, South Bend, IN: Notre Dame University Press.

Newfarmer, R., and W.F. Mueller (1975), 'Multinational corporations in Brazil and Mexico: structural sources of economic and non-economic power', report to the Sub-Committee on MNCs of the Committee on Foreign Relations of the United States Senate, Washington, DC, August.

Nyong'o, P.A. (1988), 'The possibilities and historical limitations of import-substitution industrialisation in Kenya', in P. Coughlin and G.K. Ikiara (eds), *Industrialisation in Kenya: In Search of a Strategy*, Nairobi: Heinemann.

OECD (1998), *The Internationalization of Industrial R&D: Patterns and Trends*, Paris: Organisation for Economic Co-operation and Development.

Ofreneo, R. (2003), 'TRIMS and the automobile industry in Philippines', *Technology Policy Brief*, **2**(1): 5–7.

Ohlin, B. (1933), *Interregional and International Trade*, Cambridge, MA: Harvard University Press.

Okamoto, Y., and F. Sjoholm (2003), 'Technology development in Indonesia', in S. Lall and S. Urata (eds), *Competitiveness, FDI and Technological Activity in East Asia*, Cheltenham, UK and Northampton, USA: Edward Elgar.

Palma, G. (2003), 'Four sources of "de-industrialisation" and a new concept of the "Dutch disease"', mimeo.

Pangestu, M. (1993), 'Indonesia: from Dutch disease to manufactured exports', mimeo.

Panglaykim, J. (1983), *Japanese Direct Investment in ASEAN: The Indonesian Experience*, Singapore: Maruzen.

Parry, T.G., and J.F. Watson (1979), 'Technology flows and foreign investment in the Australian manufacturing sector', *Australian Economic Papers*, **18**: 103–18.

Pavitt, K. (1984), 'Sectoral patterns of technical change: towards a taxonomy and a theory', *Research Policy*, **13**(6): 343–73.

Penrose, E. (1959), *The Theory of the Growth of the Firm*, Oxford: Basil Blackwell.

Phillips, L.C., and M. Obwana (2000), 'Foreign direct investment in East Africa: interactions and policy implications', African Economic Policy Discussion Paper No. 67.

Piore, M., and C. Sabel (1984), *The Second Industrial Divide: Prospects for Prosperity*, New York: Basic Books.

Polanyi, M. (1997), 'Tacit knowledge', in L. Prusak (ed.), *Knowledge in Organizations*, Boston, MA: Butterworth-Heinemann.

Portelli, B., and R. Narula (2003), 'FDI through acquisitions and implications for technological upgrading: some evidence from Tanzania', paper presented at the International Workshop, FDI-Assisted Development, Oslo, 22–24 May.

Porter, M.E. (1990), *The Competitive Advantage of Nations*, New York: Free Press.

Porter, M.E. (1998), *On Competition*, Cambridge, MA: Harvard Business School Press.

Prahalad, C.K., and Y. Doz (1987), *The Multinational Mission: Balancing Local Demands and Global Vision*, New York: Free Press.

Pratten, C. (1971), *Economies of Scale in Manufacturing Industry*, Cambridge: Cambridge University Press.

Prawiro, R. (1998), *Indonesia's Struggle for Economic Development: Pragmatism in Action*, Kuala Lumpur: Oxford University Press.

Putman, R.D. (1993), *Making Democracy Work: Civic Traditions in Modern Italy*, Princeton, NJ: Princeton University Press.

Quadros, R.C. (2003), 'TRIMS, TNCs, technology policy and the Brazilian automobile industry', *Technology Policy Brief*, **2**(1), 10–12.

Rasiah, R. (1988), 'The semiconductor industry in Penang: implications for new international division of labour theories', *Journal of Contemporary Asia*, **18**(1): 24–46.

Rasiah, R. (1993), 'Free trade zones and industrial development in Malaysia', in K.S. Jomo (ed.), *Industrializing Malaysia: Policy, Performance and Prospects*, London: Routledge.

Rasiah, R. (1994), 'Flexible production systems and local machine tool subcontracting: electronics transnationals in Malaysia', *Cambridge Journal of Economics*, **18**(3), 79–98.

Rasiah, R. (1995), *Foreign Capital and Industrialization in Malaysia*, Basingstoke: Macmillan.

Rasiah, R. (1996), 'Institutions and innovations: moving towards the technology frontier in the electronics industry in Malaysia', *Journal of Industry Studies*, **3**(2), 79–102.

Rasiah, R. (1999), 'Malaysia's National Innovation System', in K.S. Jomo and G. Felker (eds), *Technology, Competitiveness and the State*, London: Routledge.

Rasiah, R. (2001b), 'Industrial export expansion, employment, skills formation and wages in Malaysia', ILO working paper no. 35, Geneva.

Rasiah, R. (2002a), 'Government–business coordination and the development of the machine tool industry in Malaysia', *Small Business Economics*, **18**(1–3): 177–95.

Rasiah, R. (2002b), 'Systemic coordination and human capital development: knowledge flows in MNC-driven electronics clusters in Malaysia', *Transnational Corporation*, **11**(2): 89–130.

Rasiah, R. (2003a), 'Manufacturing export experience of Indonesia, Malaysia and Thailand', in K.S. Jomo (ed.), *Southeast Asia's Paper Tigers*, London: Routledge.

Rasiah, R. (2003b), 'Foreign ownership, exports and technological capabilities in the electronics firms in Malaysia and Thailand', *Journal of Asian Economics*, **14**(5): 786–811.

Rasiah, R. (2003c), 'Exports and technological capabilities: a study of foreign and local electronics firms in Indonesia, Malaysia, Philippines and Thailand', *Development Engineering*, **9**: 21–44.

Rasiah, R. (2004), 'Technological capabilities and export performance: a study of foreign and local electronics firms in Malaysia and Thailand', *European Journal of Development Research*, in press.

Rasiah, R., and T. Chua (1998), 'Industrial relations and industrialisation in Southeast Asia', in R. Rasiah and V.N. Hofman (eds), *Workers on the Brink*, Singapore: FES Press.

Rasiah, R., and S. Ishak (2001a), 'Market, government and Malaysia's new economic policy', *Cambridge Journal of Economics*, **25**(1): 57–78.

Reindhart, A. (2000), 'The new Intel', *Business Week*, **3**(12), 11 March, p. 32.

La Republica (1997), *La Republica Publicaciones Periodicas*, San José.

Reuber, G.L., H. Crookell, M. Emerson and G. Hamonno (1973), *Private Foreign Investment in Development*, Oxford: Clarendon Press.

Ricardo, D. (1830), *Principles of Political Economy and Taxation*, Harmondsworth: Penguin (reprinted in 1971).

Robison, R. (1986), *Indonesia: The Rise of Capital*, London: Allen & Unwin.

Rodney, W. (1972), *How Europe Underdeveloped Africa*, Washington, DC: Howard University Press.

Romer, P.M. (1986), 'Increasing returns and long run growth', *Journal of Political Economy*, **94**: 1002–37.

Ronstadt, R. (1977), *Research and Development Abroad by US Multinationals*, New York: Praeger.

Rosenberg, N. (1982), *Inside the Black Box*, Cambridge: Cambridge University Press.

Rosenstein-Rodan, P.N. (1984), '*Natura Facit Saltum*: analysis of the disequilibrium growth process', in G.M. Meier and D. Seers (eds), *Pioneers in Development*, New York: Oxford University Press.

Sabel, C. (1989), 'Flexible specialization and the re-emergence of regional economies', in P. Hirst and J. Zeitlin (eds), *Reversing Industrial Declines?: Industrial Structure and Policy in Britain and Her Competitors*, Oxford: Berg Publishers.

Santos, T.D. (1973), 'Big business and "Dependencia": a Latin American view', *Foreign Affairs*, **50**(3), 90–111.

Saxenian, A.L. (1994), *The Regional Advantage*, Cambridge, MA: Harvard University Press.

Saxenian, A.L. (1999), *Silicon Valley's New Immigrant Entrepreneurs*, San Francisco: Public Policy Institute of California.

Scherer, F. (1973), 'The determinants of industry plant sizes in six nations', *Review of Economics and Statistics*, **55**(2): 135–75.

Scherer, F. (1991), 'Changing perspectives on the firm size problem', in Z.J. Acs and D.B. Audretsch (eds), *Innovation and Technological Change:*

An International Comparison, Ann Arbor, MI: University of Michigan Press.

Scherer, F.M. (1992), *International High Technology Competition*, Cambridge, MA: Harvard University Press.

Scherer, F.M. (1980), *Industrial Market Structure and Economic Performance*, Chicago: Rand McNally.

Schumpeter, J.A. (1934), *The Theory of Economic Development*, Cambridge, MA: MIT Press.

Schumpeter, J. (1987), *Capitalism, Socialism and Democracy*, London: Unwin.

Scitovsky, T. (1964), *Papers on Welfare and Growth*, London: Allen & Unwin.

Sender, J., and S. Smith (1986), *Development of Capitalism in Africa*, London: Methuen.

Sengenberger, W., and F. Pyke (1991), 'Small firms, industrial districts and local economic regeneration', *Labour and Society*, **16**(1): 1–24.

Singer, H. (1950), 'The Distribution of Gains Between Investing and Borrowing Countries', *American Economic Review*, **40**: 473–85.

Sjoholm, F. (1999), 'Productivity growth in Indonesia: the role of regional characteristics and direct foreign investment', *Economic Development and Cultural Change*, **47**(3): 559–84.

Sjoholm, F. (2002), 'The challenge of combining FDI and regional development in Indonesia', *Journal of Contemporary Asia*, **32**(3): 381–93.

Smith, A. (1776), *The Wealth of Nations*, London: Strahan and Cadell.

Solow, R.E. (1956), 'A contribution to the theory of economic growth', *Quarterly Journal of Economics*, **70**: 65–94.

S&P (1996), *Standard & Poor Industry Survey and Dataquest*, New York: Standard & Poor.

Spar, D. (1998), *Attracting High Technology Investment, Intel's Costa Rican Plant*, Washington, DC: FIAS/The World Bank.

Sraffa, P. (1960), *The Production of Commodities by Means of Commodities*, Cambridge: Cambridge University Press.

Sung, G.H. (1999), *The Political Economy of Industrial Policy in East Asia*, Cheltenham, UK and Lyme, US: Edward Elgar.

Sunkel, O. (1989), 'Structuralism, dependency and institutionalism: an exploration of common ground and disparities', *Journal of Economic Issues*, **23**(2): 519–33.

Takahashi, D. (2001), 'Intel faces threats from rivals as the microprocessor giant's highly touted Itanium chip launch is delayed', *Red Herring* (1). PR Newswire Association Gale Group.

Teece, D.J. (1977), 'Technology transfer by multinational firms: the resource cost of transferring technological knowhow', *Economic Journal*, **87**: 242–61.

Thee, K.W. (2000), 'The impact of the economic crisis on Indonesia's manufacturing sector', *Developing Economies*, **38**(4): 420–53.

Thee, K.W., and M. Pangestu (1998), 'Technological capabilities and Indonesia's manufactured exports', in D. Ernst, T. Ganiatsos and L. Mytelka (eds), *Technological Capabilities and Export Success in East Asia*, London: Routledge.

Todaro, M. (2000), *Economic Development*, Reading, MA: Addison-Wesley.

UNCTAD (1997), *Trade and Development*, Geneva: United Nations Conference for Trade and Development.

UNCTAD (2002), 'Transnational corporations and technology development', *World Investment Report*, Geneva: United Nations Conference on Trade and Development.

UNCTAD (2003), 'FDI policies for development: nationals and international perspectives', *World Investment Report*, Geneva: United Nations Conference on Trade and Development.

UNCTC (1978), *Transnational Corporations in World Development: A Reexamination*, New York: United Nations Centre for Transnational Corporations.

UNCTC (1981), *Transnational Corporation Linkages in Developing Countries: The Cases of Backward Linkages via Subcontracting*, New York: United Nations.

UNIDO (2002), *Yearbook of Industrial Statistics*, Vienna: United Nations Industrial Development Organization.

UNU–INTECH (2002), *Survey of Technological Capabilities and Economic Performance of Foreign and Local Firms in Africa, Asia and Latin America*, Maastricht: Institute for New Technologies, United Nations University (UNU–INTECH).

Urata, S. (2001), 'Emergence of an FDI–trade nexus and economic growth in East Asia', in J. Stiglitz and Y. Shahid (eds), *Rethinking the East Asian Miracle*, New York: Oxford University Press.

USEPA (1995), 'Profile of the electronics and computer industry', EPA Office of Compliance sector notebook project 310, Washington, DC: US Environmental Protection Agency.

USITC (1993), *Industry & Trade Summary Semiconductors*, Washington, DC: US International Trade Commission.

Vaitsos, C. (2003), 'Growth theories revisited: enduring questions with changing answers', INTECH discussion paper no. 9, October, Masstricht.

Veloso, F., and R. Kumar (2003), 'The automotive supply chain: global trends and Asian perspectives', *International Journal of Business and Society*, **4**(2): 27–70.

Vernon, R. (1966), 'International investment and international trade in the product cycle', *Quarterly Journal of Economics*, **80**: 190–207.

Vernon, R. (1971), *Sovereignty at Bay: The Multinational Spread of U.S. Enterprises*, New York: Basic Books.

Vieto, J. (1998), 'Eco-efficiency in a high-tech cluster, a meta analysis of the evolving high-tech electronics cluster headed by Intel in Costa Rica', M.S. dissertation, International Institute for Industrial Environmental Economics at Lund University, Lund.

Wade, R. (1990), *Governing the Market*, Princeton, NJ: Princeton University Press.

Wallerstein, I. (1974), *The Modern World System*, New York: Academic Press.

Wallerstein, I. (1979), *The Capitalist World Economy*, Cambridge: Cambridge University Press.

Ward, J. (1999), 'Tropical chips. Costa Rica's economy shifts from coffee beans to electronics', *The Inside Line. The Industry Newspaper for the Electronics OEM*, online edition.

Warren, B. (1973), 'Imperialism and capitalist industrialization', *New Left Review*, **81**: 3–44.

Warren, B. (1980), *Imperialism: Pioneer of Capitalism*, London: Verso.

Wessner, C.W. (ed.) (2003), *Government–Industry Partnerships for the Development of New Technologies*, Washington, DC: The National Academic Press.

Westphal, L.E., K. Kritayakirana, K. Petchsuwan, H. Sutabutr and Y. Yuthavong (1990), 'The development of technological capability in manufacturing: a macroscopic approach to policy research', in R.E. Evenson and G. Ranis (eds), *Science and Technology: Lessons for Development Policy*, London: Intermediate Technology Publications.

Wignaraja, G. (2002), 'Firm size, technological capabilities and market-oriented policies in Mauritius', *Oxford Development Studies*, **30**(1): 87–104.

Wilkinson, F., and J.I. You (1995), 'Competition and cooperation: towards an understanding of the industrial district', *Review of Political Economy*, **6**: 259–78.

Wood, E. (2003), 'TRIMS and investment in South African manufacturing', *Technology Policy Brief*, **2**(3): 8–10.

Wong, S.H. (2000), *Intel's Experience in Building Linkages for SME Development, Multinational-SME Linkages for Development UNCTAD X*, Geneva: United Nations Conference on Trade and Development.

World Bank (1993), *The East Asian Miracle*, New York: Oxford University Press.

World Bank (2002), *World Development Indicators CD-ROM*, Washington, DC: World Bank Institute.

WTO (2001), *The WTO Agreement on Textiles and Clothing (ATC) 1995–2004*, Geneva: World Trade Organisation accessed at www.wto.org/english/tratop_e/texti_e/texintro_e.htm.

Young, A. (1928), 'Increasing returns and economic progress', *Economic Journal*, **38**(152): 527–42.

Zeitlin, J. (1992), 'Industrial districts and local economic regeneration', in P. Frank and W. Sengenberger (eds), *Industrial Districts and Local Economic Regeneration*, Geneva: International Institute for Labour Studies.

Index